I0458956

THE CRAIN CHRONICLES: A MEMOIR

By Gregory James Crain

Quantity sales and special discounts are available for bulk purchases by corporations, associations and others. For details, please reach out to CSI Publishing, listed above.

Orders by U.S. trade bookstores and wholesalers,

Email: ken@clientsi.com

The authors can be reached through Ken Walls.

Manufactured and printed in the United States of America, distributed globally by CSI Publishing - www.clientsi.com

Dallas, Texas

ISBN: 978-1-963986-25-9 Paperback

ISBN: 978-1-963986-24-2 Hardback

ISBN: 978-1-963986-26-6 eBook

TABLE OF CONTENTS

PREFACE

Let's start by telling you the purpose of this book. You see, it's written in a very different style. Like many people, I have lots of stories I want to pass on to my boys, Linden and Nolan. Having this book allows them and you to get a peek into my life and my outlook on the world. Although it will seem somewhat in a logical order, there will be times where I go sideways. I'll speak about items out of chronological order that happened to have come to my mind. Approximately 95% of the book was written in the span of three months. Most of the remaining time has been spent editing and revising my thoughts. The full completion has been a moving target. In fact, Boxing Day 2023 has me writing additional chapters that I've recently thought about while editing this book.

There will be a few chapters that are comical, enlightening and just general information. As I wrote this book, I realized how little information that my boys knew about my family, my upbringing and my college years. A few life lessons are shared, a few thoughts and suggestions to my two sons along with acknowledgements of valued friendships over the years.

I know, myself, I reminisce about how little I know of my parents and thought it was important that I try to explain and share my life with my two boys. In my case, you don't really know what you don't know about your parents until you become of a senior age and start to think back on your life.

I'm trying to explain that this book is personal, and it is my story. It is important that I share it with my boys, so they can pass it along to their kids, should they choose. Our family history will at least somewhat be preserved for generations to come. It is this legacy that drives me to write and share my life here on these pages.here are many things that have changed in my life during the last year. Recently, there are added medical situations that will have to be added. The moving completion date has me pushing to get this book done and frozen in time. The situation daily, weekly, along with monthly changes made completing this project a challenge, but here we are.

I hope you enjoy it. Some of it will be thought provoking, some of it surprising. Overall, it has been enjoyable for me to pass on knowledge, stories, lessons, comments and general information. I do hope you enjoy the book and always remember in life *You get what You give*.

FOREWORD

Always watching....

As children, we tend to want "things." We don't yet value what matters most in life. For some it's family, money, true love, or for the egotistical types, it's just plain old being right or self-gratification. The question is how do we develop these tendencies or attitudes about life?

Growing up on the west side in a lower middle-income family, we didn't really want for anything. My parents both worked extremely hard so they could provide the necessities for a happy life. I think if I knew now what I was watching, I might have paid closer attention.

It was a different time. It was a time when we went to the school yard to play strikeout or stayed out until midnight playing road hockey. We rode our bikes downtown following tour buses of singers and bands that were playing concerts. Crime was almost non-existent.

People made their own things. Nobody bought everything. We made our own entertainment. Going to a gym or joining a health club was for rich people.

As friends growing up, Greg and I discovered many things. We both had amazing fathers who only knew a strong work ethic and had their priorities in life of family first figured out. We built a working nautilus machine from scratch. We learned you can put a 350 Enduro Yamaha motorcycle in the rear hatch of a 1980 dodge Omni and drive home 45 minutes. We learned that animals are family.

What we didn't learn was that we were always watching.

Always watching our parents.

Always watching getting up at 5 am working until 6 pm.

Always watching getting an emergency service call at 3 AM, getting home at 8 AM and not missing a kids' hockey practice the same morning.

Always cooking the family feast so 20 people could come over for dinner on a Sunday.

You see, as kids we were always watching. We didn't know it at the time, but our lives were being taught to us as we grew up. Instilling work ethic, manners, priorities, morality, and we didn't even know it.

I was very fortunate to spend time with both of our fathers as I had a keen interest in raising birds, and Greg's father had plenty.

Greg's dad was a quiet man who didn't say much; didn't need to. I think back, and I was always watching and learning as he cleaned cages, built his own coops, or simply just sat quietly watching his birds.

We are our parents' children.

You don't have to go far to see online how proud of his children Greg must be. He doesn't flaunt it; just like his dad, he sits quietly and is proud. He's instilled in them what was instilled in him.

He's had a tremendous hockey career few know about because he's a proud man and what's important to him takes priority over his "fame." Hockey life is such a perfect acronym for life in general. As a manager or coach, you're always watching. Always trying to read the play, read the players, understand what you need to do better and win. Not lose, win.

Life throws you many curve balls. Remember your children are always watching.

When you volunteer, they are always watching. When you tip the hard-working service worker, they are always watching.

Greg might not know it, but from afar, I've been always watching.

Watching as my friend raised two strong men with ethics and morals. Watched as my friend graduated from college (with a little help from friends). Watching as my friend recovered from life's challenges to become stronger.

Your life as an author certainly was a surprise, but I think back to our childhood, and about what we both learned from our dads who could pretty much build anything out of almost nothing. Put your mind to it, and you can accomplish anything.

Your kids watched you. They are a reflection of what you've instilled. They watched you work hard, focus on family first, focus on community, with ethics and morals your entire life.

The stories of mohawks, muscles, tattoos, and much more are yours to write, and I can't wait to read the story, but....remember they're always watching, they'll still be watching....

Mike Janisse

"MACHO" is my brother. The Macho moniker came from a childhood friend of his. I say he's my brother, but a small technicality actually makes him my half brother. That has never been my opinion since the day I was told he was on his way. I could not have loved him any differently if we had the same Mom and Dad from the start.

Being brothers with a 10 plus year age difference has meant that he was the annoying younger brother. We therefore didn't socialize in the same circles (his friends were annoying also). We knew some of each other's friends but not all of them.

He has been extremely private and secretive with his revelations. Most things were kept secret for extended periods of time (much to my annoyance when the secret was out).

A few examples...

His first girlfriend (that we knew of and who became his wife) was introduced to my wife

Barb and I at a local hockey arena. I didn't know he had a girlfriend for some time!

He became a travel convenor of a minor hockey association.

He became a general manager of a Junior C hockey team.

He bought into a Junior C hockey team.

None of the above was divulged in a timely manner.

The travel convenor position was made known months after he accepted the position!

GM of the Junior C hockey team...about one year after he accepted the position!

Part owner of the Junior C hockey team...two years after buying into it!

These occurrences were important to my wife and I because we spent untold hours working with minor hockey in a variety of positions.....coach, assistant coach, manager, trainer. As a minor league coach myself, he played for me in a juvenile house league level and a juvenile travel league. Later, he took the lead and became the head coach. This time I helped him as an assistant coach with a variety of travel team age groups from Atom to Midget. The hockey connection of us coaching together is the biggest event in our relationship outside of our families.

And yet another example....

I never knew he would or had been writing his first book. I found out when he asked my wife Barb to proofread it...that was the first time he told us about it. Never knew about the second book until proofreading again was brought up...no previous insight.

For this book (third time's a charm edition), he finally asked for this foreword with me having no knowledge of what the book will be about and thousands of words into his writing. So... secretive again.

Can't imagine what and when an additional volume to his writing collection will occur next. Guess I'll find out close to the end of the rough copy with a request to proofread it!

Proud as hell of you (and your secretive endeavors)...carry on! Shouldn't be too surprised with whatever is in the future.

LOVE YOU BROTHER!

GARY

THE HEART GOES TICK TOK

Well, it looks like I am back at it on March 1st, 2023. Not sure where this will go or end and not sure why I'm writing it. This book will be about my life as I sit here today at 57 years old and begin to think about the last 57 years.

As you get to be this age, you know you are at the far end of the measuring tape. Many years ago, when I was starting out in my career, an older gentleman my current age took me aside, and we started chatting casually. He pulled out his tape measure and extended to about 74". He went on to explain that seventy-four was the average life expectancy of a male. He showed me visually where I stood on the tape measure which was, at the time, the mid 20s, and you could clearly see how much distance was between my age and the average male mortality age of 74.

He then went on to show visually where he was, which was in his late 50s. You could see the obvious difference between the years that he had remaining versus the years that I had remaining. I have always remembered this and often reminisce and show others. It's a great visual to know where you sit in basic terms of life expectancy. As you get to be my current age, you know you are at the far end of the measuring tape.

I guess the last year has prompted me to begin to think a little deeper about my life. I've had some issues with my health that continue to be diagnosed and a strategy developed to control it medically. These medical concerns started in approximately June of 2022.

Beginning last June, I had seemed to be getting very winded with very minute physical activity. Simply walking to the washroom, which is about 20 steps away, was quite a task. I became winded quickly and even had to stop halfway there. Although I have never considered myself a real fitness buff, I've always considered myself active.

After about two months of me being stubborn about it, I called my doctor's office and had a conversation with medical staff. Unfortunately, in Canada, in office doctors' appointments are very limited. I explained over the phone what was going on and explained that I thought it was some type of pneumonia. They agreed and prescribed some medication for me. After a week of no improvement, and in fact, getting slightly worse, I again called, and a new stronger prescription was given along with a puffer device.

After the third week of having no improvement, I booked an appointment to get into the doctor's office. At this point, walking only a few steps up and down stairs was very taxing with huffing and puffing and a rest required to catch my breath.

I had no idea what was wrong. I had always considered myself very active, even though overweight and not in shape. I never had any health issues. I first saw a nurse practitioner and explained my symptoms. She did an EKG on me and took my blood pressure as a standard procedure. To my surprise, she left the room in quite a hurry, later to find out during the appointment that she had called a heart specialist and explained the readings that she had seen. It turns out, my heart rate was 166 beats per minute.

The specialist called her immediately and prescribed some new drugs that would reduce my heart rate. Approximately a month later, I went to see the heart specialist. He explained that I had atrial fibrillation, a medical condition that sees the heart race upward to very abnormal rates at random unpredictable times. By this time, the medication I was put on had caused my heart rate to come down. The heartbeat was still not a normal number but had certainly reduced from the 166 bpm that the nurse had seen.

The doctor went on to explain that this was a serious situation that needed to be controlled. He explained to me that being on blood thinners for a few years due to a blood clot in my leg three years prior, may certainly have prevented me from having a stroke. The specialist prescribed another medication to remove any water from around my heart, and I had to wear a heart monitor for three days. This monitor was a small device that was taped to my chest with a small sensor taped near my heart. I wore this device for three days and went about my normal daily tasks. The monitor tracked my heart rate twenty-four hours per day.

At this point, it was September, with my next appointment booked for early October. At my appointment with the specialist who read my monitored numbers, he mentioned a procedure that may be helpful. This procedure would reset my heartbeat to normal from its current very nonstandard pattern. The heart was not only beating too fast but in a sporadic frequency. It would require me to go into the hospital, but it was a non-evasive procedure.

This procedure was called an electrical cardioversion. A high energy shock is sent to the heart to reset a normal rhythm. The hope would be that the heart would begin to beat at a normal rate and a normal pattern. The appointment was on October 30th, 2022, which was my 57th birthday. Although the specialist went on to explain that it was a common procedure, there were always risks. He had high confidence that it would work.

During the two weeks I waited for the procedure, I realized that I should let my family know what was going on. It was certainly hard to do as many thoughts flooded my brain, on top of privateness and stubbornness about letting anyone know about my serious situation. I told both my sons one at a time on different days and explained that it was not a big deal, that it was a common procedure. They were tough conversations to have, knowing how serious and possibly fatal the outcome could be. I have found at various serious times throughout the years that emotions are hard to hide. I certainly did my best to downplay the procedure, but I know my voice, along with heavy swallows and pauses may have come across differently.

I then had to tell my sister-in-law and brother. As you may expect, all of this was very difficult and emotional for me. You see, my father passed away at age 57, and that has been in the back of my mind for the last few years. Now, facing a serious medical condition, it compounded my fear and worry.

Procedure day came, and they hooked up all the wires to my chest, sedated me and within one or two minutes sent an electrical shock to my heart that literally stopped it and started it again. The entire procedure was done within an hour, and all went well that day. My youngest son Nolan was there to drive me home.

A follow up appointment had previously been booked with my specialist for a month later at the beginning of December. He again wanted me to have a heart monitor on for three days, which meant more waiting and thinking for me.

On December 22nd, 2023, I met with the doctor who provided disappointing news regarding the results of the procedure. I was told I was back in atrial fibrillation again. Although this time, with the help of medicine, I was in a much more stable condition. I was required to take two heart pills daily, one water pill along with one blood thinner pill. Although disappointing, I was a bit more at ease with the results knowing it could be managed with medication. As the condition was managed, the process of finding out why I went back into atrial fibrillation would begin.

From June through December 2022, a very limited number of people knew of my medical condition; my two boys, brother, and sister-in-law and perhaps my ex-wife. My employer, co-workers' customers and friends knew nothing about it. I would say I have always been a private person with regards to my life, having never wanted any sympathy or acknowledgement. I have always been reserved and quiet with regards to personal situations. As you can imagine, this has led to many surprises for my friends and family, some of which included the ownership of a junior hockey club, the writing of my first two books and pretty much any and all career moves and promotions.

STRESSFUL TIMES

It is now March 11th, 2023, and I'm on my way to a playoff game for the Amherstburg Admirals playing the Wheatley Sharks. We are down in the series one win for Wheatley and zero for the Admirals with our second game in Wheatley. I am headed to Wheatley where we certainly need to win this game to bring a victory back home tomorrow. As I drive about 55 minutes, I get to ponder about hockey.

My role with the Admirals started five years ago as the general manager. The role has expanded, and I am now in my second year being a co-owner of the Admirals. Originally, when I first started as the general manager, there were three owners. Now, there are two owners; me and one of the original owners from five years ago. Two previous owners sold their shares to me and my business partner.

I sit here and think that in my recent book, *Journey Through the Jungle* I had mentioned all the distinct roles I had throughout my hockey career. I wrote in one of the chapters that there was one more position in hockey that I'd never experienced. Lo and behold, nine months after I wrote about it, I became the co-owner of a junior C hockey club. As a general manager and co-owner, the responsibilities are 24 hours a day, seven days a week and 365 days a year.

As a general manager, you are responsible for all the players and all the coaching staff. You hire and fire coaches, trainers and equipment personnel and control the players who are on the team and any trades with other teams.

Now, I've never been a dictator, so I've always asked for some opinions from the staff regarding players. When we come to a consensus, the player goes on to be signed to the Admirals. We meet again throughout the season to see if the player has performed up to our expectations. If the player has underperformed, then the decision is made on whether to keep, release or trade him from the team.

As you can imagine, the full process of being a general manager is very taxing and certainly time consuming. The ownership role in our organization may be slightly different than others. As an owner, you oversee everything including sponsorships, booking the ice, fan experience, volunteers, score keeper, website and music personnel. Those responsibilities, right or wrong, were primarily shouldered by me. I will admit that I can be impatient with others, and I just want to get things done in a timely manner.

The last two years of being an owner, including all the financial aspects, have been stressful and tiring. Obviously, I put money into the team, and now I am responsible as a co-owner for the viability of that team. Add to that list of responsibilities are participation in negotiations with the town about an agreement for the facilities, and it certainly becomes a full-time job.

Although a lifelong lover of the game, it is to be noted that I also have a full-time sales career. Between work and hockey club ownership, it definitely is a balancing act that creates very long days.

These last two years were hugely impacted by Covid and its many ramifications. Mini mandates, attendance regulations from the town and the provincial government dictating vaccinations and spectator masking all had huge revenue impacts to the Admirals hockey club.

Specifically, the last year has been very grueling for me concerning what needs to be done, how it gets done and who does those tasks for the Admirals. My sales career for the last two years has been very stressful. The automotive industry seems to still be struggling from the Covid years. The inability for me to travel to the USA during those two years most definitely crushed my ability to sell to American customers. Currently, I am trying to rebuild relationships and the accounts damaged or lost during the pandemic. We all know a salesperson is evaluated on the amount he sells.

My business partner has now stepped up and realized how busy and how much work I have done for the Admirals. Communication levels have increased in the second half of this year, which is a huge positive since it was very minimal for the first year of co ownership. High stress levels can have a negative impact on your health, and that has certainly been on my mind as I navigate my heart condition.

I was excited during the summer and during our main spring camp for our 2022 / 2023 hockey season. It certainly did not start off on a particularly good note, as it seemed we were continually chasing the game. I had to make some significant player moves with the direction of the club. As I sat back and looked at our sixth-place league finish, I wondered if I made the right decisions. Obviously, not every move you make is going to be a success, but if most of the moves you make are successful then your club also will be successful.

I added a new coach into the mix after an earlier coach moved on. With a fresh marriage and new child, he just could not commit the time. I kept the head coach, an assistant coach and added a new assistant coach. I also added an additional assistant coach to primarily watch from the stands and learn. He was an ex-player who was very young with no coaching experience who had recently retired from the Admirals.

Two weeks into the year, our record was one win and two losses and a significant player unexpectedly demanded a trade. He was a fixture in our room, but for whatever reason, was not happy and wanted to be traded. A few other requests for trades and releases added to the turbulence. That trade was the catalyst that started the turmoil and unsettledness for the rest of the season.

This upheaval I believe caused the team to spiral downward to which we never recuperated. I had many sleepless nights pondering the cause of these players wanting to be released and the general lack of success with the team.

I certainly leaned on a few people outside of the hockey world to bounce some things off them and get their opinion. We discussed in depth whether what I did was right or wrong and was my thinking skewed.

As I continue to learn, some players seem to play for a different reason, not just to play the game, but they also expect enticements. I am a firm believer that these players will not be true Admirals and play for the right reasons. I can admit that the number of changes that were made by me had a major effect on the success of the team that year. Add in the resignation of the head coach towards the middle of the season, and we were facing a very uphill battle. When you put all those moves together, I would think others looking from the outside would see turmoil within the organization and perhaps some instability. I do ponder what went on that year and think whether the changes were the best moves for the team.

As I drove to Wheatley two days ago, I will admit that I had a deep discussion with my business partner about some significant changes I thought needed to be made within the organization. One was the hiring of a new general manager. After five years of being a general manager, I would hope that I am at least smart enough to realize it is time for a new face of the Admirals.

It was time for me to step back and to truly just be an owner and to allow someone else to run and build the team. My discussion with my partner also explained my thoughts and theories on the change. I asked him for his opinion and for his thoughts and comments.

In my opinion, ownership would hire a general manager who would then hire the head coach. The head coach would hire his staff and would be fully accountable. The general manager would take direction from ownership of what we expected of the general manager role. The new GM would be in control of the coaches, the players, and the building of the team. I understand everybody runs a sporting organization slightly differently, though, and that would be all ironed out during the transition.

I had a few conversations about my future and the state of the team with my assistant manager who I've known for 35 years. We both have an old school mentality. Our philosophies are in line, and our opinions of the hockey world are very similar. He and I agree on the changes of the latest generation of athletes. He also has mentioned that he would like to step back and perhaps maintain a different role that is less time-consuming.

Next was to figure out how to go about the change. The perfect solution would be to quickly hire a general manager that would grab the ball and run with it. In a perfect world, it would be great to have all the pieces in place prior to the spring camp at the end of April.

I am sure this shocked a few people including close friends, relatives and probably the junior C hockey ranks. They all know how much time and effort I have put into the Admirals. As my typical personality always prevails, answers to questions were kept brief and shallow. My decision, my business is kept to myself.

Like I have mentioned before, there are a million diverse ways to run an organization. What is the right way is unknown, there is no perfect map to the road to success. The goal is always to navigate change efficiently and move forward.

I would say the last two years drained my energy. Although hard to say, declining health along with some heart concerns, work and an enormous amount of stress led to this decision. The timing was right for a managerial shake up. A new youthful voice with innovative ideas was needed to steer the ship in the direction of success.

I certainly have enjoyed the game as a proud co-owner and general manager. I know we have made strides as an organization including the number of volunteers and community involvement. The goal is and always will be to continue to try and win a championship. I have enjoyed my time for sure, but as they say all good things must come to an end, and the fat lady was singing for my departure as the general manager.

March 13th ...one day after getting knocked out of playoffs in the first round for the second straight year. Although we got swept, the team battled, and I would say the games were closer than it appeared on the scoreboard. There was a lot of pondering those last 10 or 15 minutes of the game; thinking about what I was going to say to the team, or if I was going to make any announcement.

As the time ran down, I walked over from my usual corner and shuffled out onto the ice to go down the receiving line wishing good luck to the opposing team. I walked over to their general manager off the ice, congratulated him, wished him the best and told him he had a hell of a hockey team to keep on playing hard and he would be successful.

I walked into our dressing room where it was obviously a very doom and gloom atmosphere. I wanted to thank the Admirals players for being Admirals through the thick and thin of this year. It had been a very crazy year starting with the mass exodus of players and the changing of staff throughout the year. We competed to the very bitter end in each of the playoff games. At this point, the Crain as general manager ship had set sail for the ownership role.

TEST SECRECY

Since Christmas, I've had a CT scan, two sleep apneas studies, two heart monitor evaluations, four blood tests and was scheduled for a second EKG, along with various consultations with specialists.

The CT scan was scheduled because they found an anomaly on my spine during another scan. The results would determine if it was cancerous or only an abnormality. Wait and see was the mandate.

The sleep apnea study was completed in January, requested by the heart specialist. The review of the results of the study would have me waiting another two months until mid-March. The doctor said it was very severe sleep apnea after he reviewed the results. The sleep apnea doctor immediately scheduled me the next day to do another sleep apnea test. This study would have me wearing a breathing mask and monitored overnight. This time, the overnight lasted about five hours, which is the normal duration.

The latest test was a MIBI chemical stress test, which measures the amount of blood being supplied to the heart. Quite an interesting process, where a small amount of radioactive material is given intravenously. A scan of the heart on the first day and again the second day shows the blood being supplied to the heart, pre and post chemical stressing of the heart. The second day they open your blood vessels with an intravenous supplied chemical, and then you are taken for another scan. The results let the specialist know if there is any blockage of blood going into the heart. I was in for a lot more waiting and pondering.

It had been two weeks since my second sleep apnea evaluation. An appointment had now been booked with the apnea equipment store for fitting of a mask and machine. That will help me sleep at night and reduce the number of times per hour that I stop breathing while sleeping. Since the results indicated severe sleep apnea, I had to wait eight weeks to purchase equipment to reduce the stress on my heart. More waiting and pondering.

It was nearing one year of having my medical condition which started in July. I was eight months into this investigation to see exactly what is going on with my heart, why I went into atrial fibrillation and why the procedure did not hold. One of the heart specialists thought it was because of the sleep apnea conditions of stopping my heart 126 times per hour. The solution of the mask and machine brings that number to less than 5 stops per hour.

I try to be very patient with the medical process, however it certainly takes quite a long time between appointments. Then once an appointment or testing is done more lengthy waiting to get the results. I have stayed relaxed and again kept everything to myself but must admit the waiting is very stressful.

I continue to limit activities so as to not overexert and try to clear my head and realize I must have a positive mindset. It was just the stress of not knowing what was wrong that made me worry. I was admittedly scared and extremely cautious as it is obviously not a great situation.

On the way back from one of the multiple testing sessions, I stopped off at the gravesite of my mother and father. I do this three or four times a year. I don't know what exactly sparked the visit to their grave that day, but obviously, all the testing certainly had me thinking. It was just a casual visit to gather my thoughts, reflect and think. I stared at the gravesite with the dates and the age of the deaths of my mother and father. My father was fifty-seven while my mother was seventy years old. I sure do miss them and their knowledge.

Although I try not to think about things, obviously, it was on my mind. It's the first reason that I am writing this memoir. Just to let my two boys know about my life, to explain some things and to let them be part of some situations which I typically don't ever talk about.

It is obvious that my medical situation is very worrisome. I am usually not a worrier, but I do think about things now, mostly, about the well-being of my two boys. I am doing what the doctors tell me to do and following all the medical medications religiously. I am trying not to stress out on different things and am trying to remove some of the stress in my life, including the general manager duties of a Junior C hockey club. I have pulled back and will now just be a co-owner. I'm sure I'll still be involved but at a reduced workload.

The other thing I worried about is the results of all these medical tests. One thought that had run across my mind, is if there is going to be any reason that the doctors are going to stop me from working? I had bills and a mortgage to pay, two boys to continue to raise, help and provide advice to. I didn't know exactly how that would play out, if in fact they recommended that I don't work. I had no reason to believe there would be a stoppage of work based on all my conversations with the doctors.

At some point soon, I am going to sit my boys down and have a serious conversation and explain exactly what has been going on regarding the tests. I have just done it again, where they did not know about the MIDI scan and recent EKG test. My reservation of telling my boys is a flaw in my thinking, but I know my two boys will worry.

I don't want them spending time or energy worrying about the well-being of their father. The boys are at the age now where they can certainly make decisions and move on with their life should anything crazy happen to me. I know their tendency is to worry about stuff, though. I guess I have chosen, and I am not sure if it is right or wrong to not let them know until it is necessary.

I'm sure you've noticed in reading this book so far that I keep a lot of things remarkably close to my chest. I don't know what spurs it on. Maybe I try not to attract any attention, or maybe it's self-doubt. I'm not exactly sure, as I'm not a psychiatrist, but it is just the way I am wired. That character trait is both good and bad. It's a good thing because people tell me crazy things in the work world because they know I won't tell anybody about it. No matter how much I trust a person I could tell, I just don't. That's how I've always been, and that is why so many people feel safe telling me confidential information. They know that no matter what, it's not going to be released from my mouth. That is one thing that upsets me; if I tell information to somebody and it then comes back to me. That is on the person that would have blabbed after telling them not to say anything to anybody. It feels bad that I don't trust a lot of people. Looking back, I am not sure if I've ever really been burned like that, it's probably another character flaw of mine, but it is just safer. I don't tell people too much, as it is also safer for the person I tell. They don't have the knowledge of information that I don't want to be open to the public.

I have always tried not to get into the rumor mill. I am sure that sometimes I have, but I tried to screen through and make sure it is not a vicious rumor or anything harmful. If I was told not to tell, then it does not ever come out. It is good to be trustworthy, and I would hopefully think that all my friends and family believe that I am very trustworthy.

Nowadays with social media, it is quite easy to yap just to get some extra likes or comments or followers on your social media page. Suddenly, this person spreading the info on social media has become untrustworthy. They will go to social media just to gain popularity. I don't think that's a very good characteristic.

RESULTS

On Thursday, April 20th, 2023. I sat by myself in the middle of Alabama on a work trip. Considering what I had been through the last nine months, it was a trip that I was excited to be able to take. In the last three weeks I had received some medical results from the multitude of tests I had been doing for the last two months.

The first result I got back was from a CT scan where they had noticed a type of abnormality on my spine. After doing the scan, the results came back that the image on the scan was what they called a bone island, which was noncancerous. It's a small piece of bone that for some reason had grown on my spine. The doctor said there was nothing to worry about as it is common in many people. The doctors wanted to make sure that the image they noticed with all scans was nothing serious.

The next result I got back was from the ECG. This echo cardiogram test is where they check the health of the heart. An appointment with an ECG technologist had them push a probe all around your chest area over your heart. They record the beating patterns at different areas of your heart, with the whole procedure taking about 45 minutes. The results from the heart specialist indicated that my heart health was improving from its original state over the last nine months.

The next test we will talk about is the MIDI test. This one was a two-day test to check the functioning of your heart. They compare a heart, which is in rest state on day one to a chemically stressed heart on day two. I am glad to say that the specialist said that there were no blockages. Hearing this was a huge relief for me.

The third test I had done was a blood test. Here they checked for white and red blood cells, and many other elements within your blood. All the chemicals and blood analysis came back normal, which was a great feeling.

The fourth test result that I got back was from the sleep apnea test. This test was to determine if, during my sleep, the mask that I had to wear reduced the breathing stoppages. The heart specialist said that my sleep apnea diagnosis may be the reason I was in atrial fibrillation. As a result, I am using an oxygen machine. The difference went from 126 events per hour, to under five events per hour with the use of the machine. What this improvement change has done has allowed me to have a much deeper sleep. I did not get up as much, and my energy level began to rise. When I travel, I bring the small machine and hook it up every night in the hotel. I simply use it as a great asset and will be using a machine every night for the rest of my life, and it is not a big deal to me. I was confident that I was going to get used to the machine and determine that the machine was going to work. If that is what it takes to extend my life expectancy, then it is a small price to pay.

Currently, I know of three or four people that have the same machine. Although it sounds like it is modern technology, it has been around for the last five years. The sleep apnea doctor explained that I most likely have been in a sleep apnea mode for the last 20 years and progressively it got worse and worse. Due to it slowly progressing, you never really notice it. You never really know how well you could feel and how much better sleep you could get. That is good news and overall, the four tests that I had done came back incredibly positive.

During the results meeting with the heart specialist, he made one minor change with my heart medicine. He let me know that the blood thinners, the heart medicine, and water pills will be taken the rest of my life. He told me my heart was improving since he first saw me months ago, which is great to hear. I am not out of the woods, though, and I need to get in better shape. I must get back to walking like I used to for the last three or four years and get serious about my diet.

I will start one phase at a time, but overall, this has been particularly good news. When I consider where it was months ago, we are going to take those results and comments and run with it. Thank God that I get another chance to get better.

HEALTH

It appears that at 57 years old, my health has begun to haunt me. I have been overweight my entire life. I've struggled with my weight and, at various points in my life, reduced my weight significantly. Only a few years later, a few months later many times the weight climbed back up. Although my weight has never stopped me until recently from doing anything, it has always been in the back of my mind.

My regret is that I never took my physical appearance more seriously. It got out of control at an early age. I remember a point in grade 10, over the summer holidays before grade 11. I made it a point to get into shape and to get on a diet. Although I was never teased in high school, obviously, I was aware that I was bigger and certainly chunkier than most kids.

Walking into grade 11 after a summer of dieting and getting in shape was quite an experience. I would say though, the attitude with me was different. In fact, a few of my friends I hadn't seen all summer began to call me macho, which would be a form of endearment as I got my weight under control.

Over the years, it has ballooned back up. Now nearing sixty, it has caused some of my ailments that I have been facing in the last year. The funny thing is that when I see people from my high school, many of them still call me macho. This is ironic looking at myself now at well over three hundred pounds and not feeling very macho. If I were to advise my two boys, it would be to take care of your health and weight. Currently, they are thin, however, they obviously have some of my fat genes in them. I just caution them to always be aware and to make sure you are in great physical condition, because as you get older your metabolism slows down. In my young twenties and even into my 30s, losing weight was never a big issue. It was just a matter of discipline. I could diet for three or four months, and I would knock off weight. At the same time, putting weight back on seemed to be as easy as looking at some unhealthy foods. The big regret is that I could never just go into a normal clothing store and purchase clothes. I always had to go to a big and tall store. I remember as a young kid, the clothing classification I required was called husky. There were only a few stores around Windsor that sold husky clothing. Clothing for fat kids would be the summary of it.

It is much, much harder to control your weight as you get older. Now in my late fifties, it is a challenge. I think about what my weight has to do with the heart health situation I am in right now. Be careful guys. You only have one life to live and one body. Cherish your body, and treat it like a temple.

As you can imagine, I am continually putting on a strong face. I don't talk to anybody about my health. I keep it all internal, but by the writing of this book, it is helping me tell somebody about it. I have told my sons a bit about it. They are warriors with the rest of their lives to live, I don't want them to worry about me.

I believe with my attitude that it is what it is, I guess. If I need medication for the rest of my life, then I need it. If I need a machine to help me breathe at night, then let's do it.

I sit here and write with tears running down my eyes thinking about a million different things. Mostly thinking about my mortality. Knowing that I am the same age as when my father passed away. The most important thing I think about is that hopefully I have instructed my boys while they were growing up to know enough and have enough street smarts.

Looking over at three pill bottles and taking what will be my fourth pill today. I guess on the positive side, this is what is keeping everything coordinated and my heart working properly. Until they can figure out exactly what the solution is, then that is the way I exist. It is just extremely hard to think about the future. Knowing that you are dependent on a machine at night for sleeping and medication for the rest of my life. I hope with all my heart that we can get this figured out and to be able to get back to living.

Although I have always been heavy set, I have always seemed to be continually active, very coordinated, and healthy as a youth and adult. I now sit here with a blood pressure machine and a device that measures my blood sugar that will again be a surprise to my boys. I have recently had cholesterol pills added to my medicine diet by my physician. He stated I was on the edge of requiring cholesterol pills and that it would be a short time until they would be required. The recommendation was to begin with the pills before it was an issue.

It's a tough road as I never smoked in my life, I never drank and never did drugs. However, I did eat, and I sit here overweight and not in good enough health to get exercising. The last five years I have been very regimented, and unbelievably I have lost weight. I worked out on the treadmill on a very regular basis. Although the doctor said I can get back to normal, I just don't have a great feeling about walking on a treadmill, even though I could start slowly. It is just very daunting to know that I have put myself into this situation. Other times, I think while I openly walk around daily, what is the difference if I am on a treadmill?

Right now, I would just like the OK from a doctor to say hey you can get back to doing what you normally do. Now, I must admit that I have heard a version of that, and it is just scary. I just have not bothered to get back to the exercising that I used to do the last five years. Now I sit here and think I don't want to do it because I am worried about doing damage to my heart.

My thinking is odd and surely flawed....don't work out because I may hurt my heart. Yet, I know my heart needs me to drop the beef, so I can work out and get in shape. I must admit losing weight as I get older is certainly more difficult than when younger.

However, things have changed since January 2024 with my mindset. I have committed to get in shape and drop weight. I am happy to say that as of this mid-April, I have dropped 52 lbs. I have lots to go, but I am gaining momentum. I am wearing clothes from five years ago and adjusting my belt to be smaller.

The mind is a wonderful thing in many ways. As I dropped my first few pounds, suddenly I began to think differently. Suddenly, I had the belief of ultimate accomplishment. My two boys have been a great support, and their encouragement is phenomenal. I do have a goal in my brain, but as I do, that will be held inside. The plan is to keep going and going where at some point I am feeling great again.

As former president Trump stated, let's make Crain great again.

FAMILY DYNAMICS

I'm not sure exactly why I'm authoring this book, but as I stated above, I believe the events of the last six or seven months have had me thinking about a myriad of items including mortality. I try to keep a particularly good disguise and not let my emotions out, and I try not to show any anxiousness in front of my kids, but I must admit I am nervous.

I think the way we will start this is probably right at the very beginning with some background, and then we'll run through highlights and low lights throughout my life of 57 years. Although a fancy name is a memoir, it is again, like my other books, I just want to open my life, and let my kids know exactly what their father was all about for the last five decades.

Unfortunately, my family is a little bit different, but I will try to explain it to you. My mother and father were married and obviously had me. Both my mother and father had previous marriages and previous kids. My mother had Gary, whom I have written about in all my previous books, and my father had a son Lloyd. Gary lived with us although he was 11 years older, and we were not super close as kids. I was in grade school and my brother Gary was out of high school, married and working full time. My father's son Lloyd has never been in my life since the beginning. He lived with his mother as the situation back in the day always had the kids from a divorce living with their mothers. Although Lloyd did drop around a few times as an adult when I was a teenager. I certainly could never say we sat down and talked or had a relationship.

I called Gary my brother, and I have known him as my brother my whole life. I never bothered to ever say half-brother, stepbrother, Gary is just my brother.

It's too bad our family never had three generations alive at the same time. I didn't know my grandmothers and grandfathers because my last grandparent passed away when I was only two years old. I grew up never knowing a grandparent, whether it was a grandmother or grandfather from either my mother or father's side. It was just normal that others had grandparents, but I didn't. It was never something I really worried about, and it never bothered me. Basically, I had my mom, dad, and brother.

My mother was always a stay-at-home parent, took care of the household, prepared dinner, laundry, cleaning, shopping, and basic homemaker responsibilities. My father was a general laborer who worked at a tire company where he fixed flat tires on large semi-trucks. I would say that my father would be my inspiration for my never quit attitude. I hopefully have passed on this mentality to my boys. I must say that in the 20 years that I had him in my life before he passed, I only remember two times he ever quit doing a project. No matter how difficult the task, he always completed them. He was educated through grade 7, as is common during the depression era children were out working. He had two brothers and three sisters in his family. He lived in an area of Windsor, Ontario that the neighbourhood was called Tin Can City. I was told that this area was very much lower class, and the houses were made of steel because it was very cheap to purchase. The neighborhood was called Tin Can City because of the steel siding on the houses.

Any of my philanthropy and caring for others as well as empathy came from my mother. Caring for others was a daily attribute for my mother. My mother had four sisters and two brothers. My mothers' siblings that I remember the most were my aunt Ruth Anne and aunt Shirley. Aunt Ruth Ann was the youngest sibling on my mother's side. She was a single parent with two kids, Debbie and Richard. They did not have all the money in the world as she didn't have a job and lived on social assistance. My mom helped her out a lot, and my parents helped with housing, often moving her multiple times per year. Sunday dinners often included aunt Ruth Anne and her kids.

The uncle I remember the most was Uncle Jerry who passed away in a car accident. He was tragically run over at an intersection while crossing the road.

The other aunt I remember very closely was Aunt Shirley who had 10 kids. One of the daughters, Simonne, was my age. So, between Aunt Shirley and Aunt Ruth Anne there were four kids very close to the same age. I knew those three cousins the best, and I'm very thankful for those relationships. Sadly, my cousin Debbie has recently passed, leaving Richard, myself, and Simonne. Although I knew the other children from my Aunt Shirley, there was a significant age difference.

That is a little bit about the background and unfortunately, I don't know my four grandparents to provide any deep background on my family. My mother's father was a bus driver in Windsor Ontario, and I am not sure of my father's parents' occupation.

I would say my family was low middle income growing up. We never wanted for anything growing up. I did not have the best of everything but always had new clothes, awesome birthdays, and Christmas gifts. It was all about how you lived, not where you lived. I have always tried to keep that philosophy as my kids were growing up.

Boys Severely Jolted By Electricity

Sparks Fly As Lad
Hits Rail With Tin

550 Volts Smack Boys As They Cross
M. C. R. With Material for Chicken
Coop; Hand of One Badly Burned

WHEN he fell across the live third rail on the Michigan Central right-of-way leading to the Windsor entrance of the M.C.R.R. tunnel, Lloyd Crain, 8-year-old son of Mr. and Mrs. John Crain, of 1047 Wellington street, narrowly escaped death this week by electrocution. He was saved by a playmate, Melvin Perry, 9-year-old son of Mr. and Mrs. William Perry, 1071 Wellington street.

Demands Water
In Old Fountain

BROTHERLY LOVE

I often wonder if my brother and I were as close as we could have been growing up. I will admit it was hard especially as a young kid since he is 11 years older than me. Although Gary was a huge supporter of me in every activity, we never really hung around, and I would say it was only because of our age difference. When you think about the spread, I would have been going into kindergarten at the age of five when Gary was in grade 11. Suddenly, I was in grade three, and he was out of high school. Grade six, and he was off to get his trade school electrician's certification. Shortly after that, he got married and purchased his first home with his wife Barb.

A curious thing and a natural progression as I got older was that we became a bit closer but certainly did not have everyday conversations. Three things happened to bring our relationship closer as I read a text from him. The first thing, we got closer when my father died. We both had to help our mother in various activities, home improvements, and daily tasks. We just participated in helping her out, with no deep conversations.

The next thing that brought us closer together was the passing of my mother. At this point, it was just him and I. Going through our parents' deaths 17 years apart along with the grieving would create a different bond. I would say it brought us much closer together.

The final thing that brought us closer was the COVID pandemic starting in 2020. Our families were isolated and bound to their homes. My brother and I still today, which is three years later, text each other every day to make sure everything is fine.

AGHB...All good here bro is our comment text that goes back and forth. Yes, all good, how is the family? Love you, our last salutation to one another. During covid and now after covid, I have told my brother and he's told me, love you more than any other time during our lives.

As I write this, I'm 57 years old, and Gary is sixty-eight. Although we never had any big giant issues together, I am sure there were some squabbles here and there. He was in the role of a big brother, and I have always respected that relationship.

Barb and Gary would often bring me on vacations as they were fortunate enough to have access to trips. Gary and Barb took care of me whenever required. One time during my twenties, I got myself into a crazy situation where my financial debt was piling up from buying stupid items including cars. When I asked them if they could help me out financially, they said yes. I don't remember the amount, but it was around $10,000. It was a 100% loan to be fully paid back to them every month. I made it a specific point of always paying them back on time monthly. Obviously with huge thanks and love for helping me out of that situation.

Another life lesson that my brother and sister-in-law taught me was to be financially responsible. That included having a budget. At the end of the day, if you're spending more money than you're earning, it's going to be a bad situation. I have learned that as quickly as it gets bad, it will get worse much quicker. I would like to take a moment here to say that I love you to my brother and sister-in-law. As well as their two kids, AJ, and JoJo. Thank you for all the help and guidance and the friendship throughout my life. Obviously, losing my father at a tender age of 20 years old was hard and influenced me, and I leaned on my brother for guidance. I know that both him and Barb have always watched out for my well-being. Again, thank you and love you.

DAD'S SIDE OF THE FAMILY

My father's side of the family is a bit of a mystery. I only really knew two of his sisters. My dad was the youngest of six siblings, three boys and three girls. I recall one of his brothers passed away when I was around 6 or 7 years old and was the oldest sibling. Uncle Nelson was married, and I don't think very well off. I don't ever remember him having a job or children. I recall meeting him only a couple of times before he passed.

I would say my father's family was close but not close enough to talk every day. Occasionally, at Christmas, most of them and their families would get together, and I would get to meet my aunts and uncles, their spouses, and kids. My father's oldest sister Aunt Christina I met a few times at large family get togethers. Aunt Christina wasn't around too much although she lived in Windsor, where we all lived.

I remember my uncle Duncan a little bit more because, at one point, we lived in his house for a few months when I was incredibly young. I don't recall very many details, but I do know he was married with at least a son and a daughter. I don't recall his wife at all. His son John was closer to my brother's age. He would be at least 15 years older than me, so it wasn't like we were close. Many years later, I would run across Johnny at a horse racing track. We chatted only briefly, as we knew each other but nothing in depth. It always looked like he was going through hard times. I don't ever remember hearing that he had a job.

I was close to two of my father's sisters, aunt Sarah, and aunt Helen. My aunt Sarah and aunt Helen were two sisters who lived side by side in their own houses. They lived in the same neighborhood where they would have grown up and down the street from Uncle Duncan. I would say I was probably the closest to my Aunt Sarah. She just loved me to the end, spoiling me whenever she could. Aunt Sarah had two sons Ron and Lou, Aunt Helen had three sons, I believe. I knew Ron and Louie but not my Aunt Helen's sons.

Aunt Helen seemed serious at times. I remember when we went to her house, you could never go in the living room. I hung out with my mom and dad in the kitchen and in her backroom which was set up like a sitting room. They had two beautiful boxer dogs that I vividly remember. Although I don't recall their names, I remember they were big and friendly. My uncle Bob was Aunt Helen's husband. He owned a trucking business located behind their house.

Aunt Sarah worked for a long time at a local toy store. Yes, I did say toy store, and it was in downtown Windsor. All they sold were toys, puzzles, and games for kids. I recall occasionally, we would go to that store. I would get a toy from my aunt because she did spoil me. After the toy store, my mom and I and my aunt would go across the street to a very popular restaurant. The restaurant's name was The Chicken Court, and I remember it was on Pelissier street. Many local business workers would go there for lunch as it was a very popular place and often quite busy.

I remember when the toy store was closing the business for good, my aunt Sarah reached out to my mom. We went down there one day to visit. I recall her giving me toys from the store that she would have to pay for at a discount. I recall getting three or four different toys and proudly carrying them out to the car. What a great memory about a great aunt.

The next memory is with both my aunt Helen and aunt Sarah on Saturday mornings. My aunt Sarah, aunt Helen and my mother would make arrangements to meet at the local grocery store. My mom and I would drive there and meet them. The name of the grocery store was Dominion Grocery. Once done shopping, I would bring our groceries out to the car where I would help load the car for my aunts and mother, and in return, we would go to the store next door. Next to the Dominion Grocery store was Kmart which was basically equivalent to the Zellers of these days. They sold everything at Kmart including clothes, shoes, hardware, pharmacy, and they also had a bakery counter and a cafeteria. I don't believe they are around in Canada anymore, but I believe they have a few stores still left in the United States.

After we were done shopping at Kmart, it would usually include a trip to the bakery counter. My Aunt Sarah again would buy me what they call a bear claw, which is a Danish doughnut type of pastry. I would eat it as everybody chatted in one of the aisles or walked around doing some more shopping. After shopping at the grocery store and Kmart, we were hungry for lunch. Kmart had a cafeteria, where you stood in line, walked around a food counter and ordered food. My mother would get something very simple, and of course, my aunt Sarah would tell me to order whatever I wanted. I would most likely get a cheeseburger, some French fries, and a pop. My aunt Sarah would pay for everything as a little treat. We would all sit down at the tables and eat while everyone would shoot the breeze. Aunt Helen would ask me what I was up to and how my hockey games were going. We did that weekly ritual just about every week for what must have been five years. As I got older, I didn't go, but it was a ritual that the ladies liked to do every Saturday. Grocery shopping and having a bite to eat at Kmart. A vivid memory that I still recall fondly.

On a side note, Kmart would have what they called a blue light special. The store would announce over the speaker system that in a certain aisle, at a certain time, a certain product was on sale for a certain price. The blue light host had a little cart with the products, and a light post with a flashing blue coloured light that showed above the aisle tops. You would grab the product that was on the blue light special, and you could cash out right there at a special low price. The specials would happen once or twice while we were there shopping for a couple hours. It was quite an event to watch unfold. When they announced the special, and you saw the blue light flashing, customers would quickly gather. All the customers would hustle and see what the product was and if they wanted to purchase. Just a sign of the old times with something that doesn't happen anymore. It was a fun event for everybody to watch the blue light flashing and then hustle over because quantities were always very limited. You had to get there quickly to get the product at that discounted price.

The age difference between my father and his oldest sibling was approximately 20 years. Although there was a big age gap, they appeared to get along from what I recall. I never witnessed any squabbling among the brothers and sisters. I didn't know many of them real close, but they seemed to be jovial, friendly people. Obviously with my aunt Sarah and aunt Helen being the closest to me. I remain in contact with Aunt Sarah's grandkids and occasionally see her sons Ronnie and Louie around town. That's the story of the Crain family.

MY FATHER'S CONNECTION TO ANIMALS

My father was always an animal loving person with his first love being horses. He owned horses, trained horses, and showed horses at rodeos. Now this was all prior to me being born, but I still heard about it a bit from his friends that we had visited. In fact, in my garage, I have a few pieces of his horse equipment tucked away in a cardboard box. In my garage, I have sets of cowboy boot spurs, horse blankets and horse bits that my father used for showing horses and trick riding. Unfortunately, I don't remember ever seeing my dad ride or train a horse. Occasionally, I would hear conversations between my father and his friends regarding horses.

I remember him reminding me when I was young about my name. He explained that I was named after his friend in the horse business, Mr. Greg Wright. Greg went on to own and race many horses in the standardbred circuit across North America for many years. Apparently, he was exceptionally good and a recognizable name in the horse racing industry. Greg Wright and my dad had a chance to go to what was called groomers school. This meant they learned different details about maintaining horses and became registered groomsmen, which is a certificate to care, race and raise horses. As I understood it, my dad did not end up going to the school. I am not sure the reason, but Greg went and became quite successful in the standardbred horse racing industry. An additional fun fact that many would not know is that my godfather was also a friend of my father and was a horseman. I do remember visiting him a few times over the years. His name was Bill Rocheleau, and he lived in the country. I distinctly remember going to his farm and that the water in the bathroom and kitchen spelled like sulphur and had stained the sinks. It's weird what you remember as a kid.

The next thing that I have an animal memory of is of my father raising pigeons. He had a friend who I called uncle Bob. They were long-time friends back to his horse days. These pigeons were called fancy pigeons, where you raised them for their looks including colour, size, and feather quality. We had a pigeon coop in the backyard when we lived in Windsor. A small little housing area, where the birds could come inside the coop and out to a small flying area that was covered with wire. He had many distinct types of these pigeons. These ones were not like you see on the streets of major cities called homing pigeons, although that will come up shortly. I remember often in the summer months especially, we would place the pigeons in a crate and travel to different shows and community fairs around Ontario. You would show your pigeon in a cage to judges against many other pigeons of the same breed.

You could win ribbons and trophies at each show, which was quite a thrill for me when I was young. I remember, at one point after my father's passing, we were cleaning out different storage boxes, and there were at least 50 trophies that we had won over the years with his show pigeons. Uncle Bob that I speak about mostly showed chickens and a few pigeons. He also lived in Windsor at the time when it was legal, and no one bothered you if you kept your pigeons in the coops. The family would get in a truck with the chickens and pigeons loaded into cardboard boxes with air holes. My mom, me, uncle Bob, and my father would head down the highway to the local show. We would set up on a Friday night, where we would put the birds in their cages at the fair. Saturday morning those areas were closed off to the public to allow the judges to look at the birds. They would decide which pigeon or chicken was the best in the show and hang the ribbons on the cage. If you've been to any of these fairs, you also notice that horses are on display with pigs, sheep along with ducks, pigeons, and chickens. I got to see many distinctive styles of pigeons, chickens, and animals while walking through the many livestock and fowl barns at these shows. Some funny looking, normal looking, some short, some tall. That was my exposure to different animals and a great hobby for my father.

At one point, he got tired of raising show pigeons. It was at the time when we moved out of the Windsor house for the very first time. When we moved to Lasalle, he was reacquainted with a childhood friend who lived down the street. His last name was Langlois, and they used to call him Cricket from what I recall. Anyway, this gentleman was a pigeon owner, but he raced his pigeons. Nowadays, you may hear about these homing pigeons because Mike Tyson, the famous boxer raises them. These are the pigeons that are quite common sitting on the sidewalks of major cities looking for scrap pieces of food and corn. It wasn't long after a few nights chatting with Cricket that my father was into raising and the racing of homing pigeons.

He built a pigeon coop, but this time the pigeons all stayed inside the coop until he let them freely fly around the house for exercise. When training the homing pigeons, you would box them in a distinctive design wicker cage. Next, you would drive away to a location in the countryside, let them out of the box, and they would fly home to their home coop.

Training sessions would start out by taking the birds down the block, and then a few miles away, and then 50 miles away, and finally a training length of 90 miles from their home. Eventually, they learned the skill of coming home, hence the reason they are named homing pigeons. These are the types of pigeons that you would hear about in old war stories that delivered messages from one place to another during war times. Racing pigeons is the same idea, where they would return home as fast as possible.

There was a local racing pigeon club located in Windsor where the members would show up to a building on Friday night with their pigeons that were going to race. I remember it was a small club with a simple garage to meet in where the guys who raced pigeons would gather on training and race days. It was all very official because there was money bet and exchanged for the races. They would make small bets in old English currency. The club members would put the pigeons into large baskets for their travel to the location where hundreds of pigeons would be released simultaneously. On Saturday morning, a driver and his helpers would bring all the crates of pigeons to whatever length the race, whether it was a 50-mile race, 200-mile race or a 500-mile race. Yes, that is true, a five-hundred-mile race with pigeons. At the proper moment, they would all get set free and the pigeons would fly home as fast as they could, often taking hours and sometimes arriving at their home coop the next day, depending on length of the race.

On each racing pigeon's leg was an official rubber band. The pigeon racing bands would be taken off when they returned to their coop. The pigeon would fly into the coop where my father would grab the pigeon and remove the specific band. The rubber band would be placed in a capsule and then placed into a time clock that created a timestamp on a roll of paper. The owner would rotate the timestamp printing lever so there is an actual time stamp on a piece of paper. The pigeon owners would wait around for a few hours at home for all the pigeons to return. Eventually, all would gather Saturday or Sunday afternoon and bring their time clocks. The clocks would be opened from the secured place they were in prior to the race. The race official would eventually figure out who won the race and how long it took each bird to fly home. Next, they would find who made a couple of dollars and who lost with their bets.

Now the curious thing, my dad would develop his own champions through breeding. We never had the money to go buy champion racing pigeons for hundreds of dollars. At the time, he would raise a flock of racing pigeons. He did this because he enjoyed the activity and obviously enjoyed animals. He won several races and was certainly the unknown guy racing against the guys with the money and years of experience. It was all about having a keen eye and closely watching the birds for different tendencies. He would remember which pigeon was a fast one for a certain length of race and which one was not so fast. Then he tried to have the fastest one's breed with each other. Eventually, he got a strain of pigeons that were surprisingly fast without spending a lot of money. Many in the racing pigeon community would simply buy a winner for hundreds of dollars. My dad, it seems, always liked to be the guy who raised the animal to be a champion and would never just buy from somebody. He always liked being the underdog in those types of situations.

Now, I do recall there is a bit of a crossover. Before we left Lasalle, we got rid of the pigeons, and my father built a small area down in our basement where he raised canaries and finches. When we moved back to Windsor, he continued raising canaries and finches. He built a new and much fancier building; aviary was the correct name. The aviary had cages with different areas to raise canaries and finches. It was the same idea as the fancy pigeons in that they were raised for their looks and colour. Again, my father raised them and never bought the champion. There would be various canary and finch shows across our local Essex County. You would bring them to a local show where they would be judged to win ribbons and trophies.

I remember he would travel around to visit other canary or finch breeders found around the area. They would chat casually with him, and sometimes he would buy a canary for maybe $10 at the time. Then, he would raise them and breed them and ultimately, try to produce a champion.

That is where I got my first bug of animals and what it took to raise animals. I never spent hours and hours with my dad to learn the skill of raising pigeons or raising finches or canaries. However, my good friend when we lived in Windsor would often spend hours with my father to learn how to raise birds. He was really interested, and he would spend a few hours here and there chatting casually with my father in his pigeon coop or aviary. Often, he would just help feed and water and assist my father in packing things to go to the next show. I never had a lot of interest in doing those tasks or learning about the birds. Primarily, it was because of the timing, I was in my mid-teens at the time, and in my eyes, it was not cool to hang out with your dad. Raising pigeons, canaries or finches was not part of being cool. You know, 35 years later, I wish I'd spent way more time with my dad to learn new skills, including caring for animals. I can speak a little bit about it, having listened to him talk to his friends who would come over for coffee. They would chat casually about raising birds, pigeons, or horses. It was quite an experience and certainly different and not mainstream. If you were to ask your ten closest friends about raising animals, they would look at you like you had three different heads. When you talk about racing pigeons or canaries to the vast population, those are birds that you see in a pet store sitting in a cage.

I wish I would've known more about my dad's horse raising and showing part of his life. Obviously, it was before I was born, but it is a cool aspect that I do, in fact, have a couple of items from when he was in the horse business. Horses are a bit more mainstream versus birds and chickens. I would say that he was an animal person. My love for animals stems from him, even though I didn't take part much. As I grew up, we always had tiny Chihuahua dogs often only weighing two or three pounds. I don't recall any reason we had those little dogs, but we always seemed to have one running around, sleeping on your pillow, jumping on your lap and just being a tiny dog. Contrary to widespread belief, they were not yappy little dogs. They were well behaved, which was not common with the little yappers.

I do recall a couple of times my father having been gifted other dogs. I guess with his love for animals someone gave him a retired racing greyhound dog at one point. That was back in the early nineteen eighties when that breed of dog was less popular than they are now. Nowadays, you have rescue organisations that obtain greyhounds after they have retired from the racing industry down in the southern USA. I don't know where he came from or how we got him, but I remember we may have had the greyhound for a week. One day it was out in the backyard, and the next thing you know, he was missing. We suspected someone stole him.

I also recalled when we lived in LaSalle, for a short, abbreviated period we had a big fluffy dog called a Chow Chow. Again, no idea how we got it, but we had him for a few months. I seem to recall we were doing one of my dad's friends a favor while they were gone on vacation overseas. I am not exactly sure, but we had the dog for probably a month, and then we didn't have it anymore.

FARMER CRAIN

This chapter is about an old farmhouse along with forty-seven acres located in Bothwell ON. that my mother and father owned for about 15 years. Sometimes, we would all go up on the weekends. Mom and I would have events including hockey, so we did not go up every single weekend. Dad would drive to the farm after work on Friday and return on Sunday evening to go to his regular job Monday morning.

My dad worked a full-time job during the week and was also on call for any tire repairs throughout the week. Often, he would work a full shift, and he would get calls throughout the night to repair tires on the highway. I don't know how many hours a week he would work at his regular job, suffice to say it was surely over 60 hours a week, and it seemed he was always on call. He would work extra hours during the week to allow him to get the odd weekend off to maintain the farm in Bothwell.

I remember hearing that, at one point, my father had transferred up to the local Uniroyal store located in London, which was about 40 minutes away from the farm. We moved up to Bothwell to live when I was three years old. From what I understand, we only lived there for less than a year and eventually moved back to the Windsor area.

A couple of cute memories that I recall. We were living there for a summer or were on vacation at the farm. We had an old barn with a few chickens and some geese. I distinctly remember I had gone out to the barn by myself. As a little kid, I thought it would be nice to go and pet the geese. Lo and behold, the little buggers ran me down the laneway back to the house. They were squawking and hissing behind me, trying to nip at me. Let me tell you, those geese can be mean, nasty, and very intimidating feathery cobra chickens.

Another memory from the farm is that my mother and dad, I remember, went to a livestock auction where they auctioned off pigs, horses, goats, sheep, and other farm animals. I remember for some reason my mother felt sorry for this small black coloured pony being auctioned. The pony was obviously mistreated, and my mother ended up buying it for $15. My dad had been in another location at the auction and did not know about the purchase until later. We were just there watching the auction, and the next thing you know; my mother had bought a pony. I recall there was a rule that all animals sold had to be checked out by a veterinarian before leaving the auction building. I remember my mother and dad having a conversation that the examination and the medicine was well over $100 for all, which was a crazy amount of money. I am guessing nowadays it would be well over $1000 for a $15 pony. The next pony adventure was to get it back to the farm. One small issue is that we had no horse trailer to bring the pony home and obviously, we were not prepared. The solution was to walk it home using our car. We had a rope hooked onto a bridle which goes over the pony's head. My mother held the one end of the rope through the open car window. We slowly walked the pony back to the farm located a few miles away driving on the shoulder of the highway.

It's a bit fuzzy, but I know we owned it for a while, and we called it Midnight. I don't think we owned it exceedingly long. Obviously, we didn't live at the farm, we were just up there visiting on weekends. When we were gone, my dad had a neighbor feeding and watering all the animals daily.

I remember going up there on weekends occasionally, with my father and my mom. I can nearly remember the whole entire route to the farm in Bothwell. One thing I do remember is at one-point enroute there are many oil pumps up in the Bothwell area, and I remember naming one road Stinky Road. It was a dirt road, and you could smell the oil being pumped in the field near the dirt road. It was only about 20 minutes before we got to the actual farm. It was like a milestone for me to know we were close to the farm, old school GPS.

The other thing I remember on the way to the farm was a small old-fashioned confectionery. Imagine an old cluttered, neighbourhood confectionery that sold the essentials that were necessary. It was cramped with small aisles, wooden floors, old rickety floors and doors and a pop machine. At that time, you could purchase a Coca-Cola in an actual glass bottle from a cooler. You would put your coins in it, and you would reach into the cooler and grab a bottle of Coke. The bottles were small there, about six inches tall but they were a treat going to the farm after we were done going down Stinky Rd. We would stop and grab a pop and chips or a chocolate bar. My dad would give me a couple of nickels, and I would get the pop from the cooler.

That is the memory of going to the farm in Bothwell. The house was a 2-story house however from what I recall, we never used the upstairs. My dad had a bed in the kitchen area when he lived up there on the weekends. Just a bed in the kitchen area because there was a wood burning stove. The upstairs had three bedrooms with no furniture. There was nothing going on upstairs at all. There was another room downstairs from what I remember that had another bed. Upstairs had kerosene burning lights. You could put liquid in the lamp, and you started the flame with a match and then it would burn all night. I don't remember ever using upstairs. We even blocked it off so the heat would stay downstairs when we were there at the farm.

The other thing I remember is that the farm had a garage that I thought was super cool as a kid. The garage must have been for a mechanic as there was a pit where you could change the vehicle oil. The repair person would've walked down under the pit before someone would drive over the top of it. I always remember that garage door being locked, as my parents didn't want anybody to fall in the pit. Just above that garage was another room, and I remember having chickens and pigeons up there. You walked into it from the outside, and you had to crouch to walk around. I must admit I am not sure exactly why we had chickens and pigeons upstairs, but I know it was not for exceptionally long.

Here is another interesting tidbit from the farm days. There was no running water. We had a fresh water well with a manual pump outside of the garage. You would pump the well using a long handle moving it up and down, and it would pump water from the deep well out of the spout. You would need to fill up buckets if you were taking a bath or cooking, putting the pot on the wood burning stove to heat. Yes, a wood burning stove to heat up a bucket of water and then my mother would throw it in the bathtub, and I could have a warm bath. We did not live there long and certainly didn't live there steadily. We lived back in Windsor before I ever went to school.

The farm has always been a great memory for me, and I wanted to share it with my boys. My boys were eleven and eight at the time of my great idea. The boys and I always used to go for car rides around our area. We would find parks and different things to occupy our time. During my divorce, the time spent with the boys was precious to me. Although custody was shared, it was important that there was a sense of normalcy for my kids.

One day I had the bright idea to find the Bothwell farmhouse and show the kids. Sure, enough, we jump in the car and start the adventure. I remembered just enough of the route to eventually get us there. I stopped a couple of times at various places and tried to explain to the person where I was trying to go. I would look for landmarks that were 40 years old, sometimes they were there, and sometimes they were gone. I had thought the highway was Highway 77 or Highway 79, but eventually with many wrong turns, I eventually found it.

The farm looked different then when we owned it 40 years ago. It was still yellow brick but now there was a porch on it. When we eventually located the farm, it was obvious that it was the house that we used to own. The farm's big barn was gone, the garage was gone. The front of the house had fresh style windows, and it had a porch, but it was the house. We drove down the long driveway to view it closer. Then I left the boys in the car and walked up and knocked on the door. A gentleman came out, and I explained my long-winded story that we owned it 25 years ago at the time. He seemed very cordial and believed my story as he walked off the porch and towards the driveway.

I explained there was a barn back years ago and a garage and about an old water pump. Lo and behold, the gentleman told me to grab the kids, and that he was going to show us something. The kids got out of the car, and we walked to where I remembered the well was previously. It was the actual pump that I used to pump up and down to get water. It was not working, but it was still there. It might have been just a piece to look at, but sure enough the old pump brought back a flood of memories. I think it was more of a thrill for myself, but the kids did get a kick out of it. Occasionally, they mention the farm and ask, where is that farm where you used to live? That is the story of the little yellow farmhouse in Bothwell.

Towards the end of ownership, we would simply rent out the property to another farmer who would come in and farm the acreage. The funds from selling the farm provided enough money to purchase our house in Sandwich West. I remember my mother and father having a conversation about the purchase of the Sandwich West house, and they were worried about the high price of the house at the time. Since we weren't using the farm much, and almost not at all in the winter, it made sense to sell it and apply the money to the purchase of our dream home.

NO LOYALTY

Just to set the table on this one, my father and mother owned a duplex in Windsor. They had kept our house in Windsor after we moved to Lasalle into our dream home; a three bedroom brick home, with the basement completed with a great living area and a large yard.

My dad was a labourer his whole career, and he worked in Windsor at a company called Uniroyal. He repaired tires on semi-trucks, passenger cars and anything in between. To say my father was hardworking would be an understatement. He worked 45 hours a week during the day shift, and then he was on call during the evening. On call meant you would carry a pager, which was a device to alert the carrier of a message from someone. The pager would beep and vibrate, he would call the answering service, and they would tell him where the vehicle was located to have the tire repaired. There were no set hours to be on call regardless of time or functions that he may be attending. He would put on his work clothes and be off at all hours of the night to repair a tire. At the time of his passing, he had more than 35 years at the same company.

He was 52 years old when the company went through restructuring. They felt the need to rid the company of their senior labourers. Anyone over 50 years old was permanently laid off. We were approximately three years into a brand new home. My dad had a minimal education level of grade seven or eight, and his skill was fixing tires, which meant that employment by another company would be extremely difficult.

Suddenly, our family income and any ability for my father to provide for his family was eliminated. He went from a very meager income to unemployment payments of a few hundred dollars a month. This was quite devastating for a proud family man. He had never been unemployed in his entire life and now would be facing a limited amount of money to feed and house his family.

My father heard from other employees across the country that had the same situation happen to them. They were all over 50 years old with no job and income to support their families. They had to learn how to file for employment.

After talking to some fellow Uniroyal employees, they banded together and hired a lawyer. After more than a year of being unemployed, it was determined that the company committed age discrimination, and a settlement was reached. From what I understand (I was only 15 years old at the time), there were no monies given back, but the company allowed everyone to have their jobs back in the same position at the same wage.

During that year of unemployment, my father was hustling to earn any extra money possible at the time. He knew tires, and he had connections in the tire industry. He would pick up any used discarded tires and bring them to a local rubber manufacturing plant. They would, in turn, give him a few dollars for the used tires. These local companies that he had worked with for 30 years really helped my father. They knew the situation my father was in and would simply give him the tires to get a couple of bucks. Now, when I say a couple of dollars, I mean it was very minimum. I remember hearing conversations of him making an extra $20 or $30 a week. At the time, in the early eighties, we had to watch what we spent. With only a small unemployment check and a little extra cash on the side, we scraped through.

Now, please understand none of this affected me. I never heard much about it. There were never any conversations. I never heard that we cannot do this, or we cannot have that, or we need to watch our spending. The little knowledge I have gathered was by just walking into conversations between my mother and father who never spoke of family financial stress. Basically, my mom and dad were dealing with this situation. Once the lawsuit was settled, my dad went back to the same position that he had started more than 30 years prior.

I can only imagine the stress level at that point going to work each day. I never remember him complaining, whining, or hating the company. He just dealt with it and went on to provide for his family with the situation he was given.

The one thing I do remember was he ended up back at Uniroyal at the time I would've been in Grade 13. All the emotional and financial stress changed our lives forever. My parents sold their dream home in Lasalle, and we moved back to the duplex home that luckily, they had kept over the years. My aunt lived upstairs while we had the main floor. I would say that it was a saviour having that home. Getting a few dollars for rent from a cousin and his family who lived downstairs in the duplex while we lived in LaSalle certainly supplemented my father's lack of income. Family upstairs and family downstairs renting from my parents. Ultimately the family was helping the family.

All the same neighbours were there, my friends that I had stayed connected with while living in LaSalle were still living in the neighbourhood. For me, it was not a big adjustment, but I would guess it was an adjustment for my parents to move from their dream home back to Windsor.

There was no fanfare and no sadness. We just moved forward. At 17 years old, you don't know everything you do as a 57-year-old. I cannot imagine how I would feel being unemployed for more than a year after working for a company for more than 30 years. I would think that it was an incredibly stressful time in my father and mothers' life.

Fast forward 15 years. After experiencing that situation, I was going through a divorce and in a highly stressful time of my life. There was no sense in complaining, whining, and moaning. I just did what I had to do. In one way, it was similar, yet in many other ways, extremely different from my parents' situation.

You learn from your experiences, good or bad. I am now thinking that being in the middle of that situation taught me many things. I think it would have taught me to just roll with the punches. Don't play the blame game, and just do what you must do to get through it. At that young age, you certainly are not aware of a learning point. You are in the middle of it and may not understand all the intricacies. I am thankful that I learned from that example and have used that philosophy throughout my life.

PASSING OF THE PATRIARCH

This chapter will be very emotional in a bunch of ways. I have spoken a few times in my various books about the death of my father. In this chapter, I go deep into the weeds. I remember it like it was yesterday. My mother and father had decided, uncharacteristically, to take a trip to the Chicago area to look at some canaries and finches similar to the ones he was raising. It was the long weekend of our Thanksgiving, which happens to be in October. They had a little old pickup truck. It was still only a few years after my dad had lost his job and then went back, and life was somewhat in a normal state. Little did we know, our lives were about to radically change.

They had left on Friday and were planning to return on Sunday, but they actually returned on Saturday. I recall it was on Thanksgiving weekend because there was a local restaurant where I went to have Thanksgiving dinner by myself. All my friends and family were having their traditional dinner with their families. I didn't want to go anywhere as a guest, so I just had dinner by myself at a local restaurant.

I remember when they got home early from what I thought would be an all-weekend trip, it seemed odd. I asked my mother what was going on, and she replied that my dad was not feeling very well. Dad had a sharp pain on the left side of his back that was causing a lot of discomfort. I have mentioned many times that my dad's a tough character, so for him to turn around and drive back five hours, it was serious. It must have been a painful situation. It may have been the next day or later that evening they went to the emergency ward at a local hospital. The medical staff had a look at the situation and determined that it was profoundly serious.

They rushed my father two hours away to the London hospital that could deal with medical emergency heart issues. Obviously, my mother got a hold of me and my brother from the hospital. We raced up to the London hospital. When Gary and I got there, my dad was settled in his bed and was in a state of a medically induced coma. I remember there were four beds in a room, and he was in the last bed on the left-hand side closest to the window. The doctors explained to my mother, myself, and my brother that they were doing testing on him, and they believed it to be some type of heart issue, but they were not exactly sure what was wrong.

We all stayed at the hospital until the next day. My brother, mother and I were told things were progressing, but they still had not determined the reason for the pain. However, my dad was in a much safer and less serious condition. It was a definite sense of relief to know my father's health was improving. That evening, we again stayed at the hospital, sleeping in the waiting rooms. At one point, on the third day, a nurse came to the waiting room and explained that they were still not exactly sure the reason for his pain. He was in a much better state, though, and he would be released later that evening to go home. They would be bringing him out of the coma over the next few hours. I remember visiting my father in his room, and he was looking much better, although very worn out and tired. We had a short visit, and I continued to wait in the lobby until he was to be released.

I remember the doctor coming through the waiting room lobby doors five or six hours later and taking my mother aside. I was genuinely concerned at this point. Obviously, the doctor explained the sad news to our mother. We knew by mom's face that something was going on and immediately jumped up and went to talk to the doctor. He said that, out of nowhere with no warning signs, my dad had an aneurysm of the aorta and had passed. The aorta is the main artery that carries blood away from the heart. When it ruptures, it creates massive internal bleeding. What I understand is that when the aneurism occurs, if untreated, it's almost always fatal. He had passed very quickly after the undetected aneurysm occurred.

Obviously, we all were in shock after hearing the news and not a lot was said to each other in the waiting room. We were in a stunned state of confusion, with many emotions and certainly, some crying. After we regrouped, we all walked in and said our goodbyes to my father. He would pass away at the tender age of 57 years old. I remember driving back home with my brother as the driver, my mother in the passenger seat, and myself in the back seat of his Ford Bronco 2.

My brother called his wife from the hospital to tell her the news. Once we came home, we were still in a state of confusion and stunned. I remember several times in the next day or so going from anger to crying in the shower for 20 minutes so that no one could hear or see me. The next day we had to make the funeral arrangements. This is the time where it hit me with the reality that I would never see or talk to my father again.

Funeral arrangements are where you must pick out the service, the pallbearers, the procedures, and coffin, as an example. I remember being very direct with the funeral person and making sure that everything was going to be perfect. There should be no errors, omissions, or deviations to the family requests. I sit back now, and I would be 100% confident that I was, unfortunately, rude to the funeral director.

When it came to the day of the funeral, I was one of the pallbearers, along with my brother and my father's first son Lloyd. Unfortunately, I don't recall the other three pallbearers.

However, I do recall the trip to the cemetery. The driver of our funeral car was an old grade school friend from the neighborhood in Windsor, and there was a bit of a calm effect having an old friend there. I remember a little portion of the ceremony at the gravesite, where it was the first time I had ever seen anybody grab flowers and gently toss them onto the lowered casket in the ground. I remember there was a bit of a get together at my brothers and sister-in-law's house. I specifically remember sitting in the back seat of the limousine next to Lloyd, where he said something that I thought was stupid at the time. The last time I have ever spoken to or seen my father's first son, Lloyd, was at the funeral of our father, some 38 years ago.

I only got to know my father for 20 years, but he left me with a lifelong imprint. I was 20 years old, and suddenly, it was my mom, myself, and my brother. My brother had moved away with his wife, still in the local area but no longer with my mom and me. This experience toughened me up and certainly matured me quicker than normal. I would like to thank my father for providing me with a foundation that I have, in turn, tried to pass along to my two boys.

Often, I sit here and think about what my father would've thought of my two boys. I know the answer. He would be damn proud of my two sons. His imprint has been passed on to his grandchildren. Obviously, I wish my two boys could have experienced their grandfather. However, there seems to be a generational thing in the Crain family. I did not get to experience my grandparents at all, and my two boys did not get to experience my mother or father. That's why it is so important that they know their mother's parents. They got to know their mother's father up until five years ago when he passed. So, they did get to know their grandparents, just not on my side, unfortunately.

The love of my father and mother is permanently displayed in ink on me. I have a tattoo on my shoulder of a horse's head and praying hands. The horse's head represents my father. There's a horseshoe around it, which represents good luck. Inside the mane of the tattooed horse is a set of praying hands representing my mother and her caring way. An attitude of strong will and never quitting has been absorbed. Dad, I love you dearly, till we meet again.

MOM'S FAMILY

This brings me to describe my mother's side of the family, especially regarding the use of alcohol. Her two brothers and one sister were all alcoholics. They were in and out of rehab throughout their adult lives. The youngest brother I got to know for 20 years here and there is certainly a nice enough guy but with demons he was fighting daily. He was in and out of marriages, had many girlfriends and didn't seem to have much contact with his children. In fact, I don't even know the name of his kids or even know how many he has.

What I do know is that a few times my caring mother would get called from a local bar. They would explain that my uncle was intoxicated and causing trouble. He was in a state that he could not walk or talk, so she had to go pick him up. My mother took him to rehab multiple times. The staff would come out to the car where my uncle was in the back seat slumped over drunk. Many of the staff would recognize my uncle and knew him by his name from previous stays. The staff would get him into the detox process where he would stay for 45 days. Many times, from what I remember, he would complete the rehab program and come back into society where he would be welcomed back into the home of his girlfriend.

A few months later, my mother would get a call from his girlfriend saying that her brother had not been home in two days and was somewhere on the streets. All those situations certainly worried my mother, but it became a regular occurrence.

My mother's other brother also was an alcoholic. Unfortunately, he passed away in a house fire when I was seven years old. I can't comment too much about that situation, but I did understand that he was a cook in the military, at one point.

Now, for about 40 years, I heard about an aunt that I never met until 25 years ago. This aunt had moved to another province and isolated herself from the entire family. She moved out to the west coast of Canada and never had any communication with her brothers or sisters. My mother's youngest sister somehow got hold of her. They began to communicate through letters. There were no cell phones at that time, and there certainly was no money to pay for long distance phone calls.

After a few years, they began to contact each other through phone calls. My mother and her sister were eventually brought into the communication loop. They all began to have calls with their older sister after nearly five decades of very minimal communication.

My brother and his wife were not wealthy, but they had good jobs and huge hearts. They caught wind of the situation that our aunts and our mother were communicating with a long-lost sister. They arranged out of their own pocket to have her flown in to visit my mother and her two sisters and their families.

I remember meeting her. I was in my thirties at the time. My brother and sister-in-law thought it would be a great idea and planned for all the sisters to go to Las Vegas for a few days to have a little bit of fun and see some shows.

During the two week visit, everything seemed to be cordial between the sisters, however, apparently, there was much more to it. The sister that moved out west also was an alcoholic. Upon her return home, I understand she had written a letter to my aunt saying she wished she had never come.

Her letter said she was glad that she never had a relationship or communication with her sisters and their families. She thought their families were all bad people and always flashing their money. She ended the letter, from what I've heard, saying to not bother ever contacting her again.

As you can imagine, the three sisters, my brother and sister-in-law and I were in shock. We were upset, disappointed and angry. I heard rumour that my aunt had tried to reach out to her and never received any reply to letters or phone calls. She went back to isolation from her sisters for the second time.

I write this knowing that my mother had at least three siblings that were alcoholics. I never saw my mother drink. She was not a drinker nor was my father. Occasionally, my father would have a beer with a friend that came over. I never saw either my mother or father just sitting at home having a drink by themselves. I believe my mother's choice of not drinking was due to knowing that her siblings were alcoholics and did not want to risk anything to do with that type of lifestyle.

She had seen all the damage that alcoholism could do to them and their families. None of them had any relationships with their kids and all were divorced. I guess subconsciously, she saw all the hurt that addiction caused and chose to never get into drugs or drinking. I never got into any drinking binges, and I would think that by witnessing my family's issues with alcoholism, I made a very conscious decision to never get into that situation.

MOTHER MEMORIES

This chapter will be very emotional for me to write. My mother, Donna passed away in 2002 when I was 34 years old. I had been married for three years with one son, Linden.

I wish I knew more about my mother's history; but I do know a few things. She was born in Windsor ON. Canada and had multiple brothers and sisters that I spoke about previously. She had a previous marriage to an American citizen and had lived in the states. Her first husband's name was Lou, and my brother Gary was the product of that marriage. I don't ever remember her working. She was always a stay-at-home parent to me. I understand, though, she was a restaurant waitress when she was a single parent.

I do recall going on visits with her and Gary to their relatives in the states a few times a year, often for a Christmas or an Easter gathering. As a young guy, I am again 11 years younger than my brother, it was just relatives we were visiting. It did not matter to me whether he was a brother, stepbrother, half-brother, half uncle or half cousin. Those kinds of details never bothered me as I didn't really worry about it, maybe because of the age, maybe because it was just my mentality. They were just family members as far as I was concerned, whose father was whose, a father, brother, and sister and all that kind of silliness did not concern me.

My mother, with her general giving nature, was a caregiver to anyone she came across. She cared for her brothers, her sisters, friends, and her family. I wish I could recall the birth order of her siblings. I believe she was born towards the middle of the family. I don't recall what her father and mother did for a living, or even where they lived, but I guess somewhere in the Windsor Ontario area.

My mother's education was that of mid high school and taken in Windsor. It's a bit upsetting that I don't know any of the history or heritage of my mother, although I know her birth last name was Mackenzie. I remember her joking at functions with her siblings that their ancestors were kicked out of Scotland, kicked out of England, and ended up over here in Canada. I have no idea if that was just tongue in cheek or was a long lost fact.

My mother was always a mother, wife and then a homemaker. She would make dinner, lunch, and breakfast for the family with her caring nature. I remember her being a little bit stern at some points when it was required.

I would say my dad was easy going in every aspect. In our family household, the mother would deal with the situation and if that was not working to her satisfaction, she would let my father know. At that point, you knew it was serious, and to smarten up, fix the issue and apologize. You did not want dad involved.

My mother grew up in the same kind of atmosphere as my father. I don't remember her ever speaking of wealth or anything like that. Each of my parents had many siblings. I am guessing back in the day; it was tough going financially.

I would say my parents lived lower middle class and then perhaps became middle class later in their lives. Although my brother and I never really wanted for anything, I do recall my mother had to budget their money. They had to do some planning for money for vacation or any expenditures like a TV, washer and dryer, and furniture. My mother led a casual life; she was not into glitz or glamour or anything fancy. I remember at functions or weddings she would occasionally wear a basic dress, more often wearing slacks and a blouse. I would say that her favourite attire at home was a simple T-shirt and sweatpants.

I recall that my mother's favourite thing to do was go fishing off the docks at the waterfront located around Windsor. We would go and purchase worms or minnows, pick up my uncle if he were around at the time, and go fishing. At the very least, she and I would go down to the local fishing hole and sit there in hopes of catching some fish.

You didn't see women fishing often. There were mostly guys fishing, myself and then my mother. We never kept the fish. We would often give the caught fish away to other fishermen. We did not clean them or eat them; it was just a pastime. We would sit on the dock, relax, and simply fish. Sometimes, I would get bored and walk around talking to people, looking at what they had recently caught, and she would just simply sit there all quiet by herself and fish. During the summer months, we would go fishing two or three times a week, and I would say much of the time it would be her initiating the activity.

Some of our fishing stories were quite exciting. I remember one time we caught a big giant snapping turtle, 20 inches in diameter, out of a local watering hole. Another time, my uncle mentioned to us that he, unfortunately, had snagged a dead body in the Detroit River.

I don't ever recall fishing on a boat with my mom or dad. She was not a swimmer. She seemed afraid and always concerned about the water. She would always be worried about me on the dock or at any beaches.

Occasionally, when we would go on a summer vacation, we would bring our rods, reels and tackle box. My dad would fish for a little bit, although certainly not an avid angler like my mother.

He would drive us to where we would want to go out of town to go fishing. We would toss the frog around for a few hours and then head back to the campsite.

Another vivid memory that I have is my mother's cooking. I'm upset for not paying more attention to it now. I would say her cooking was top notch, but there was nothing fancy about it. Basically, the only seasonings were salt and pepper and maybe a bit of onions here and there. Christmas dinners were always extremely delicious with a full complement of food; vegetables, mashed potatoes, turkey or ham, cranberries, and pumpkin pie.

Curious enough, my father would oversee the cooking of the turkey. My mother did everything else including setting the table, washing dishes after a big Sunday meal or a meal for the holidays. My mother's gravy was one of the things I sure wish I knew how to make. I don't remember it being anything complex, but I sure do recall the great taste. Now unfortunately, I buy gravy mixes in a little packet and add water. My gravy tastes okay, it gets the job done, but it certainly is not homemade gravy from a nice roast beef, or an oven turkey cooked by my mother.

The other thing I wish I could duplicate is her meat pies and pumpkin pies. My mother's pumpkin pies were not made special. She even bought the pumpkin filling in a can. I do recall that she would occasionally make her own pie crusts and fill them up with the pumpkin filling or her own meat pie filling.

She always liked flowers. I remember her spending hours and hours gardening, including pulling weeds out of her flower beds, of which she was extremely proud. I don't recall ever growing vegetables, it was always flowers, and my mother's flower beds were the highlight of the neighborhood. The grass cutting was always completed by myself or my dad.

The one unfortunate thing that I am a big advocate against is that she was a smoker. She smoked her entire life. At that time, it was common for 15 or 16 year-olds to smoke. She smoked until the very end of her life. She had an air pump to assist her breathing for the last four to five years that she had to carry with her because her lungs were failing. She did not die of lung cancer, but eventually, her lungs failed. It was a dirty habit that she tried many, many times to quit. However, she could not beat the beast of smoking.

My father also smoked from an early age and ended up quitting sometime when he was nearing forty. He quit cold turkey with no assistance, no courses or no visits to the doctor. He just simply stopped smoking.

I do remember my mother smoking a brand called Rothmans sold everywhere you could purchase cigarettes. My father chose to roll his own cigarettes from scratch. He would buy the cigarette wrappers separately from the tobacco. Once he had the contents, he could roll them by hand or use a small little mechanical machine often sitting at the table for an hour or so making cigarettes for the week. I remember him rolling his cigarettes for the last 10 years or so that he smoked.

I guess watching my mother's health dwindle over her last years caused me to hate cigarettes. The proper word would be despised. I never liked the smell, I did not like the look of them nor the discolouration it caused on fingers, clothes, and the interior of houses. At the point where I was growing up, the popularity of smoking cigarettes was beginning to dwindle. As everybody knew, it was a huge health issue for the population.

I am pleasantly excited that my two boys don't smoke at all. I don't believe they ever tried to smoke. Unfortunately, the boys' mother smokes. Although she has tried multiple times and has been successful quitting, the addiction part of smoking has always gotten back to her, and she continues to smoke.

I sit here as I write this and summarize that my mother lived a life of solitude for approximately 15 years after my father passed away. For the last five or six years, she received a small stipend from her old age pension, a benefit from our government. I don't believe my father had a pension at Uniroyal. If he did, it was the bare minimum.

After my father's passing, it was very evident that she would not be able to afford their house in Windsor. She sold that house and purchased a trailer home out in the country. There are lots of comments about living in a trailer home that are not positive. Many think it is the last resort before being homeless. Many think if you can't afford a house, you live in a trailer home.

At the time, she purchased the trailer home just outside of Windsor in a nice area with other trailer homes in a primarily adult community. There was nothing fancy, but her new home was all rebuilt with a nice size yard. The money gained by selling her house, which sold for well under $100,000 at the time, would allow her to live a bit more financially comfortable for the remaining years of her life, which turned out to be 15 years.

It was just her and I living in the trailer home. Again, she kept up her flower bed, although her health was starting to fail. During the last years, she could not maintain everything as she once did since she was on an oxygen tank her last five years. She did travel locally with her own car to visit friends and to do her own shopping. I also remember her in the initial stages of osteoporosis, which affected her back.

In her last five years, I would say she looked like a very frail old lady. She was in her early seventies when she passed. Unfortunately, I believe smoking took its toll. Her life for the last

15 years was no piece of cake. She continued to move forward, running our household as she always had. She never complained, but I know it was hard for her. Her resilience and strong mental attitude was a great example for me. I am confident that it is where I get some of my mentality. When stuff happens to you, just move on. Don't sit there and dwell on it or make excuses. You just proceed and do what you need to do to accomplish the task at hand.

I was in my early 30s before I moved out of her house. I'm sad when I think about it. Here is a woman that was married to my father for more than 20 years. Suddenly on her own, in charge of doing everything, she was a pillar of strength and grace. My mother was not a big social butterfly, preferring to keep to herself most of the time. She loved to watch television. Occasionally, she and one of my aunts would go to a local bingo game, maybe once every couple of months. I would say that was her biggest excitement. She couldn't go every day, like many people do that play bingo, obviously because of finances. But occasionally, she'd splurge and go for a night of bingo that probably cost $15 for a full night out. I remember going a few times when I was younger, just for her to have some company. I recall winning a jackpot one time, and that was some real excitement for the Crains. It was a $600.00 jackpot, and I'm sure I split the money with her.

Since I lived with my mother while I was a young adult, I paid her rent. Since I had a job, it was obviously the right thing to do. When your mother, who has provided everything for you, has a need for monthly money, you do it. So, although it was, I'm sure, very minimal, I did try to help financially, even though she never asked me for it. It was always a priority for me to give her a few hundred dollars to help pay for my expenses while living with her.

As I think about it and look across the street here, one of the other favorite recreations when she lived in our house in Windsor was to visit with a neighbour. There was a single lady named Edna that was probably 20 years her senior who lived across the street. The two happened to meet one day, I guess probably started chatting about flowers, and they eventually developed a friendship. They were like the neighborhood watch of the time. My mother would go over to Edna's front porch where they would sit and have coffee after coffee until all hours of the night during the summer. It would be common that at two or three in the morning, they would just be sitting there chatting about anything and everything in the neighborhood and about old times. I don't recall Edna ever coming over to our porch. It was funny that my mom always went over to Edna's porch.

Funny story about Edna, who was a big football and baseball fan. When I would go across the street to see my mother and her, Edna would often have a football or baseball game playing on a transistor radio. She actually was the first one that taught me the rules of football and exactly how it was played. Crazy that I learned the rules of a sport from an old lady. Thanks, Edna.

HEART OF A MOTHER

When I was in the seventh grade, my mother started feeling sick and began going to a general practitioner. Then, she started to have appointments with a heart specialist. Various tests and specialist appointments determined that she had to have open heart surgery.

We brought my mother up to the London Hospital where she was scheduled for open heart surgery. At the time, you could not stay at the hospital overnight, but they had dormitories. So, my father and I stayed at what they called a dormitory, but it was one of the nurses' homes. Nurses offered their homes to patients' families while they were working. It was only $25 or $30 a day and was just a two minute walk from the hospital. Obviously, in this situation, it is important that you are near the hospital.

The surgery turned out great, but it was determined that she had an actual hole in her heart. She became what other heart surgery patients refer to as a member of the zipper club. The surgeon medically breaks your breast bone to gain access to the heart. They create an incision from under your chin, at the bottom of your throat down the chest approximately 18 inches. You could see a little bit of a scar towards the top of her chest. Obviously, I couldn't see the whole scar, but it was a significant start. The zipper club is a nickname because the full chest scar is very reminiscent of a zipper.

Recuperation from the heart surgery had my mother performing various lung and heart exercises over the next three months. I recall her using different machines at home to expand her chest and to make sure her lungs and heart were working properly. Obviously, meetings and appointments with the physicians over the next year eventually led to a clean bill of health.

As I sit here and write this chapter, I begin to think that this serious heart surgery on my mother was nearly fifty years ago. Fast forward to my recent health condition, and I again get emotional. Although the issues with our hearts are different, I wonder whether hers was caused by smoking and mine by obesity, with the commonality that both involve the heart.

Although my memory is a bit foggy, I will try and recall as closely as possible the end of my mother's life. As I mentioned, my mother needed to use a portable oxygen tank for the last few years. I don't recall exactly the circumstances, but what I do recall is that myself, my ex-wife and our oldest son were living just outside of Amherstburg at the time.

I recall my mother had gone by ambulance to the hospital in Windsor. I remember receiving a call from my brother about it and rushing there. I guess I don't really think about it, or perhaps subconsciously choose not to think about it, but the details are still a bit blurry. Knowing the outcome and circumstances is not something I want to remember.

I met my brother at the hospital where my mom was admitted. She was in an intensive care unit bed with three other patients in the room. She was in the first bed on the left side of the room. The nurse's station was immediately across from her bed, and there were various machines hooked up to my mother. Beeping noises and visually looking at medical screens with a heartbeat scrolling are still vivid images for me even all these years later. It is a memory that never fades, and even seeing anything similar in movies triggers the memory.

My brother and I stayed at the hospital and eventually, later in the evening, my brother had to go home to his kids and his wife. I stayed there, where they gave me a room to sit and sleep, if possible, throughout the night. I just curled up in a chair and dozed off to sleep. Then, suddenly a nurse had awakened me towards the middle of the night, somewhere around 3:00 am. The nurse explained to me that my mother was not doing very well. She explained that her body was beginning to shut down. That meant that vital organs such as kidneys, pancreas and liver were beginning to stop functioning. I remember walking over to my mom, who was heavily sedated at the time. I looked at the intravenous tubes in her body, breathing masks, and heart monitors and began to cry.

The nurses came over to talk to me, so I put on my game face on and listened. They explained to me that her body was shutting down rapidly, and that I needed to decide whether they should turn off the machines that were keeping her alive or continue to keep her breathing by machine. They explained that they would need to add a different solution in the intravenous bag and that the end would be a slow, painless process.

I remember calling my brother and trying to explain to him exactly what was going on, and that we needed to decide on what to do for her. My brother and I made the decision then to stop all the intravenous meds, and let the natural process take over so she could pass away without any pain. I was the messenger that told the nurses our decision. I stayed beside my mom's side while the nurses began the process, with my brother arriving at the hospital shortly after her passing. We obviously consoled each other. I remember holding her head and gently rubbing her leg, letting her know that I loved her.

Here I was 32 years old at the time, married, with a young son. Both of my parents had passed away. Obviously, it was extremely hard to watch my mother pass away but knew there would no longer be any pain, and that she would be with my father again.

My brother and I had to make the funeral arrangements. All the while, we both kept a stoic face. We both had our lives, families and wives and had to continue without her. She had been the leader of our families for the last 16 years. Even though we were now dealing with our own grief, we had to continue with our own families.

I don't really recall all the details of the burial of my mom or the funeral arrangements. My brother and I had to sell her home and settle her estate, distributing proceeds to both of us. Now, I am talking a total of less than $15,000. The money was not an issue, and there were no squabbles or disputes between Gary and me.

It's crazy that I sit here writing about the passing of my dad and my mother with detail at points and fogginess at others. In both situations, reminiscing with tears rolling down my cheeks whimpering uncontrollably.

An attitude of caring and helping has certainly been absorbed from my mother. Mom, I love you dearly, till we meet again.

THE FAMILY UNIT

Many of my relatives' have not had the same fortune as me. A few relatives are living paycheck to paycheck, sometimes bouncing from couch to couch for sleeping arrangements. Although you would love to help every single one of them, you also have to realize in life that, at some point, it becomes enabling.

I watched my mom help her sister with living quarters, and I'm sure with food here and there. Many Sundays she would invite her sister and kids over for a meal. I recall my two cousins had never seen real milk, they had to drink powdered milk as it was a cheaper cost. At the dinner table, they would drink glass after glass of milk. I remember watching this and thinking of how many glasses of milk they would drink at dinner. I would eventually ask my mother about the milk, and she explained to me about the powdered milk.

I also think about the great Sunday meals when we had them over. We would often cook roast beef, mashed potatoes, salad, vegetables, bread, and a dessert. I'm very sure that they did not often have these types of meals at their house, and they were very appreciative. They were always excited that they were coming to their aunts' house to have a great meal. My aunt did the absolute best she could with her income, and her two children were raised with huge hearts.

My other aunt with the ten children was a stay-at-home spouse, and her husband had a full-time job. Again, the unity of family dinners always took place on Sundays. In those days, aunts and uncles would visit each other with their kids for a few hours on the weekends. Large family get togethers at Christmas time were quite common in our family.

Fast forward 50 years, and very seldom do I see a family eating at the dinner table. It does not seem like you hear of families visiting each other. I remember as a young kid going with my mom and dad to visit my dad's friend where they would sit in the kitchen having coffee. I'd be in the living room watching TV or playing some games, reading a book, or doing puzzles. Those types of visits were quite common and part of learning social skills. It was all around our family and part of growing up as I remember it. Nowadays, that is one thing that is missing inside the family unit. The love and affection between families and siblings and your relatives seems to be different now. Again, I'm not saying this is true with every family, but it's just an observation that I've noticed. I watch when my kids have friends over and see them playing on their phones. They have the TV on while watching a sporting event and two or three of them are sitting in their chairs or on the couch relaxing and texting like crazy.

The other thing you notice is that kids in this generation very seldom talk on their cell phones. I notice that if they were arranging something between their friends, it was only through texting. There is no more calling on a phone, and there certainly is no going over to little Johnny's house, tapping at the door, and asking for little Johnny so they could have a quick conversation.

It's crazy to think how much family and friend communication has changed over the years since I was a young kid. We would walk over to the house of our friend and have a conversation to see if they wanted to hang out and do anything.

It's just simply something different, and who knows how it will be in 20 years. I can only imagine that, at some point, communication may be done telepathically. Maybe you just think about something and look at somebody, and they know what you're thinking without verbalizing. Personal communication in the future should be interesting.

WHERE O WHERE

I grew up primarily in Windsor Ontario Canada where the first house I remember living in as a kid was on Pelissier St. in the downtown area of Windsor. The next one was a little bit to the west side of Windsor on McEwen Ave. The third one was a big jump for the family in moving to the town of Lasalle, just outside of Windsor.

I lived on Pelissier St. from kindergarten to grade three and attended Victoria public school. Next, we moved to McEwan Ave. where I went to school from grade three to grade seven at JE Benson public grade school. Our next family move was to Lasalle where I moved schools to Sandwich Public through grade 7 and 8. Grade 9 through grade 13, I went to Sandwich Secondary School while still living in Lasalle. After high school, I went to St. Clair College where I earned my technologist degree in industrial engineering while living in Lasalle for my first year and back in Windsor for years two and three.

My days at Victoria public school from kindergarten to grade three were basically uneventful. I walked to school, which was a quick three blocks away. During my time at Victoria, we lived in a duplex that we rented. One of the memories I do have from Victoria public school was the time I wore glasses. I remember a bunch of my friends and I were fooling around in the schoolyard. I collided with someone, and my glasses shattered.

The next event I remember was having a yo-yo that looked like a #8 cue ball. A kid stole that yo-yo from my locker, and I remember going home without it and telling my dad. He asked where the yo-yo was, and I said I didn't know. A few more fatherly questions, and I eventually told him someone took it. I remember my father going down to the school with me and him asking me who I thought took it. I told him, and he went and asked the kid and got it back.

The last event I remember from kindergarten to grade three was riding my bike in the schoolyard after school. There was a big sandpit used for a long jump at the time, and I was riding at the edge of the sand. The wheel slipped out, and I fell off the bike and carved up my knee. There was blood everywhere; it was my first big scrape. I don't remember even getting it stitched. I probably had my mom put on a bandage, and all was good.

It's funny how, throughout your life, there's things that stick out. Sometimes, they're very minor things like I just described but are implanted in my brain. I would say you never know what a memory may be at the time, but years later, you still remember it vividly.

The next stop on my youth timeline was when we moved to McEwen Ave. Again, the house was on the west side of Windsor, and this time it was an upper and lower duplex. Grade three to grade seven were big development years where I would meet many lifelong friends. One of the friends I met lived four doors down from my house. His name is Mike Janisse. Fast forward to our age now, me being 57 and Mike just about turning 60. Our friendship is still intact after 45 years.

Many years after I met Mike on McEwen, we ultimately married sisters. So that made us brothers-in-law. Seven or eight years after our marriages, we both were divorced and remained friends.

It's kind of funny when you think about our friendship because we have never separated. His two boys and my two boys got to grow up together. Mike and I basically grew up together, and now two generations of the Janisse and Crain family are growing up together as cousins.

Grade three through seven on McEwen was primarily fun where I started to play lots of sports. The grade school I attended was seven houses away and where I would spend hours and hours playing basketball, road hockey, baseball, hide and seek, and strike out.

A few of the memories were good ones and a couple were bad ones. Right across the street was my close friend named Daryl Doe. We used to play in his backyard and build tree forts in the summer, and in winter we skated on his backyard ice rink. This is where we first learned our construction skills and skating technique.

The next thing we used to do at Daryl's house was hang out under his back porch. It was located at the back area of his house. We had what we called a fort, which was a small crawl space. We spent time together hanging out talking about our next adventure. We decorated the fort with many objects we found by going up and down alleys. We would walk near our neighborhood finding items that were tossed away. Old pieces of carpet were valued treasures along with framed pictures we would hang up on the wooden walls that were underneath. We always did it by ourselves with no help from parents. Our parents knew there was no mischief going on in there. It was just a cool place for a few neighbourhood friends to hang out. It was our own little restricted area.

We used the fort all the way up to grade seven. As we got older, we outgrew the uniqueness of a fort. One thing we did find exciting was walking up and down different alleys finding furniture, trinkets, and old Playboy magazines. As you can imagine, it was a big thrill for kids 10 years old to look at a few Playboy magazines with some minor nudity in them. How different it was then. Now kids simply search for pornography on their cell phones.

One hobby we had involved making money. We would search alleys as we walked up and down and looked for pop bottles. At the time, a glass pop bottle was worth $0.10 and was refundable at any local convenience store. On the weekends and on garbage night, we would go up and down alleys and collect pop bottles. The bottles that we collected allowed us to go immediately to the local corner store and cash in the bottles to buy candy and hockey cards. We collected the cards, and we also had a game that we could play with hockey cards. I'm going to tell you about what we used to do with the hockey cards which were extremely popular back in my youth. As I tell you, I looked on the Internet for the value of hockey cards from the seventies, and some were valued at thousands of dollars. What we would do is go to Daryl's house to his unfinished basement and play hockey cards. There are multiple games that we would play with our own collection of cards. We would throw them across the floor and against a wall to try to make them lean up on the wall.

As you can imagine, throwing the cards against the wall for many games would damage the corners of the cards. At the time, they'd be of no real value other than to collect them to see who could get the most cards and the most popular players. We would often play another friend in the neighborhood to see who could win the most cards. That is where I started my love of hockey. It was collecting and playing cards against the wall. I would always have favorite players, and you always tried to collect some which we would never use against the wall.

We also played at the school yard all the time. A few doors down were older kids who were in high school, and we were in grade school. So, for young kids like me it was cool to hang out with kids in high school. One of these memories is my first brush with the police.

One evening (I don't remember if it was during the summer or during the school year), but, regardless, we were playing in the school yard with the usual neighbourhood kids, including the older kids. There was some kind of function at the school where someone had rented the gym for a few hours. There were cars parked inside the school yard off the road. While we were playing, one of the older kids noticed there were some tennis rackets sitting in the back of a car. I watched but stayed away. I was at least smart enough to know that some mischief was about to happen regarding the car. Sure enough, one of the older kids opened the car door and grabbed two tennis rackets, balls and shorts that were sitting in the car and took off running towards his house.

As a young kid, I didn't know what to do, so I ran home to my house. The next evening, we had a knock at the front door from police officers. I recall the two officers were not wearing uniforms and introduced themselves as detectives. They asked my mother for me using my name and asked if they could speak with me. You could imagine my trepidation as two officers came into my small house and began speaking with me about the incident that happened at the school the previous night. My mother and father sat on the coach listening to my story, as they were unaware. I had not told my parents anything had happened that night and just came home.

The two officers began to tell me that there was a break in to a car and items were stolen and asked if I knew anything about it. I was brought up to always tell the truth, so I began to tell the truth. I explained what happened and what I had seen and what went on as far as I knew. The officers thanked me, took their report, and left. I did not hear anything about the incident for a few days.

You can imagine how I felt after the officers went and spoke to the culprits as well; hanging around in a neighborhood knowing that you had just spoken the truth. You basically just ratted out some older kids regarding them breaking into a car and stealing stuff. There certainly was a lot of anxiety knowing what I did and not knowing what the ramifications would be towards me from the older kids. It turns out that the officers went down and spoke with the older kids and got the items back. Although I don't know the details, I don't believe there were any serious police issues with the older kids. I would think they would have been given a stern talking to and read the riot act to which they would never do any of that kind of mischief again.

It seemed that from grade three to seven, I truly developed a love for the game of hockey. My parents enrolled me in organized ice hockey. Although not particularly good admittedly, I was the only one in our neighborhood that played ice hockey. Daryl was a baseball fanatic and enjoyed playing baseball. Mike never really played any organized sports. Another neighbourhood friend was Brian Eagle who played football in high school and lived across the street from me. We all would casually play a little bit of basketball, road hockey and various sports.

I recall another memory that is kind of embarrassing and now has me thinking about the situation years later. I remember being a chubby kid and occasionally would get teased. I was athletic but had extra pounds which, unfortunately, 50 years later I have the same situation. Occasionally, I would get teased in grade school. I remember a kid teasing me during recess multiple days in a row when I was in grade six.

I finally stuck up for myself and told him to stop and that if he teased me again, I would punch him in the mouth. Well, he certainly said it again to which I pounded him in the face, and he ended up getting a severe black eye and bloody lip. I don't remember being suspended for it, but I would think I most likely received the paddle for fighting in school. All that said, there was no more teasing.

The next event I remember is a kid stealing my eraser for which I made a big deal out of it. I told him to give it back, and he said he didn't steal it. The next thing I know we had lined up an after school fight in the back alley between the schoolyard and my house. I remember all the buzz going around the school that I was going to fight this kid. The school bell rang, and we walked out to where we are four doors down from the back of my house. Well, one of the neighborhood kids had told my mother that I was going to be fighting. My mother walked down the alley to watch two kids in grade seven standing there yapping at each other, not even pushing and shoving. I remember my mother saying that if I was going to fight then get on with it. Well, in my eyes that gave me permission to fight, so we started to fight. I ended up giving the kid that I thought stole my pencil eraser a bloody nose, fat lip and a black eye. Now, the curious thing is that I remember walking home and the kid that was my combatant walked past the front of my house, and I was feeling some serious remorse.

Some of the neighborhood kids began saying how much trouble my opponent would be in because he got into a fight. Hearing this, I started to feel bad about giving the kid a little bit of a beating. As kids often do, a week or so later we were chums again, but I do remember feeling bad about fighting this kid.

Another situation I remember was involving two girls. The girls were older than me, and as I recall, they were certainly bigger than me. I don't know what really started the issue other than them mentioning that I had said something about them which I know 100% I certainly did not. I didn't even know these girls. In fact, I had never seen them before. These two tough girls grabbed me on the sidewalk and walked me down behind an apartment building and started laying a beating on me. They were punching me in the stomach, kicking me in the legs and pulling my hair. I was raised and always told to never strike a girl, so the best I could do was protect my face and take a couple of blows in my stomach. After a few minutes they rushed off, never to be seen again.

I remember walking home terribly upset and crying at the time. A couple of my friends saw me and asked what went on, and I explained that these two girls jumped me and started punching me. I explained that all I could do was defend myself. Well, that was enough for my friends to have a plan, and I was suddenly a tough guy again. We walked around the neighborhood looking for these two kids where we were going to administer revenge. We never saw the girls again, and we didn't even know if they were from our neighborhood. I got a feeling it was a case of mistaken identity, and the girls grabbed the wrong guy. Anyway, we were just kids, so yes, I got roughed up by two girls.

EARLY CHILDHOOD VACATIONS

A great memory while growing up on McEwen were various vacations. My dad would save up money during the year so that we could take off on vacation during the summer. We traveled with a small 17-foot camper that he had rebuilt in our backyard, pulled by a van or a pick-up truck. Ours was a basic trailer with two beds. It did have a fridge and stove, and at the other end of the trailer, was a bed for me. There was no washroom, no shower just the very basics, it certainly beat sleeping in a tent. We pulled it with a 1979 GMC Vandura van that my father had redone the interior with two benches and a bed where I would sleep while we were travelling down the road. There was a third seat in the middle that my dad had mounted between the driver and passenger seats. A funny time lapse, at the time you had seatbelts that foolishly no one used, with an AM FM car stereo for music. By this time, my brother who was 11 years older was gone from the house living by himself. It was myself, my mother and father as the campers. Now my father always used to enjoy starting the big trip a little bit later in the evening, when it was dark, and he did it for a few varied reasons. The first reason is that there is less traffic on the road. The second was when he got everything cleaned up and readied and everything loaded. The third reason was that it would be easier on me because at some point quickly, I would be falling asleep.

The first vacation I remember was going out to eastern Canada. In that trip, we travelled hundreds of miles each day and each night we would find a campground and set up camp with the trailer. We usually pulled over sometime later in the afternoon so there was a little bit of daylight to set up the trailer and have dinner. I would go for a swim while my dad unhooked and positioned the trailer. The next day, sometime earlier in the morning, we would hook up and drive all day and do the same thing again. On this trip, we went as far as Prince Edward Island for our vacation.

The first event on this eastern trip was travelling through Quebec, Canada. I distinctly remember going into a restaurant which back in that day was primarily French speaking. I can recall my parents were trying to order in English, and the server had said in broken English that she did not speak English. So, we would point to the items we wanted on the menu. This same server only minutes later, began speaking in English to the next table. I don't know if it was a tourist issue or perhaps an only English-speaking prejudice. It upset my parents enough that we just walked out of the restaurant and were on our way out of the Quebec province. Nowadays, that situation would be called language discrimination.

The next event I remember was travelling around Prince Edward Island. That entire trip from Windsor to Prince Edward Island would have taken I'm sure, at least two weeks pulling a trailer with a van. I remember Prince Edward Island and driving around what was called the Cabot Trail; a perimeter road that went around the entirety of the island. I do remember our van had a transmission issue and would no longer function properly. We pulled over to the side of the road and were towed to a garage where the transmission was repaired quickly, the next day. I do recall that Prince Edward Island had very red soil and obviously lots of farms as they are famous for the growth of potatoes.

I remember while in PEI we found a beach somewhere as we were driving and enjoying the scenery. I wanted to swim in both the Atlantic and Pacific oceans. It was the Atlantic Ocean out east, and I was determined to somehow swim in it. I remember that the small beach we found had a small little food shack in the parking lot before the beach. It was a cold, chilly day with the wind blowing. There was nobody on the beach as the Atlantic typically is not the warmest of oceans, but I was determined to go swimming in it.

I recall that, at the food shack, I ordered a lobster sandwich. I have never had lobster before but maybe my parents were familiar with seafood. I ate it and then we went on our way, and I changed into my swimming suit in the van, and then we pranced down to the water. I remember walking into the water, which was crazy cold with nobody else on the beach. It was one of those dark and gloomy days, but I was stubborn enough wanting to say that I swam in the Atlantic. At that time, I would have been probably in grade 7 so I would have been 13 years old at the time. My parents were back on the beach as I had walked out into the water to go for a swim. Basically, I fell into a wave and went underwater where I could not be seen. My mother with her caring attitude ran out into the water thinking that I may have been in dire need as I got pushed down into a wave. She was not a swimmer at all, zero swimming skills but tried to assist. Suddenly, as she was trying to help me, she got swept by a wave and fell. We eventually both got up with no issues at all, but I remember that picture of her running out there not being a swimmer to save her goofball son that got knocked down by a small wave. Obviously, it was a scary situation to see her kid fall and go underneath the water, and I am sure at the time looking out, it probably seemed like I was underwater for hours. Her mentality was that she had to run out there and save her child no matter the situation.

One thing years later, I always remember my parents saying that we should've gone to Newfoundland and Labrador, which would have been a big boat ride from the mainland of Nova Scotia. That was one regret I remember us all having that we never did that last piece of the eastern trip.

Now, a curious thing is that my father's first son, Lloyd, lived in Halifax with his first wife. I remember my mom and dad making arrangements to visit him as we were somewhat in the area. He would have been in his late twenties, and apparently, as the story goes, he was in the Navy. Which may have been a bunch of tall tales. We went over and visited him and his wife. I don't think we stayed there overnight, we just visited. He is just basically a guy that I never knew, and I certainly did know that he was my father's son from his first marriage. A curious thing I do remember is that they had a big chess board, and I had been learning how to play chess. It was made from nuts and bolts and the chess pieces were five or six inches tall on this large chess board.

The next year, we were off to the west coast and the Calgary Stampede. At some point, when you're driving out west, you're driving through the Rocky Mountains, and it's exactly as described. It's mountains and not hills out there in western Canada. Winding two lane roads that are obviously, exceedingly high elevation with steep sides on one side and more mountains on the other side. I remember one evening after supper, it was getting dark as we pulled out of the campground to get on our way. I remember my father a few hours after we left slamming on his brakes and skidding to a stop. I jumped up from my van bed and hustled up to the front and watched a mother moose and two calves in front of the van. They were walking from the steep side of the mountain across the road in front of us and down the other side. If you have never seen a moose, and that is the only time I have ever seen a moose, they are huge and can weigh nearly 2000 pounds. They were ten feet in front of our van, and the mother's back was higher than the top of our van. Those are massive, massive animals, and it's scary in the middle of the night to suddenly be awakened by a slamming on of brakes to watch three moose walk in front of you. In fact, in the Canadian province called Newfoundland and Labrador, there are several deaths a year with cars and or motorcycles running into moose. The vehicle doesn't win the collision with the moose, which usually dies. The cars are usually totaled and often the occupants of the front seat unfortunately perish because of the huge crash.

On this western vacation, our goal was to go out to visit my father's nephew who lived in the Calgary area with his wife. We headed west with the same van, same trailer that I have described. Now, I must admit, going west in Canada is very, very boring until you get to the Rocky Mountains. I remember hours and hours of just wheat fields on the sides of a very straight highway. I would spend hours trying to play board games with my mother or drawing in the back of the van. I think, at the time, I did a lot of drawing in a little sketchbook. I also listened to music on a Walkman, which is the predecessor to the iPod. That trip would take 30 hours if you drove it straight, but thankfully, that never happened.

It took us three or four days to get out that far. I do recall a couple of different events during our western vacation when I was in the 14 year old range. The first event I do recall is we were driving through the Chicago area, which I have never really looked at on a map to see if that was the case. I remember the traffic being crazy with back-to-back cars. Being from Windsor, you never see that on the highways around here, but I remember it being bumper to bumper and looking out the back of the van and seeing a vehicle maybe five feet from us, which was something abnormal for our everyday driving.

Another thing I remember about the trip going west was stopping at a famous lake called Lake Louise. I am so grateful that I got to see Lake Louise because the colour of the blue as we rode horses around the lake was unbelievable and still vividly etched in my brain nearly 50 years later. I recall this very historical and famous area called Lake Louise like it was yesterday. What

I recall is that Lake Louise is situated towards the bottom of the Rocky Mountains. The Rocky Mountains were a horseshoe around the lake, with one end of the lake having a glacier called The Crowfoot. So again, it was a touristy thing to do, but as I have mentioned previously, my dad was a horseman in his younger years and a horseback riding tour was on the agenda that day. I am going to guess the horse path was several hundred feet above the actual lake, and maybe even higher. There was a little ledge on the mountain side for the horses to walk. It was not very wide from what I remember; maybe five feet wide but a well used horse trail. The horses knew exactly what they were doing. My mother rode a horse, I rode a horse, and my father rode a horse, and you followed the horses in front on the tour. Basically, you just sat on the horse while you were looking at the beautiful scenery as you rode around the lake which was several hundred feet below us. Now, when I try to explain the colour of Lake Louise, take it upon yourself to look at pictures on the internet and see the blue colour. It was indescribable, but I will do my best. It was a bright, brilliant blue like I have never previously seen. It is believed that the rock composition made it appear that beautiful blue. It was a crazy blue that once you have seen it would be etched in your mind for the rest of your life. I remember riding the horse just looking around, on the one side the mountain on the other side the lake. It was a little bit intimidating, but the horses knew exactly where to walk. There is no real horse riding other than being on the back of a horse where you had a guide at the front and a guide at the back. At the end of the trail, there was a small area where there were cars in a parking lot at the bottom of a glacier. As the guide explained to us, the name of the glacier was Crowfoot. If you looked up on the side of the mountain, there were people skiing on the glacier. He went on to explain that the glacier was sliding down the mountain side at a rate of an inch every year and would eventually fall into Lake Louise.

I remember another thing we did on this western vacation was to travel to a famous rodeo called the Calgary Stampede. There you got to see all the horses in a rodeo and Chuck wagon races, which is the famous part. The other crazy memory is we eventually made it our destination to visit my dad's nephew. I remember visiting him and his wife at their condominium where there was a small Kermit the frog stuffed animal sitting on the back of the couch. Obviously, they were adults, and I was just a young kid. I recall starting to pick it up, and they had said no, no, no, no, don't pick it up, but of course, I grabbed it. This stuffed Kermit had a great big set of testicles I saw as I moved it. It was quite a laugh for the adults and embarrassing for me. I put it back and did not touch it the remainder of the visit.

For a few summer vacations, we drove in a convoy with another family, which were my cousins, all the way to Florida where we would go camping. We had a simple camper, and my cousin's camper certainly was not comparable to ours. Theirs was about a 30-foot-long trailer with microwaves, bathrooms, showers, and couches.

That same trip, after getting permission from my parents, I invited one of my friends in our Windsor neighbourhood to join us during our vacation to Florida, because it was only myself, my cousins, and my parents. My friend Mustafa and I, along with my parents, traveled down to Florida for a couple of weeks camping and enjoying the Florida life.

Mustafa Booze had three sisters and a brother, and they lived five houses down with their mother and their father. The father we never saw, but the mother named Hanieda was very friendly and loved all the kids and neighbours. Across the street from us was a family from India. The family was very scholarly. The two boys and the sister were chess champions through grade school and throughout high school. My neighbourhood in Windsor was quite diversified, having people from India, Lebanon, Italy, and Canadian born families. We all spent time together with zero care regarding anyone's ethnicity, just all friends having fun.

Somehow my cousins made last minute arrangements so we would be camping at the same campground as them. Now, they are seasoned about camping, and they had a spot in Florida at a campground in Kissimmee, FL where they frequently camped. At that location Disney World was only 45 minutes away. There were other touristy things to see such as Gatorland as one of the attractions. I am sure we would have done some other things, but I do remember visiting those two amusement parks. I recall playing all kinds of billiards at the campground clubhouse as well as spending hours in the arcade.

It is odd the things or events you remember from years gone past. Now I sit here and think of what my boys have remembered over their young years. Something I may not think is memorable or even an event they may recall for the rest of their lives.

Again, for whatever reason I remember, we did not go to British Columbia or Vancouver Island, the most Western province in Canada. It was always a comment that was discussed over the next years, that we should have gone to British Columbia. We almost travelled exactly coast to coast in Canada, but we are a bit short in each vacation. The memories that I have just described are unbelievable and something I would never change. I am incredibly lucky to be here 45 years later, remembering these special moments. Lobster lunch, mother trying to save me in the Atlantic, moose walking from the left side to the right side of the van, Lake Louise, the glacier, and Kermit the frog.

What I've described is a trip out east, the trip out west, and the trip down south to Florida. Huge memories, lots of fun, and I would like to pass on some of those memories via this book to my kids.

LASALLE KID

In grade seven, it was determined that the family were going to move to LaSalle, Ontario. LaSalle was about 20 minutes away from Windsor with bigger houses, a nicer area and removed from the city. I reference to where I lived as Lasalle, but at the time, it was named Sandwich West Township. My parents had saved up enough money to purchase a 3-bedroom house with a basement and a large yard.

I remember the prices were approximately $50,000 for a house in Lasalle while houses in Windsor were $30,000. It was my parents dream house, and they were all very proud of the house. I was certainly proud of the new to me house with the 3 bedrooms and basement. We moved to Sandwich West where I went to Sandwich Public School for grade seven and eight. In grade school at Sandwich Public School, I met many new kids, some of which I am still friends with today more than 40 years later.

Grade seven and eight was where I had to take a school bus to school for the first time. That was a whole new situation that I had to learn to navigate. In the city, I lived seven doors down from my school, and I had never seen, witnessed, or even heard about kids taking a bus to school. In Windsor, you simply walked to your school regardless of where it was located from your home.

You remember me talking about always playing basketball in the schoolyard for hours and hours. I was a short fat kid who could not run and couldn't jump. However, I sure enjoyed shooting and dribbling the basketball which would later impress the gym teacher in grade seven at Sandwich Public School. I remember playing basketball in gym class after moving to Lasalle. I had entered my new school playing basketball as an activity. The teacher noticed during gym practices that I could certainly shoot the ball; he asked me if I wanted to play on the basketball team. Now here is a little short fat kid that could certainly shoot the ball during gym class, was slow and certainly couldn't jump any higher than a piece of toast. And yet here I was on my first basketball team because of my dribbling and shooting skills. I don't recall playing very often to tell you the truth, maybe a few minutes here and there. The team was full of the cool guys who had been at the school for years, the athletes and the super jocks. The two years that I was on the team, I had lots of fun and enjoyed myself even though I hardly played. That was the beginning of learning how to play on a team, which is a skill I use today in life.

I don't remember any huge events in grade seven and eight, maybe I had my first crushes on girls at that age. I don't recall who they would've been, but there were certainly a couple that were raving beauties, in my opinion as a grade seven kid. It's funny, 45 years later I do occasionally run into those grade school kids from Sandwich Public School. We chat casually and have a few laughs.

The next phase is high school where I went to Sandwich Secondary School and again had to take the bus to school. I went to high school for five years of secondary school and graduated from Grade 13. These are the years that you're suddenly growing into a mature teenager but certainly not an adult. I will say as an adult that my high school years were memorable. I have certainly seen many movies where kids come of age and may experiment with different things, try different things, and certainly do different things. In the movies, they do a lot of stupid things and yes, I certainly did a few stupid things here and there. Those were the years back in the 80s when there was no social media, and there were no cell phones. Any evidence of my stupidity is only from the memory of those who witnessed it, and that's a good thing.

Basically, all your memories could be forgotten or remembered as you saw them happen and as you chose to remember them. I think back to all the crazy stuff we used to do, and I am certainly thankful that there was no social media. Nothing could be broadcasted across the world showing the crazy things myself and my friends did through our high school and college years.

In grade seven, my dad bought me a motorcycle dirt bike to have some fun riding. We had lots of areas in LaSalle that were unpopulated with grass fields and trails down train tracks. I would ride for hours, just myself or with a couple of friends. I would meet up with buddies, and we would travel the trails through LaSalle on our dirt bikes. You were not allowed to drive on the road or on the shoulder but to get to the trails we certainly had to drive on the shoulder.

I remember in grade 8, I was 14 years old and had a friend from school who used to go dirt bike riding occasionally. Now that I think about it, there was one event that would impact me for months...literally. Yep, one of the stupid things I did was think I was Evil Knievel and could jump a big, large pile of dirt that was set up to jump. Well, I didn't land correctly, and the foot peg crushed my ankle as I landed the jump. I ended up breaking my ankle right behind my friends' place. His house was nearly a mile down the road from mine. Now remember, we couldn't drive down the shoulder, so I had to push my bike home over a mile with what turned out to be a broken ankle. When I got home because of my stubbornness and knowing I would get in trouble, I didn't bother to tell anybody. I put my bike away, and limped into the house and laid down on the couch. Laying down on the coach was very unusual for me and would eventually get noticed. I would go to my bedroom when no one was around so they wouldn't notice me limping. Two days after I initially broke my ankle, my parents noticed me doing nothing at home on what was now the weekend, which was again not typical. They must have either seen me or suspected something and asked me to show them my ankle. My ankle was ballooned up like a basketball with black and blue bruising. We ended up going to the emergency room where an X-ray was taken, and a cast was put on.

Normally, a cast is on for six weeks, and of course, that timeline didn't work out for me. After six weeks of wearing a walking cast, I went to get it removed by the doctor. He told me it had not had enough healing time. You see, I had played soccer and taken showers without covering it up. As you can imagine, I went to get the cast taken off, but the heel was all broken down and the cast was incredibly soft to the touch. My doctor promptly informed me that I would be in a new cast for another five weeks. In total, I believe I was in a cast for nearly 12 weeks. All because I did something stupid and then didn't bother to listen to the instructions on proper care of my cast.

During my years growing up, I can remember attending three grade schools and one high school. School years were fun filled. In the five years that I was in high school, there were lots of fun times. Exciting and crazy stuff happened as well as personal growth during those post-secondary years. At the beginning of those five years, you go into high school as a little pimply faced grade schooler in grade 9. At the end, you graduate from grade 13 and are a bit more ready for the world.

In Grade 9, there were 120 new students from other grade schools. Some of them I had played sports with, others I just knew from around town. In high school, you learn quickly about the pecking order of the school where Grade 13 students get to do primarily what they want while getting an education. The grade nines need to watch everything they do or don't do. I'll start off with a few bad school memories and then we'll go into the school memories which are much more fun.

We were all assembled into what was called homeroom, kids with last names starting with the letter B and C were in my class. You sat in homeroom in the morning just before school started for opening announcements and attendance and the playing of Oh Canada. You are in that class every morning for the next four or five years with the same people. Sometimes, there would be a few new kids that moved into town. Basically, you were in homeroom for the next four or five years, depending on if you want to go to grade 12 or grade 13.

After homeroom, everybody would take off and go to their respective classes, attending six classes a per day. As grade 9 continued, I got to be a bit more confident and comfortable with the homeroom classmates; so much so that a little joking around and giggling in homeroom class was the highlight of your day. One day, a friend of mine and I were fooling around in class pretending to pass an imaginary basketball ball and take imaginary shots on a fictitious net.

I am not sure exactly what caused this stupidity, but we were doing it and getting laughs from the remaining class. Everything was good until the homeroom teacher noticed the antics and called us out. We were told to walk around the room up and down the aisles, and we could bounce our imaginary ball and pass our imaginary ball around while waiting for opening ceremonies. A bit of an embarrassment tactic that certainly worked. Those antics never happened again.

SNOWMOBILING ADVENTURE

This little adventure was almost forgotten while I was drafting the book, but as the weather gets colder it seems to spark my memory. It was an adventure my father and I took while I was in high school. One of my friends' fathers happened to be one of my dad's friends throughout his adulthood. Although they weren't very close, they were certainly on a first name basis when they would meet. You don't have to be in contact every day to have a good friend, and this was the case with my dad and Mr. O'Neil. The O'Neil's family owned a farm out in the countryside for generations.

During the summer, my dad purchased a snowmobile on one of our small vacations. We figured out a way to put it in our van and ultimately brought it back home. We didn't know anything about snowmobiles but knew a little bit of the basics. We went out and bought snowmobile suits, gloves and a helmet, and suddenly, we were ready to be snowmobilers. Locally, there is a small creek called River Canard where we could snowmobile. We would load up the snowmobile into the van and drive down to the creek which was 10 minutes away. After unloading our snowmobile from the van, we would tour around the creek for miles and miles.

During this time, I was probably 15 or 16 years old and in high school enjoying life. The weather was much different then, it seems that River Canard always froze solid. Often during Christmas break, we were skating on it, playing hockey, and riding snowmobiles.

One day, although I don't remember exactly the reason, my dad and I were over at the O'Neil's house shooting the breeze during the winter. I had previously mentioned to my friend that we had bought a snowmobile, and he mentioned that they had a few snowmobiles for the family, and we should go riding one day. They did not ride out of the local area, as they would travel hours away from home. They would load up their snowmobile trailers with two or three snowmobiles, and the entire family would take off to northern Ontario where they would go snowmobiling for the weekend. That was a new concept to us since we would travel about 10 minutes to do our snowmobiling. During the conversation, Mr. O'Neil mentioned to my dad to join them and go snowmobiling with their family that upcoming weekend.

As new snowmobilers, we didn't really know what we were getting into, but it certainly sounded like fun. The next day, I remember my dad calling the other family and said sure we'll go snowmobiling. They made arrangements for the time that they were going to leave. Ultimately, we packed up the van, using a makeshift ramp we made so that we could load the snowmobile easily into the van. All our clothes were packed, but we didn't know where we were going to stay, which seems to be a theme when the Crain's go on vacation. We drove to the O'Neil's farm and eventually both families took off for our sledding adventure. Although I don't remember exactly how far we went, I believe it was four or five hours away. The O'Neil's had their van pulling the trailers with three snowmobiles on it and their entire family. Our van had my dad and I and the snowmobile loaded in the back. Eventually, we arrived at our destination which was a snowmobile resort. It was a resort where you rented rooms for the weekend. There were restaurants, washrooms and a huge dining area with a beautiful fireplace.

There were snowmobile trails that were groomed by machines through the forest area. This looked awfully fancy for the Crains, but we were willing to give it a whirl. I remember my dad went into the chalet hoping that he could rent a room so that we would have a place to sleep that evening. There were no rooms, of course being last minute, and no pre-planning by the Crains. Well, we didn't want the evening arrangements to hinder a wonderful day. We didn't even know if we were going to stay for the full weekend. We went on and enjoyed a momentous day of riding snowmobiles with the O'Neil's riding the trails and stopping for lunch. The O'Neil's were regulars at the resort, so they knew exactly where to go through the town and which trails were good. We just basically tagged along and enjoyed our time. I remember the trails were groomed, and every 20 or 30 miles there would be a small warming hut where you could go inside and warm up. Often, there was a small wood stove in the hut, so you could sit there, have a snack that you had brought and warm up. You would take off your helmet and gloves, sit there, shoot the breeze and enjoy the time with the other family.

Later in the day, we traveled back to the chalet to get ready for dinner. Obviously, my dad had thought about whether we were going to stay overnight. We came up with this idea that we would stay in the van overnight. Now, I don't know what temperature it was, but it was rather cold that day. He had brought a small electric heater, so maybe he was anticipating staying overnight. We borrowed electricity from the chalet and a long extension cord, and we hooked the small heater inside the van. We had sleeping bags, blankets, and pillows, and we were ready for the evening. Obviously, safety was a factor with electricity and having a heater, so we had the two of the windows cracked open for ventilation.

We set up our bed on the floor, jumped in our sleeping bags, took off our outer clothes and slid into our pajamas. Each of us was inside our own sleeping bag, all bundled up and ready for a night of sleeping. In the morning, we heard a little bit of rustling outside, and we were ready to wake up. The van was cold even with the heater, but it had kept us from freezing. It was certainly cold in the van, nonetheless. I remember it was time to get out of the sleeping bag and jump into our jeans, put our socks on, our shoes on, and get ready for the day. I remember it was so cold it felt like your eyeballs were frozen, and they were watering. The next adventure was how to get out of the sleeping bag and into our jeans. Well, as you can imagine, our jeans were frozen, shirts were frozen, and socks were frozen. It was quite an adventure as you jumped out of the sleeping bag and got into a pair of frozen jeans in record time. Next, you grabbed the cold socks you had tried to warm up before you put them on, your T-shirt, and threw your coat on, which was also frozen. Finally, you grabbed your snowmobile boots and jumped outside. We were surprised at how cold it was, but we got ready and went into the chalet for breakfast and to spend another day snowmobiling.

Now, can you imagine a father and son sleeping in a van in the middle of winter with a small little electric heater, freezing their butts off but having a fun time while snowmobiling. I think back and begin to laugh. Now we often complain about a hotel not being up to our homestyle standards and it not being as fancy as home. We spent the weekend sleeping in a van in the middle of winter, jumped into frozen clothes to run to the chalet to go to the washroom. Anyways, a bit of a goofy story but certainly a memory between my father and me.

GIRLS AND GIRLFRIENDS

Girls and girlfriends are a crazy topic for discussion. In grade school, I would say starting in grade six, I started noticing girls and had a few crushes. I was not one of the top-notch athlete jock kind of guys or super good looking in grade school. I was a fat kid but always had a good relationship with the guys and the girls. In high school, it was the same thing. I was a bit chubby and more on the shy side. I would say overall I seemed to get myself into the friendzone with girls quite often.

I didn't have a lot of confidence with girls in grades 9 through 11. Friends and I just hung around with girls, some of the guys would have a girlfriend, however, they would still hang out with us. But overall, it was a mix of friends. I remember in grade 12, a bunch of us guys along with a few of the cool guys and some of the jocks thought we would not bother going to the grade 12 prom.

The prom was always a big function for graduating students. The prom had a dinner where the girls and guys dressed up and then there was a huge student only party after. Obviously, not going was okay for me. It wasn't a big deal. It meant the guys and I probably did something dumb and sat around and played pool and had a couple of pops. Grade 13 was something different, so again, being a shy guy with a lack of confidence, I was slow out of the gates. I always had a good relationship with the girls. I wasn't a nerd, and they didn't think I was an idiot or anything like that. It was a lack of confidence I would say. A bunch of my friends started to ask girls, or they had girlfriends, so that was a given that they were going to go to the prom. Crazy me, I started too late...maybe three or four weeks before the prom. I think about it now, and it was kind of stupid. Who would even think about asking so close to the function. I remember basically shaking in my boots but got up enough courage to call a couple of girls that I had known from a few of my classes. I thought I really had a good relationship with them. Maybe we sat beside each other and were kind of buddies and would see each other at parties and chat. No one would make a romantic advance, especially me, which kept me walking down the friend path rather than the boyfriend path.

Anyway, by the time I got around to calling, the girls had already been asked. I asked four or five girls, and each time they would say no because they were going with another guy as friends. Whoever had asked the girl got to go with her to all the festivities, and at the end of the night, go their separate ways. Now that was the story of my high school...all too often in the friend zone. I had opportunities as they say as a young teenage boy in grade 12 or 13 to advance around the bases for a home run, but I would say I never felt confident about it. It often would never happen, so you could say I didn't have any girlfriends throughout high school. I had enough courage a few times to take a girl out for dinner or have a date with her, but again, I ended up in the friend zone. Nothing became of it, and any chance of a relationship would fade off into the sunset. It was all my doing rather than any girls' issue with me. They always accepted me, but it just never happened.

It was the same situation throughout my college years, even with all the parties and shenanigans. I just never pursued having a girlfriend. I was not the hound dog as they say and didn't pursue girls for the purpose of having a girlfriend. I wasn't much of a dancer, so I never did that whole dance scene. My friends and I would hang out, have a couple of pops, watch everybody, chat casually, and enjoy ourselves. We would watch bands and keep to ourselves, having everyone come over and hang out with us. Maybe that we were the cool guys who didn't appear to care is what drew the crowds around us. We never really pursued girls. It was the thrill of them coming to us. Our goal was not to get a girl for a friendship. I try to think of a few of my friends who ended up with girlfriends in high school or college, and they would have a girlfriend for only a few months. Now that being said, I do know of at least three or four couples to this day that are married to their high school sweethearts.

That is awesome to hear in these times...a marriage of 35 years. Currently, the divorce rate is over 50% for couples, which is a sad state. I mean I think about myself. I was lucky enough to have a mom and dad living together for 20 years before my dad passed away. Then, I look around at my close friend. He and I were divorced after only a handful of years of marriage. We each had two boys during the marriage, and now unfortunately, our sons have been raised in a divorced household. I look at my other friend Mike St. Germain who got married within a month of me, and he is happily married to the same beautiful wife. His marriage has lasted close to 25 years. The duration of the marriage appears to depend on the individual couple.

I guess one take away from this is that many teenagers are very self-conscious, and I would surmise that only a very few have true confidence. As you watch your kids growing up, you watch and realize their confidence levels. They often don't realize that whoever they may have an interest in is most likely in the very same situation of maybe not feeling so confident. They don't think they will ever have a boyfriend or girlfriend, so when you get that whole mix, basically both are equal.

So, to anybody reading this book, make sure you build self-confidence. Everybody needs to be loved, and everybody can be loved. Just be yourself, and love will come to you. Don't force it. Obviously, you can pursue it, but it's kind of a natural progression in life. I would think that there are more people not confident in their pursuit of a relationship than there are those who think they may be the best thing since sliced bread.

My words of wisdom, along with my experience, would tell you that if there's someone that you fancy, and you want them to be a boyfriend or girlfriend, don't be afraid. Begin the process of pursuing them, and tell them your intentions. You never know where it could go. Just maybe they could be feeling the exact same way.

PARTY BOY

As the years went on, you got to develop tighter friendships with classmates. You would spend time together during school, after school, and on weekends. A few of those friends from high school I am still very much in touch with and occasionally we meet up for the holidays. In grade 10, I was a 15-year-old who thought he was mature. This was the age where you began to be aware of parties in the neighbourhood. There were parties every weekend where there was alcohol and drugs. Now, even in grade 10, alcohol was consumed by many under agers. The drinking age in Ontario is nineteen, however, that didn't stop the alcohol from flowing in high school.

One Friday night, I remember going over to a long-time dirt biking friend's house. The plan was to leave from his house and walk down the street to go to a party that we had heard about from friends. Sure enough, I let my parents know everything was good, and they dropped me off at my friend's house. I told them I was just going to be hanging out for the night at his house. A few minutes after I was dropped off, we left and walked to the party which was a block away.

We walked into the house as grade 10 kids, at a party with mostly older kids. Everything was cool and quickly somebody passed a beer to each of us. I had consumed less than a 1/2 a bottle of beer when the phone rang in the house. Remember, there were no cell phones and no texting. It was just good old-fashioned landline phones. My friend's sister had called because my mother had called my friend's house and asked for me. Now, this was very strange as it had never happened before, so something was up in the parent investigation. My friend's sister called the house where the party was and let my friend know that my mom was coming over to his house shortly to pick me up. We scrambled home and were there in time when my mother unexpectedly and certainly out of character drove over to pick me up.

I got in the van, and everything was okay. It was only a five-minute ride back home, but there was a lot of conversation with my mother, including a lot of inquiring. Everything seemed normal, but she definitely had a lot of questions. No suspicious questions, just a lot of talking as I walked into our house and immediately walked to my bedroom. Out of respect in our house and in many houses, you always took your shoes off before you went inside. In this case, because of my nervousness of having drank a half a beer, I didn't bother to take my shoes off, and it was noticed. It wasn't long after going to my room that I was called out to the kitchen area to sit down and chat with my parents.

They asked me if I had been drinking, as I was raised properly, I told them the truth that I drank half a beer at a party. Obviously, they were disappointed, one for lying about the party, saying that I was just spending time at my buddy's house. Second for having alcohol three years earlier than legally permitted. The punishment was to never hang out with that friend again because obviously, he had made the same bad decision, and together we both were making bad decisions. I respected their wishes and never hung out with him again. That meant no more dirt biking or even saying hello in the hallway.

Our friendship ended that night and only recently, I would say 40 years later, we saw each other on the street and had a casual conversation. I still remember my mother's saying she did not want me to ever hang out with that friend again. Some 40 years later, it was still etched in my mind. All these years later, and I still hear a little whisper from my mother about never hanging out with that kid again.

That experience did not end my partying, however. I definitely attended my fair share throughout high school and college. A small group of friends and I would go to parties where consuming alcohol was normal. I do recall most of the time I was the driver since I had a van, nothing super special, but built up inside. My parents owned the van, but I was fortunate that I got to drive it when I wanted. At the time, modifying the interior of vans was always the cool thing, and my van was nicknamed the shagging wagon. I will leave that for you to research.

That van is famous for a bunch of distinct reasons, both throughout high school and years after in college. I took it to drive-in theatres with a bunch of friends and girls. We used to take it back and forth to school and to the city of Windsor from LaSalle. I have always enjoyed driving because I had ultimate control of what I did, where I went and when I went.

It was always fun, and we all enjoyed watching bands and live performances around town. We had an abundance of bands in our high school playing several types of music, from rock and roll to punk rock to hardcore music. The bands would play at various venues around the town of Windsor mostly on Fridays or Saturday nights. My friends and I would support the bands each weekend. We enjoyed watching our school's high school bands, with many of them having quite a following around the city.

The venues that these local bands played were always in the Windsor area or nearby. I would pick up the guys and their girlfriends and drive into Windsor to watch the bands. There were a few memorable incidents I can recall.

The first one was at a Chinese restaurant located in downtown Windsor. It was a restaurant during the week and a concert venue on the weekends. During the day on the weekends, half the restaurant was for dining, and in the evening on Fridays and Saturdays, the remaining half was for the bands.

The restaurant's name was The King Wah located near the corner of Ouellette and Wyandotte. I don't really know how much Chinese food they sold, but I can sure tell you that Fridays and Saturday nights were jammed with crazy high schoolers. There was always a charge to help support the band. I'm sure they were only paid a few hundred dollars for their gig. Kids would come to the venue. pay a couple of dollars and head over to the band side of the restaurant. The security certainly wasn't very tight, but they did always want to get their money at the door. The restaurant got the door money, and a portion of the total may have gone to the band. The restaurant also would get the money from food and alcohol sold. I can tell you there was no one checking to be sure the alcohol buying patrons were of age. It was great fun going there and supporting the local music scene.

One crazy thing about The King Wah was that there was an alley directly behind the restaurant. The restaurant was in downtown Windsor. Every Friday and Saturday night when we decided to go down to watch the band, it was always an adventure. A couple of friends and I, along with a few girls, would all head downtown in the van. We were 17 or 18 years old at the time, adventurists and partly dumb. The restaurant sold beer for those of age, and as teenagers, we were always concerned about our alcohol budget. Restaurant beer was expensive in our eyes.

What we would do was grab beer and jump in the van, and the girls would grab a magnum of the cheapest wine and sit in the back of the van where, at the time, there were no seats. They would sit on the carpet floor in the back. I was always the driver, a modern-day Uber. The van had a couple of seats where my passengers would sit, while others were in the back on the floor. We would drive into Windsor and park directly behind the restaurant in the alley. Admittedly, we did a few stupid things, but I can say we never had open alcohol drinking in the van while we were driving. The girls would get all loaded up on their cheap wine once we were parked, and the guys would have a couple of pops. We would then put a few bottles of beers in our pockets to bring into the venue. The kitchen door was always open to the back alley because the kitchen was so hot.

We would hang in the van until we noticed nobody was in the kitchen. At the right moment, we would open the screen door, run through the kitchen, and get into the crowd of spectators watching the band. We would do that just about every week. Occasionally, we would get caught and kicked back out to the alley. We then would have to go around to the front door and pay a few dollars to get into the restaurant. We used the kitchen entrance more often than the front entrance for sure. Now, we were not stupid enough to be drinking while driving, but we certainly were stupid to sit in an alley and drink beer while underage and then run through a kitchen without paying to watch a band.

Some of the foolish things I did as a teenager, not thinking anything of it at the time, now has me shaking my head all these years later. The band was always done around midnight, and we would often go searching for late night food. It was usually pizza. I would then drop everyone off at their houses and head home.

In those days, drinking and driving was not a big societal issue. Reminiscing as I am writing this, I am thinking about how many times, as a teenager, I drove after having a few beers. I can honestly say that I was never a big drinker, however, I would have a few drinks and then foolishly jump in the van with my friends and go on our merry way. It was a stupid idea at the time and 50 years later, it is still a stupid idea. That is not recommended in any way, but truth be told it did happen.

It's funny as I write this thinking of all the craziness of high school and college. My two boys Linden and Nolan often make comments that I was perfect and an angel in high school and college. So, this will be their very first time knowing a little bit more about their dad and all his teenage antics. There will be many things in this crazy book that will shock everyone. However, sharing my stories will help you understand where I got some of my knowledge. Yes, I was a teenager once and made bad decisions just like many other teenagers.

The one thing I have always tried to teach my two sons was to make good decisions. I explained a few times that especially on McEwen Street there were kids who were not angels and hung around in our group of friends. They would do stupid stuff, but I was always aware that just because they're doing it doesn't mean I have to do it. My father always used to tell me to always find a way to remove myself from bad situations.

An example to get out of the situation would be to say...I got to get home...I got something to do. You never had to confront them, or tell them their idea was stupid. They could make their own decision. It was most important to get myself out of those situations. Now, obviously after years of removing myself from many bad situations, everything has turned out good.

I don't think I was a bad kid by any means, especially compared to some of the guys that I hung around with all throughout school and college. Some of the parties and concerts we went to were wild. There were drugs back in my day, however, but it was mostly marijuana and hashish. Those were the go-to drugs for a few of the guys. At parties, the use of hashish was always done through a process called hot knifing. Someone would grab a kitchen knife and put a chunk of hashish on the knife, heat it on the kitchen stove and then inhale the smoke. I certainly saw it used but never participated because I always thought it was dumb.

I didn't look down on people that did drugs, but you always knew it was not the best thing to be doing. I chose to sit around and drink beer instead. I heard about cocaine in my older college days, but I never saw anybody use it in high school. As far as my friends went, I don't believe any of them ever did cocaine as far as I know. There were no drugs like fentanyl or other opiates like we see today on our streets. Those drugs were not even thought about or invented.

One way I avoided the heavy drug scene at parties was to not partake in drinking on a regular basis. Certainly, I would have a couple of pops when we went out but never excessively. One thing I never did and don't ever do is just sit at home and have a beer after a hard day's work, a frustrating day at work or a long week. The only time I have ever had drinks is in a social setting. I chose that scenario for a few reasons. One reason was I never understood how somebody enjoyed the feeling the next day after a hangover. The second reason was I never liked feeling so drunk that I really didn't know what I was doing or saying.

That situation happened one time that I recall, where a couple of friends and I went out and I had too much to drink. On our way home, I threw up in the cab. I would say that is the only time I remember being in that situation where I had no real control over myself.

I have always told my boys, and I still say it today, you need to know your limitations. Even now, you never see a case of beer in my house because it's nothing I genuinely enjoy. I would rather just have a cold glass of milk to which people often laugh at me. I don't judge people that have cases and many bottles of liquor at their homes. I wonder how they can afford that because I believe a 24 case of beer is nearing $60 Cdn. I just never understood it, but if people do it that's fine. I have always cautioned my boys that when they get to be of drinking age, that it is not an incredibly good feeling to be out of control because of drugs or alcohol. When drugs or alcohol control you in any situation or life, it always leads to problems.

STAY CALM HAVE FUN

I was not always the wild guy that I talked about in previous chapters. I have never smoked cigarettes, and I was 25 years old when I took three puffs of a marijuana cigarette. I did not feel any effects from it and have never touched pot again.

I still can't stand it, but I guess at 25, I just wanted to try it. There was no real reason and no real thought other than just to do it and have the experience. To this day, I don't agree that marijuana is not a gateway drug to other drugs. Now, I do realize that there are some additional benefits according to what you read and hear. If there was some medicinal value to marijuana, which I guess is still being debated, then why someone wouldn't just eat or consume what they call edibles is a mystery. In 2025, in our small town of Amherstburg with 22,000 people, there are three cannabis stores located downtown. Two of them are within a block and a half of each other. It seems that any municipality that you drive through certainly has at least one kind of cannabis store now. It is legal to sell and consume it currently, but I worry about the long-term effects.

A fairly new hazardous habit kids are facing today and probably have been for the last 10 years or so is vaping. I believe that vaping teaches dependency or habit to be more specific. You can buy assorted flavors, and from what it looks like, you inhale it through a cigarette shaped device but it is an odorless vapor. You can taste it, but you can't smell it. I'm not a doctor, but I do wonder what all this juice and liquid they put in these vapor machines is doing to their lungs. What long term damage is it doing? You think back 50 years ago, and they had advertising for cigarettes that made smoking cool. Many actors or actresses were advertising smoking on television and radio. Now, 50 years later, you don't see any advertisements regarding cigarettes. There are hundreds of thousands of people dying from lung cancer every year. Fortunately, cigarette smoking is on a decline since the population now understands the damage it causes to the human body. In fact, I don't know of anybody in my immediate circle that smokes.

I never experienced it, but when I got into the workforce 35 or so years ago, you were allowed to smoke. Many smoked inside their offices where it was common to see an ashtray, and you could see people sitting at their desks having a smoke while working, and it was no big deal. You also could smoke in restaurants at that time. Nowadays, to smoke a cigarette, you need to be outside any building, and I think a certain distance away from an entrance door.

All the health issues that you hear about from smoking has me wondering if, in 30 years, vaping will be the same. It's always been a concern of mine. I have never agreed with vaping or marijuana and certainly always voiced my opinion whether I was asked for it or not with my kids. I would make it a point that they knew my opinion. If I see anybody vaping, although not directed at them specifically, I let them know what I thought of marijuana and vaping.

Another thing that will shock the world is a couple more drugs in high school that were tried. I thank the Lord that I was never addicted and never had an urge to do them again. I did not enjoy any of them and only experimented with them once. I remember playing high school intramural hockey, which was just a fun league where we played against the teachers each week. A player was talking about this drug in the dressing room one week.

I don't believe it was a hard drug, but it was illegal, and it was called speed. You took a tablet, and it would give you all kinds of energy. I was curious and tried it one week before our intramural hockey game. You felt like you were skating a million miles an hour. Other than that, it didn't seem to have an effect on me.

Also, during high school, I once tried a drug called blotter acid at a party. It was a little tiny piece of paper a quarter of the size of your smallest fingernail. What you did was put it on your tongue, and the hallucinogenic drug would get absorbed into your blood stream. It would start to take effect shortly after it was on your tongue. Acid was a more serious drug for sure, and I knew a guy who used to do it all the time. I talked to him and told him I would try it but only a half dose.

So, I tried it one evening at an outside house party, and it was a weird crazy feeling. I remember just standing there staring off into space, just feeling tingly and different from any normal experience. I could still function, but it was delayed, no feeling or emotion. It was a situation where I was not cognizant of anything I was doing, just staring off into space. Its full effect seemed to last well into the next day. I still had some residual effects for a few days because I remember I felt a little bit weird and off kilter.

I can raise my hand and say those were my three experiences with drugs.

PUNK ROCKER

During grade thirteen of high school, I was 18 years old and decided to try being a punk rocker. It's the same today... kids try to have their own identity whether with crazy hair, crazy clothes, or crazy music. I laugh as I did all those things in my late teen years. A couple of friends and I were of that mindset for a few years. Listening to crazy music was a natural part of the punk rock scene. We listened to music from bands including the Sex Pistols, the Cramps, and the Ramones; all pioneers in the rebellious punk rock band scene. We dressed up like punk rockers thinking we were so cool. Myself, I remember having tie dyed pants and a dress jacket that I had splattered with multicoloured paint. My friends and I would wear high Dr. Marten boots, army pants, and army jackets. We thought of ourselves as true punk rock kids. In those days, it was all about being different. In fact, I remember one night before we all went out, a couple of guys and I had a crazy idea about haircuts.

My friend shaved one guy's head entirely clean of hair, so I got the great idea to shave my head into a Mohawk. We passed the clippers and began our front porch hair styling party. When we were all done, I had myself a mohawk, and my friend's head was bald. We were ready to go out for the night as punk rockers.

In the punk rock scene, there were a bunch of different people who would meet up at the bars. We would mostly watch music together; many were dressed like me. Others wore standard normal clothes. There were others who are now referred to as goth, where they dressed up with makeup and wore black clothes and had dark black hair. Really, it was just a room full of teenagers dressed as they wanted enjoying music. After the bands were done, we would walk up and down downtown Windsor. It seemed that everybody would look at us like we were a bunch of freaks. They had the right to look at us like that because we did look like freaking idiots who were acting like idiots trying to be cool.

Now, back to my first punk rock haircut, parental viewing. After a night of partying and watching bands, I remember coming home somewhere near 2 o'clock in the morning. The house was laid out so you walked past the kitchen table and then down a hall to my bedroom. I recall taking off my shoes and walking past the kitchen where my mother was up having a cigarette at the kitchen table. I continued walking down the hall to my bedroom. I don't remember even saying hello. I just walked by not thinking anything of it. The next thing I remember after getting settled in bed is my mother yelling down to the bedroom where my father was asleep. She shouted to my father, "Lloyd, look what your son has done." He got up, went to the kitchen table, and I was beckoned to come out of my bedroom.

They both looked at my mohawk, shook their heads, and my father proceeded to give me a speech which I still remember today, as it was true. My father explained that the things you do as a teenager are often remembered years later. I was always respectful and explained that it was the cool thing to do. I mentioned that a couple of friends and I shaved our heads, and that it wasn't a big deal. There was never any shouting between us. My parents were respectful to me and I to them. I will leave that for future reference. As you can imagine, it does come up again.

Well, it wasn't even two or three days later that my dad called me down downstairs and he said, " If you're going to have a mohawk haircut, it might as well look good." I remember going down in the basement and sitting down in a chair where he had a set of his old horse clippers. He trimmed the mohawk, so it was nice on the sides and in the back. I remember my mom coming down and just yelling at him about what he was doing, supporting this stupid haircut on his idiot kid. He just said he just wanted the hair to look half decent instead of like a bum and a fool.

My mohawk and my blue shagging wagon van will rise again years later.

Here is another memory that I recall taking place while at a bar watching a band. This bar scene was the same setup as the one where I would drive the friends and park in the alley. This bar's name was the Coronation, and it was located on the waterfront in Windsor. It was an old established dumpy bar owned by a lady named Stella who lived upstairs. Stella was in her late seventies. She would sit at the bar with her dog Bruce and watch us young kids act like idiots and she would drink draft beer all night. At the time, everybody said she was a little bit crazy; not having all her senses (which we now know could have been a mental disorder or dementia). The rumor had it that every dog that she owned in her adult life was always named Bruce. Nobody ever remembers her having a husband or kids, just her dog Bruce.

We were regulars in this bar, and we had a favorite table where we'd all sit near the stage. Everybody that came to the Core (as it was nicknamed) usually knew each other. It was the same punk rock scene that would watch bands at different bars around Windsor. As teenagers, purchasing beer was always expensive for us with limited budgets. The weekends that we would go there, whether a Friday or Saturday night, we would walk in dressed like punk rockers with long trench coats or army pants with big pockets. The deep pockets were perfect to conceal the bottles of beer we would sneak into the bar. We would spend the night buying a few bottles of beer around the table. The service was not that great, and the servers didn't really care.

All the empty beer bottles would just sit on the table until the server would clean up the table at the end of the night. As usual, they did have a door attendant that would collect money and check ID. As you can imagine, back in the early eighties, a fake ID was easy to produce. If you could show something resembling a birth certificate with the correct age, you would get in without any hassle. After a few weekends of going to the Coronation and purchasing beer while watching bands, we had an idea. We obviously couldn't afford to sit there and get drunk because it would cost too much.

A few idiots in our group (including myself) had a great idea to just bring in bottles of beer. We would hide them in our pockets or in our trench coats, and we just had to get them into the bar. There was no frisking or clothing searches for weapons or contraband. All we had to do was get in, and we would have our beers ready to pull out of our pockets while watching the show. Well, for whatever reason, we had Heineken beer in our possession for the evening's festivities. Heineken was a higher end beer and not too many bars sold it, certainly not the lowly Coronation. We figured everything was good. We were enjoying the band and had a couple of pops. Heineken, if you don't recall, has a green bottle, which is quite different from the typical brown beer bottles that were sold at this venue.

After a few pops, there were brown and green beer bottles on our table. It wasn't long before the server noticed that those green coloured bottles were not purchased from the bar. Sure enough, the door attendant and bouncer came around the corner to our table. He told us that bringing in beer was not allowed, that we were acting like idiots and to get out of the bar. It was not like we could dispute the claim. The evidence was sitting all over the table. Naturally, we all got up and left without any fanfare. So, there again, something harmless but illegal and at the top of the stupidity list. As they say, you play stupid games, you win stupid prizes.

After reading the few paragraphs above, it certainly sounds like we were a bunch of boozehounds getting drunk every weekend, which was not the case. As an adult, I would be shocked if I had one beer every year, so I am not an alcohol hound for sure. To me, it didn't matter if my friends sat there and got loaded, I would get them home safely. Although I was not necessarily the designated driver each time, I was the driver that would get them back to their place.

Here is another silly situation with the old blue shagging wagon. The incident started at the King Wah restaurant where we were watching a band for the evening. My friend, rest his soul, asked if I could give him the keys to my van because he needed to grab his wallet that he had left inside.

Of course, I thought nothing of it, but he was on the wild side, so I should have known. I gave him the van keys, and he had unknowingly left the bar and went to a house party. At the end of our night watching the bands, we proceeded to leave the bar, only the van was gone.

I remembered I had given my keys to my friend, and it was obvious he had taken my van. After talking to a bunch of different people in the restaurant, I soon realized where the van was located. It was apparent that my friend and the van were at a party.

I got someone to drive me and a few friends to where the party was and drop us off. They were headed to the party anyway, so it was no big stretch. I walked in, and at this point, I am very agitated at my friend for taking my van. I walked into this strange house with strange people I didn't know. I finally found my friend in the house. He obviously could tell I was super mad, tossed me the keys, and ran out of the house. We got in my van and went home with no thought of how my friend was going to get home after doing this dumb thing and not really caring.

The next day we met up, and he knew I was still angry. He apologized, said he was sorry and that he would never do it again. Obviously, we got over it, but I told him he would never borrow my vehicle again.

Another event I recall was me and a couple friends joyriding around town one weekend. We were not drinking and driving, simply cruising with my van. We went to one area in the surrounding town that had a huge hill that was parallel to a small dirt lane. I figured it would be a cool idea to drive down the lane with two tires slightly in the air; two tires on the lane side of the hill and the two wheels that were on the side of the hill now in the air. I was driving down the lane on the side of a hill that got steeper and steeper and had the van tilting at quite an angle. A bump later, and we were driving in a forward motion and had the van up on two wheels for a few moments while I drove. Now, I don't believe we were in any crazy danger, though perhaps I'm still being stupid about it. It was cool that I got to drive my van with two wheels off the ground like a stunt driver in the movies. A dumb idea and foolish thoughts by teenagers yet again. We all survived with no harm and no damage to anything but a memory 42 years later. I remember this because I often drive by the same hill and reminisce about that stupid stunt.

ROCK STAR

My claim of being a rock star was halted quickly and before it started. The stoppage was all about the timing of the unfortunate passing of my father. A little background information of my musical career. Although I played the saxophone in high school for a couple of years, it was only because I needed the credits. There was no ambition, eagerness, enthusiasm, or any care during music classes. I did the bare minimum, never practiced, or brought the saxophone home. I left the class with just a passing mark and eventually graduated. Sometime after grade 13, a couple of friends and I decided we would have a band. If you recall in the previous chapter, I was into the punk rock scene. I would say the only instrument that I could have played would be the drums. I remember banging on my knees and tapping different things as a kid. I seem to have a little bit of rhythm, in my opinion, but I don't know if I ever had the coordination required to be a real drummer. The impromptu band had a legitimate musician who was in a real band and two other friends. One was a singer who had never been a singer before, and one was a guitar player who had recently learned how to play guitar.

I remember going over to the real musician's house for a couple of weekends practicing. I recall playing the drums for so long during a few of those sessions that I had blisters on my hands from the drumsticks. The legitimate musician was a drummer, so he showed me a few techniques and the basics. He played the bass in our crazy band. We had written a couple of silly songs and tried to do some covers of a couple of other songs. I don't even remember what they were, but I know they were punk rock songs. I recall us somehow getting an opportunity at a punk bar to play a set. Unfortunately, the weekend that we were going to play was the weekend that my father passed. There was no chance of me ever playing for that set as I had some serious things to deal with in the passing of my father. I can laugh that I never had the opportunity to be a musician for that one set of a few hours.

I certainly did not have any talent, but the other guys had mild talent and the true musician had all the talent. The drummer, which was me, didn't have any talent but was willing to do it just for the experience. In the punk scene, you didn't have to be good, you just had to be there and be loud, wild and dress crazy. The singer would be yelling and screaming obnoxious lyrics, the guitar player would be full volume and the drummer would be banging on his drums loudly. Our bass player with the talent would lead the task of getting the rest of us to play like musicians. It would be the perfect fit for a guy with no talent.

Anyways, it never did happen. The real regret in all of this is that I didn't bother to learn any instrument. I do remember taking a few lessons for drumming as a very young kid at the Canadian Conservatory of Music. At the time, they gave you a small board with a rubber face on it. When you had to practice basic drills you used the rubber pad, it was extremely boring. It did not look like a drum. It was a piece of board with rubber on it. So, it lasted about three lessons, and that was the end of that adventure.

I wasn't quite done with my musical aspirations after the punk band dream. I remember when I finished college, I moved into my buddy's house in Oakville. He was the guitar player in the punk band, and he turned out to be a skillful player. I decided I would learn how to play the bass guitar so that we could jam. I rented a bass guitar for a month and tried to practice. My enthusiasm quickly faded and there was no real practicing. After a month, I brought it back to the music store from where I had rented it and that was officially the end of my music career. There was a little bit of a regret, I must say, because I certainly do love all genres of music from rock'n'roll to blues to instrumental.

COLLEGE YEARS

College in my family was never thought about and, from what I understand, I was the first to get a college diploma. My brother Gary worked at Chrysler after high school for about a year and then left to be an electrician tradesman. He was an electrician for more than 30 years before he retired from a local salt company.

I was okay using my hands but would say I never really took a liking to doing anything with my hands. A fun fact is that throughout high school, I wanted to do something with robots, perhaps making them move or repairing them.

It's funny that you don't really know what you don't know at the time. I do know that robots were the buzzword, something new that was all automated, so that's what I wanted to do. I can tell you in the next 30 years after I graduated college, I never once fixed or moved a robot. I could never operate a robot or program a robot, so I guess I didn't succeed in fulfilling my high school ambition.

During my first year of college, I didn't hang out with anybody, I just walked around like an idiot. I dressed and acted like a punk rocker with a mohawk haircut and wild clothes. I basically remember not talking to anyone in my first-year college. It certainly was not conducive to meeting new people, I must admit. I went to my class and sat by myself, went to the library and sat by myself. I kind of just did my own thing. I would get out of class and hang around the guys I knew from high school.

During my first year at St. Clair I was making money at Chrysler throughout the summer. I paid my way through college, so to supplement my tuition, I would apply to receive money from the government. The program was OSAP, Ontario Student Assistance Program, where post-secondary applicants could receive financial aid. I believe, at the time, college enrollment was about $800 for each semester.

After students identified and chose a course of study, they went to orientation the first couple of days. I knew I wanted to be in a technical field, something like engineering and not math, sciences, or accounting.

I remember one presentation by a gentleman who ended up being my main professor. He talked about how the style and size of the ketchup at McDonald's was calculated. An engineer had to determine the optimal amount of ketchup required for the consumer. I am not sure why that impressed me, but I guess it did. The discipline I chose was industrial engineering technology.

At this point we still lived in Lasalle, my dad was in his early fifties at the time, and I was 18 years old. The first year was basically a waste for me. I enrolled but did not attend every class. I certainly remember never really studying or putting forth an effort that would get me good marks. I did enough to barely pass the first year. I put in very little care or effort. Honestly, I was just there for the college lifestyle and not so much an education.

I remember the first-year carpooling with a kid that I would pick up in my van. At that point, because the college was small, you could park close to the building in a parking lot. I remember on Fridays I had a three hour break between my first class and the last class of the week. As you can imagine, that last class was not well attended by me or my carpooling friend. We would often meet at a local bar to have a couple of pops at lunch and never end up making it back for the last class. In my eyes, I was getting a head start on the weekend. He ultimately dropped out of college after the first semester.

An option that was used on test day, when I was feeling ambitious was to go to my van that had shag carpet and pillows and take a few hours nap. I remember justifying it to myself because I would've had to drive back home, which was probably only 15 minutes away, but in my little pea brain it didn't make sense to drive 15 mins both ways to attend a one-hour class, and then drive another 15 minutes back home. It did not make sense, so instead I got to take a little afternoon nap in my van.

A couple of other items come to mind during my college years, and it was the hosting of a raffle in our second year. A few other students and I came up with the idea of holding a raffle to make some money. We got the approval of a professor, telling him that we would be raffling off moose milk which is a slang name for a basket of liquor.

In our college, we had five or six foreign students from a very wealthy country. They were very studious and never hung around us, but they had unique non typical Canadian names. The grand plan was to sell raffle tickets to as many people as possible. On one half of the ticket was a section with a ticket number and area where you would print your name. The other half of the ticket had the same number which the purchaser of the ticket would keep. Those stubs were put in a large bowl to which we would pull out the winner who would be the proud owner of a big basket of moose milk.

We sold about $800 worth of tickets, and along with that, there were many tickets that were fictitiously filled out with our foreign students' names. The names were non-Canadian so nobody would know they were fictitious; the plan was almost complete. The raffle looked very legit as we stood up in the cafeteria at lunchtime, pulled out a ticket and announced the winner. As you're probably anticipating, the winner was nobody that purchased the ticket. It was one of the foreign students or a version of a foreign student's name that won the raffle. So, here we are pulling out the winner as a fictitious person that would win. Ultimately, we would not have to give them the prize because they were only a fictitious person, and we could keep the money.

Once the raffle was completed, we decided the best thing to do would be to go to a local town about an hour away in Chatham Ontario, rent a couple motel rooms, and stay a Friday and Saturday night. My friends and I headed up on a Friday night. We had some fun Friday and Saturday at a local bar that was within walking distance of our hotel.

As you may or may not be surprised to hear, things got a little crazy. I was not involved directly but definitely guilty by association. The guys I was with decided to have a fire extinguisher fight, so they grabbed a fire extinguisher and sprayed each other up and down the hallway. They then brought them into the two adjoining rooms.

Later in our evening, somebody had locked the adjoining door between the two rooms, and we couldn't go back and forth. In a drunken stupor, one of the guys kicked a hole through the door between our adjoining rooms. One Saturday evening, we had two bed mattresses soaking wet because of a fire extinguisher battle, a busted door and a few other dings and wall bruises in our two motel rooms.

We were smart enough to take mattresses off the beds and place them against the wall while turning up the heat and opening the windows to let them somewhat dry out. Now, if you've ever been in adjoining rooms, there are two doors, one on each side of both rooms. During all our commotion, hotel staff came up and knocked on our door. Luckily, they knocked on the door of the room that did not have the damaged adjoining door. Then, they knocked on the other hotel room door, but before they did that, we had a little bit of a conversation in the hallway while the guys in the room switched out the adjoining doors, so now the second room the hotel staff went in to inspect showed everything was good. We had thrown both the mattresses down, but they didn't check if they were wet. Nothing appeared broken or wet during their inspection, but I would think they suspected something was going on.

The next morning, we had to pay for our rooms. I don't remember exactly whose credit card was used. I think, at the time, we were too young to use a credit card, so we used one of our parents' cards to book the room. After our weekend escapades of getting stupid in a hotel room, we had to worry they would find the damage and charge the credit card. Whoever was the owner of the card never mentioned anything to their kid, and I never heard about any extra charges. There were no charges to us, no fines, no criminal charges. We got away with some real stupidity having a fire extinguisher fight in the rooms, soaking mattress, and door damage. We were like professional partiers, and we put it all back together again like Humpty Dumpty. On Sunday morning, we packed up, left the scene and luckily everything was good. Could you imagine the fines and embarrassment now with cameras everywhere along with the social media today? Wow, the eighties were good to me.

As I've mentioned, my first year of college was a bust for multiple reasons, including me being a very immature 18-year-old. I did not really grasp the concept of post-secondary schooling, and that it was up to me. There was nobody hounding me, my parents were not familiar with it, so they didn't really get it. I was paying for tuition myself, and they were simply happy, trusting and assumed I was doing what was required to get through college.

In my second year, I began to buckle down and got through with slightly higher marks but still maintained a bare minimum GPA that would allow me to eventually graduate. The problem was, you could pass all your classes, but there was a potential that your GPA would be too low to graduate.

In my third year, I took my classes but also took first year classes again in the hopes of getting my grade point average high enough so I could graduate. After the first semester of my third year, the time came to think about a career. Students were starting to apply. We had learned about building resumes and were almost finished with school. This timeline kind of shook me because now suddenly getting a job was no longer years away but only a few months away.

I did what all diligent students were doing. I put together a resume and started applying for jobs. Shockingly, after my third year first semester, I received a job offer in the Mississauga, Ontario area. Here I was, a student with not particularly good grades who had not received his diploma for his degree, and yet was offered his first career job. I had to decide on whether to move approximately four hours away to take a job which would mean I would not earn my college degree.

I took the job offer, and with my stubbornness and don't quit attitude, I took a couple of courses at the local college. I took courses at night while working and eventually my grade point was high enough to graduate. Ultimately a three year program took me four and a half years to complete with graduation in the fifth year.

I sit back and think that that first year of stupidity cost me probably $30,000. The don't quit attitude got me my industrial technology diploma, and it was the first in our family. One caveat is that during my first year of college, my father unexpectedly passed away. After my third year, I moved away for my job leaving my mother by herself. During my second and third year, it was only my mother and myself at home. My brother was well established into his marriage with no kids at the time. I was still living with my mother when I got the job offer, and in my infinite wisdom, decided to move four hours away from my hometown.

I remember I only moved away for a year, and that was into a condominium with two long-time high school friends. The brothers had purchased the condominium because they had also taken jobs in the area after graduation. The three amigos, two brothers and Crain living in a 3-bedroom condominium in Oakville, Ontario. We will get into those Oakville antics a bit later.

The one thing I remember about moving away for that year is coming back every couple of weeks to visit my mother. At that point, she lived alone so I had some guilt but damn, I was having fun living with my friends as an adult. I remember once letting my mother know I was coming back for the weekend, and she told me she wouldn't be home much because she was working. Yes, I just said my mother was working. She had taken a job at a local donut shop to keep her busy.

She probably worked there half a year and was probably in her 50s at the time. She hadn't worked a job for well over 35 years, and it didn't sit well with me or my brother and sister-in-law.

After about a year living away from my family, I came back to Windsor where I took another job. It was a bit of a better job paying about $1000 more per year, which was a significant difference in my eyes.

I was certainly glad to be back at home caring and being there for my mother. I wouldn't say I was a momma's boy, but I was remarkably close with my mother. Once I came back, I explained to my mother that she didn't need to have a job, and ultimately, she did resign.

So, the above was a little bit of craziness I experienced in my college years. As the saying goes with a little Crain twist, I was at college for an enjoyable time and a long time.

HAY LOFT DIRT BIKE

Here is a crazy adventure between myself and my long-time friend Mike Janisse. Two kids living in the city a few houses apart, and we decided that we needed to have a dirt bike. I was in my first year of college, and Mike would have been in his third-year of college. Our family had recently moved back from living in LaSalle after my dad lost his job. I was somewhat familiar with dirt bikes since I had one while I lived in LaSalle.

At the time, I owned a small red four door Plymouth Horizon hatchback car. One Saturday, Mike and I had a great idea of going for a ride to see what we could find for a dirt bike. Again, this was typical of many Crain adventures throughout my life. We just started driving out in the county, no destination or detailed plan, just driving through the county looking for a dirt bike to buy. We drove around, up and down different county roads and didn't find any dirt bikes that were at the end of someone's driveway. We had stopped and had lunch, and we began to wonder if our adventure would ever lead to a dirt bike. We started to drive into small towns further out in the country, and eventually, we found a tractor store that sold tractors and farming equipment. Our great idea was to go inside and see if by chance they had any used dirt bikes for sale. Two young guys walked into this farm equipment place and headed to the counter. We asked the gentleman if he knew any place that would have any dirt bikes for sale. The gentleman said no, they didn't sell dirt bikes, so we turned around and were off for our next tour of the county. Ultimately, after another hour or so, we found another place very similar to the first farm equipment store. This time we walked in, and the gentleman at a counter said, "boys you might be in luck."

He explained that there was an old barn at the back of his property, and he thought there was a dirt bike up in the hayloft. He wasn't sure if it was there, and if it was in one piece or missing parts. If we were interested in going to have a look, he would send somebody out with us. We were excited and certainly took him up on his offer to walk out to the barn and see if we could find a dirt bike. Mike and I walked out to the barn with one of his store helpers. We looked up into the loft but couldn't see anything because it was deep, and we couldn't see the very back of the loft. We climbed up the old rickety ladder that brought us up into the loft and had another look. To our amazement, we noticed an old dirt bike laying down, sitting in the back corner of the loft in front of junk and straw bales. There was a dirt bike there, but we couldn't really get to it to have a good look at it. We climbed back down and went back to the store's front counter and talked to the gentleman to let him know we were interested in having a look. The gentleman said it was going to take time to pull the motorcycle down and that he didn't really have a lot of time to do it and didn't want to spend the effort unless we were interested in buying. We were basically at a standstill. We had to show interest before he would bring it down from the loft. We end up offering the gentleman $100 for this dirt bike, sight unseen. He said that seemed fair and grabbed a forklift and had his guy clean out the loft area and eventually got to the dirt bike. He put it on the forklift and brought it down to the barn floor. We now had a $100 dirt bike. We looked at it but didn't know what we were really looking at other than it appeared that it was all together. Two wheels, gas tank, handlebars, and the engine; it looked like a dirt bike to us, and we were good to go.

The next adventure was to get it home to Windsor. As you recall, I had a four-door hatchback car. We just bought a full-size dirt bike for $100, and we were probably an hour and a half away from home. Well, in our stubborn way, we folded down the back seat of the horizon, opened the hatch and loaded the full-size motorcycle into the back of the car. We had picked up the motorcycle, laid it down inside the car as much as possible and pulled the hatch down as far as it would go. We roped the hatch down so it wouldn't bounce around or smash into the dirt bike.

We jumped into the horizon and were on our way home. We got home with no issues, unloaded the machine and were proud owners of a dirt bike. Although neither of us were mechanics, we knew that you should take out the spark plugs and put fresh gas in the tank. We didn't know if it was a two stroke or four stroke. Eventually, we found out that it was a two stroke, meaning you had to mix the gas with oil. After a few days of fiddling around and replacing the spark plugs, we got the crazy old girl started. We rode it up and down the alley a few times. That was the beginning of the riding adventure, or maybe the end of the adventure of our dirt bike. Shortly after the dirt bike purchase, I moved to Oakville and the dirt bike was at my house, but obviously Mike grabbed it whenever he wanted. There's no real ownership, we didn't have insurance, it was just fun riding it up and down the alley.

While I was in Oakville, Mike had to put more gas and more oil in the tank. He mixed the gas in the oil but didn't realize there was a certain ratio that was required. Ultimately, he didn't know anything about that ratio and mixed too much oil into the gas, and it never started again. He had a friend who was a teacher in the mechanics department at our local college. Mike donated the bike to the college for them to be able to take it apart in the mechanic's class, rebuild it, do whatever they want, but we donated the bike and that was the end of the adventure. We came, we saw, we conquered. We found a bike, bought a bike, transported a bike, got it running and donated a bike all within three weeks.

A silly little story about two great buddies. On an adventure bound and determined to find a dirt bike and to get it home. Sure enough, we succeeded in our adventure, and we still laugh about it some 40 years later.

THE PINERY ESCAPADES

The famous story of the Pinery is about to be revealed. Friends and family have heard bits and bytes of it. Now it is time for the full story. Back in my second year of college, the boys and I decided to go camping at a popular campground located three hours away from Windsor. None of my friends really had any extensive experience with camping, and I only had experience with a trailer. We were adventurous, and it was going to be an exciting long weekend in May.

After a small amount of planning, the weekend was set. I was the driver with my 1979 grey two door AMC Concorde car. Four others and I filled the car with our camping tents, sleeping bags, food, and our alcohol. We were meeting a bunch of others at the campground, so we didn't have to worry about forgetting anything, we would just simply use someone else's who brought what we forgot. I want to say we left around 2:00 o'clock in the afternoon after we packed everything, jumped in the old Concorde, and headed down the 401 highway toward Grand Bend, Ontario. The campground was a provincially owned campground named the Pinery, located a few minutes from a summer resort community. We had heard stories previously about the campground being extremely strict and kicking people out feverishly. Young, foolish and the word invincible come to mind quickly.

At our age, we were certainly a little dumb and naïve and figured we were different and much smarter than the others. We travelled three hours to the campground and waited in a huge, lengthy line up due to the May long weekend. It was an immensely popular weekend for campers including family campers, partiers, and college kids. We finally got to our campsite and began the festivities. My group was on one campsite and across the laneway was another campsite with friends of ours. Our sites were all pre booked, so we were in the same area. We could spend time together and share the food and cooking. We arrived there around 6:00 o'clock in the afternoon.

We figured out how to put up our tents, but certainly not very well, I am sure. Next was to set up our picnic table and cooking area. We had our items set up the best we could by non-campers, and we were ready to camp and party all weekend. While we were doing this, of course, at that age you need to have music and have some pops. As we set up our campsite, we all consumed alcohol, played music, and had fun. We walked back and forth between the campsites across the road with beer to help our friends with their set up. Somewhere around 7:00 o'clock, the campground warden gave us our first visit. He talked to one of us and explained that there was a noise bylaw broken, and it would not be tolerated. We needed to turn down the music, or there would be fines. So naturally, five idiots started yapping to this gentleman telling him we were just trying to have some fun and to leave us alone. He reminded us again that it was a government campground, and we needed to abide by the laws of the campground and the province. This visit was our fair warning to smarten up. Remember the above young and dumb comment, we didn't.

Eventually, we turned down the music while he was there and waited for him to be out of sight. When he took off, of course, we were the rebellious ones, we turned up the music volume and had some more pops. It was apparent that he was going around trying to tame the entire park. Somewhere around 7:30 pm which was less than an hour after his first visit, he came back this time with a pad and pen in hand. His second visit was not as casual, and he began to give out tickets. The first ticket he gave out was for a noise violation, and was around $70. The next ticket he gave out was that there were two cars parked on our campsite, which was a violation and another $80. The third ticket was for moving the car across the lane way onto our friend's campsite. The person that was driving, had a beer can in his hand while in the vehicle and did not think anything of it. He jumped in the car and drove it fifteen feet and parked the car in the other campsite. At this point, the third ticket was given out for having open alcohol in a motor vehicle. As you can anticipate, we are two hours into our camping, with too many beers and liquor, so we began to yap. Of course, when he handed all the tickets to us, we crumpled them and threw them to the ground, to which we got a littering ticket added onto our previous stack. At this point, there is no return, no way to get back to a normal state. Eventually, he left, and of course we grabbed the tickets and paraded around the campsite like they were a badge of honour. We unfolded the crumpled tickets and stuck them into a tree with a knife, what we thought was a proud display for all passersby to see. About 15 minutes later, we have the warden along with the OPP visit our campsite. We now get another ticket for damaging a tree or some version of that bylaw. Given the circumstances, it was a fine total of over $500 in less than three hours.

The warden came over and explained that we were now kicked out of the park. He explained that our behavior was not going to be tolerated, and we had 15 minutes to pack our belongings. We explained to him and the OPP officer that we had all been drinking. The officer had a solution. Again, they explained that we now had about 10 minutes to pack up all our belongings and to not bother being organized. We were told to get our belongings into our car quickly, or else we would be removed without having any of our belongings. The OPP officer brought each of us into his vehicle to be administered a breathalyzer. I was the only participant that was under the legal blood alcohol limit to drive. I was the chosen one and was going to drive home.

We scurried around our campsite, grabbed all our stuff, jammed it into our car and into the trunk. We jumped into my car and got in line. The OPP cruiser was first, we were second in line and behind me was the warden. We drove through the park and eventually out the exit. He drove us across the street to a parking lot to which we noticed there were many other cars that were in the same situation. A parking lot was a place to reorganize your car after you got thrown out. There were ten or so cars doing the same thing, repacking their cars and their camping trailers. We repacked our car and began our journey back home.

A little summary of our three hours at the Pinery in Grand Bend, Ontario. We accumulated over $500 in tickets, got escorted out by the OPP and kicked out of a provincial park. Four people are in my car that were too intoxicated to drive. Luckily, I was sober enough to drive. We headed our way back to Windsor where there were more festivities.

Now being a long weekend, some of our other friends who did not bother to go to the campground were having a party. We left the parking lot somewhere near 8:00 o'clock by the time we were done repacking, and we then drove comfortably home. Our next mission was to get home in time to attend our friend's party. Sure enough, after we filled up for gas, we drove back and made it to the party in our hometown of Lasalle near midnight and continued to party. Obviously, I was the designated driver at this point, so my friends got to party.

I enjoyed a good party, and the Friday at the Pinery was one to be remembered. We got to camp for about three hours and go to a hometown party. Now, divide $500 in tickets between five idiots. The last Pinery adventure caused us to pay over $100 each for fines. As college kids, that was some serious money. So, in the next couple of weeks, we gathered all the money and eventually paid the fines. Fast forward to one year later, same campground, same long weekend. This time I did not go. Luckily, I was working. Again, my dumb friends did not learn their lesson the first time. The same scenario happened, and they got thrown out the first night. Again, another $400 in fines and a trip back home after a few hours of camping at the Pinery.

Dumb things you do in college, and one we still talk about today. It was not enough to get the first ticket, we had to keep going, play cool guys, and call the warden a bunch of names. All these antics to eventually get escorted out of a Provincial Park with over $500 in fines.

OAKVILLE BOUND

This is a crazy part of my life that has never really been discussed other than with the people that were directly involved. As you just read, I moved to Oakville to take my first real job. At the same time, my two good friends Mike and Brian St. Germain had graduated university, and they had taken jobs in Mississauga. Timing, as it turned out, was perfect as they purchased a condominium together and were willing to rent me a room for a very minimal fee, for which I was extremely grateful.

The condominium purchase was to be completed in three months, but our jobs started in two weeks. In the meantime, we had to have other accommodations for those three months. A long-time friend of my mother's lived in Toronto and was willing to allow me to live temporarily at their family's condominium. This would be my very first experience with condominiums in a high-rise apartment in Hyde Park Toronto and living away from home.

Their son Chris had moved out, and their youngest son Jeff, who was my age, was busy with life and working. Uncle John and aunt Shirley were also both working at the time and enjoyed a busy social life, but they were gracious enough to allow me to live there for three months. They had a den area with a fold out sofa where I would sleep. In the morning, I would take a shower, put everything back as it was and get dressed. I had a small area to put my clothes in and a television in the den area. We lived like a family, but I always felt a little bit like I was intruding. I must say that was certainly just in my mind. There were great dinners and breakfasts every day. I was treated like part of the family.

The one cool thing about living in the high-rise condominium was that the view was just phenomenal. You could stand at the window area, look out for miles, and see condos and other high-rise buildings.

It was a fun time for those three months that I lived there, and I did a lot of growing up. Those three months gave me the opportunity to explore Toronto on my own after work, at night or on the weekends. I really enjoyed finding unfamiliar places to go in the many different areas of the giant city of Toronto. I would also go back home on many weekends because I missed home. It was my first time living by myself, and I didn't want to wear out my welcome. I was trying to get out of the condominium as much as possible, finding things to do and places to explore. The one thing I remember is I would buy my own groceries for lunches to help with the expenses. I had a parking spot that was located underneath the huge building. You had to unload everything into the elevator, go up to the floor and then unload to your home. It was something little, but I had never experienced it. At home, you pull in your driveway at your house door and take everything inside.

The one thing I do regret living at my aunt and uncle's was my departure. It wasn't meant to do any harm, it was just to leave without fanfare. I've done this a few times before in my life. I was a bit spontaneous and acted before it was well thought out. On my last day at my aunt and uncle's place, I was excited and finished packing up all my items in the morning and headed off to work. I left them what I thought was a great note thanking them for their hospitality and generosity and wishing them all the best. Thinking back, and after receiving a call from my aunt Shirley, me leaving that way was rude. It was a cowardly way to say thank you, and I should've had the courtesy of sitting down with them, given them hugs and thanked them properly. Instead, I took the uncomplicated way and just wrote a letter and basically left.

Obviously, 35 years later, it still kind of bothers me. I don't like long goodbyes, and I wanted to go without any fanfare or emotions. I chose just to pack up quietly and leave a note and be on my way to the next chapter. I will admit, it was not a very adult way of managing the situation and disrespectful to their entire family.

The next chapter in my life was living with my two friends in Oakville Ontario. I lived there approximately a year, and the amount of fun we had could be packed into decades. As I have done in previous chapters, I'll give some highlights and low lights of the year with the gang.

The first thing we must establish is the lay of the land. Mike was the boss of the house. He was the organized one, and the one that would make sure that Brian and I were doing our share of the chores and upkeep. He would be on us when we began to slack.

Brian and I were easy going and had the "I will do it tomorrow" mentality. Mike has always been patient with our antics throughout our friendship. We have always all gotten along very well and certainly had lots of fun. When we moved in, we rented trucks and all chipped in to share the expenses.

Mike, and I didn't smoke, but Brian was a smoker, and the biggest bedroom somehow was negotiated to be Brian's room. The way that large room was negotiated was that there was a sliding screen door to the outside in Brian's bedroom so he could keep it open to get rid of the smoke. In fact, his bedroom was at least twice the size of the other two bedrooms. I had the smallest bedroom, however, it didn't matter to me since I was just a tenant in their house. There was a one-bathroom upstairs where our bedrooms were located. The main living area on the first floor had a small living room, kitchen, and hallway along with a door to the condominium hallway. You could simply walk in the sliding doors from the parking lot into the living room area, which was very convenient.

Their cousin Johnny, whose parents Mike and Brian had lived with in Brampton, moved into a condominium across the parking lot with his friend. Johnny had a girlfriend who would stay over at his place. Tracy was a great person, and we would often carpool together back and forth to Windsor since she lived in Windsor and would come up on the weekends.

The stage is now set with the cast, the three amigos and their cousin Johnny, all living within 100 yards of each other. We were all on our own for the very first time in Oakville, Ontario, about 30 minutes from the big city of Toronto. On different weekends, Mike would organize an outing to go to a hockey game or perhaps a basketball game in Toronto. We would all jump in a vehicle and drive into Toronto and try to purchase tickets.

Along with Johnny, we got to meet several of Johnny's friends and acquaintances. Often, there would be a half of a dozen of us lunatics that would get together on the weekends. Brian and Mike worked at the same place, and Mike was in a supervisory role over Brian so you could imagine the dynamic at work.

We would sometimes be going to local bars in Oakville. Other times, we'd drive into Toronto to have a couple of pops at some other bars. We found ourselves in the Toronto or Mississauga area I would say two or three weekends a month. Mike would be the guy that would organize everything, including grabbing tickets and checking event schedules. He would say, "hey why don't we do this tonight, or why don't we do this on Saturday?" If Brian and I weren't going home, and we had nothing else to do, we were ready to go. It was always a good time. We would invite Johnny and his crew along, and we'd have a great evening.

Mike and Johnny were avid Toronto Maple Leafs fans. I was a Red Wings fan, and Brian was a Montreal Canadiens fan. You can imagine all the ribbing and joking during Saturday night hockey events we'd watch on TV. It was always especially exciting if Toronto, Montreal, or the Red Wings were playing.

Periodically, we'd have the guys over for a poker night. The real gamblers in the house were Mike and Brian. I would often just sit at the table and try to play, but ultimately donate $20 for a half hour or so, losing miserably. Those guys knew what they were doing and how to play poker, so they would play for hours. We'd BBQ since we were on the first floor with easy access. Just outside the sliding doors was our barbecue on our tiny patio. We would BBQ hamburgers and hot dogs and occasionally, we'd play big shots and have steak and potatoes. Occasionally, we'd do the same thing over at Johnny's. Tracy and Johnny would have us over when Tracy was there, and we'd do the same kind of activities, including sitting around the house, watching TV and having a couple of pops. Sometimes, the guys would have too many pops and end their night sleeping on the couch or floor.

One weekend, I recall Mike organizing a Saturday afternoon for us to go watch high school basketball in the big city. High school basketball in the Toronto area was the best basketball around Canada and often those Toronto teams would come down to play the Windsor teams and simply destroy them in tournaments. The area we went to that was hosting the tournament was a very low-income area with a criminal element that was all over the local news. A tough high school was hosting the tournament that weekend. I would say we were a very visible minority inside the gym. It was so well attended that we had to park a few blocks away and walk through the neighborhood with our eyes wide open. We watched an afternoon of high school basketball where some of the players were being recruited for Division One NCAA scholarships. It was great to see the excitement of the fans who were primarily students supporting their high school teams. The quality of competition was at an unbelievably elevated level. At the time, I would say 90% of these high school players could dunk the ball. In fact, there was a ritual at one point in warmups where both teams would try to outdo the other team with some crazy wild music and exciting slam dunks. The crowd got excited when each team would score. The volume and excitement of the cheering was unbelievable. I still recall that it was just one afternoon in a tough neighborhood for three guys that had no concern watching some basketball.

One of the things that still lingers is the condominium parking situation. The building was located on the top of a hill, and part of the condo purchase included two parking spots, obviously one for Brian and one for Mike. There was no third parking spot that would have been mine, but there was a parking lot immediately outside of the building.

Of course, with my Crain stubbornness, I would park in the parking lot where visitors were supposed to park. There were many warnings from the condominium association about my being illegally parked. Eventually, it led to parking tickets from the association. I started to understand, after paying for many tickets, that I had to park down a crazy hill. Walking down the hill was not an issue during the summer months, however, walking back up the hill after a long day's work was always a pain in the ass. There was nothing worse than working 12 hours a day, coming home, just wanting to relax and having to walk up this mountain as it always appeared. You can imagine how many times I wiped out on that hill in the winter and got soaked every time it rained. I laugh now, but man was it a pain in my side. Of course, the guys would always give me a good ribbing like, "hey it's a little icy out there today. Have a good slide down the hill this morning."

Mike was always tidy and organized and would be on Brian and me about cleanliness when required. Brian and I would use all the dishes and all the utensils without washing them. They would stack up in the sink and on the counter after about a week of eating. The condominium didn't have an automatic dishwasher. Instead, it had manual washers named Mike, Brian, and Greg. Mike being smart to our game and knowing how we were, kept all his dishes and utensils to himself. He would use whatever he needed, wash them, and put them in his own cupboard. Brian and I would use everything available and stack them up in the sink until there was nothing else clean. Eventually, Brian and I would require a dish and then the debate would start. Who was going to do the dishes, me saying most of the dishes were Brian's and Brian saying the dishes were mine. We would then have some kind of contest to see who was going to do the dishes. We played cards or played rock paper scissors or something childish. Often, we came to the resolution that one would wash the dishes and one would dry. Who would put the dishes away was the next great debate. I sit here and laugh now how doing those dishes was always a wild experience. One dish washing situation had us acting like idiots. I was washing a knife and Brian reached over, and I ended up accidentally cutting his hand. We headed off to the emergency room for a couple of stitches, where he had to make up some kind of excuse so I wouldn't go to jail.

Sure enough, that wasn't enough hospital drama after one emergency visit. The next week, Brian and I again were washing dishes when Brian reaches into a glass to clean the bottom, the glass shatters, and he cuts himself. Off to the emergency room we go for a couple more stitches. It was me driving him there both times, and I remember thinking whether the hospital was going to be a little suspicious about this poor guy cutting himself all the time. Nothing was said, he got sewn up, and all was good. We still have a few memories about dishwashing adventures. What craziness.

Three letters: bbq. Boy, did we have some fun barbeques. We would have everybody over, and of course, Brian and I being the class clowns would be the cooks. We would make some very obscure looking hamburgers with the meat. A few were obscene, others silly like houses or donut style hamburgers, and sometimes a few phallic symbols. Just a couple of clowns doing dumb stuff for fun.

I remember trying chewing tobacco. For some reason, Brian and I figured we were going to try chewing tobacco like baseball players. Brian was a smoker, so he was used to the taste, I guess, but not me. We did not know anybody who chewed tobacco, but a weekend dare got the ball rolling. I remember grabbing a pinch of chewing tobacco and placing it under my lip, where I thought it was supposed to go. It was in my mouth about three seconds before I spit it out. I have to admit that was the most godawful taste ever. I spent the next hour rinsing my mouth, spitting, coughing, and brushing my teeth. It was the worst taste ever. I'll go on the record saying I have no idea how anybody can use that stuff without throwing up. Mike just sat back, smiled and shook his head at our stupidity as he watched his brother and idiot friend do something dumb.

At one point, immediately next to our condominium unit, a couple of girls moved in who were going to college. We were just out of college and university, so we were all basically the same age. We got to know them and became friends, occasionally hanging out with them. There were usually girls involved in our activities, just in case anybody out there reading this was wondering. So yes, we dealt with the girl situation next door as you can imagine teenagers would deal with it.

Another learning experience during this time was when the guys and I bought hockey tickets from a scalper for the first time. The Toronto Maple Leafs played only a half hour drive from Oakville at the Maple Leaf Gardens. We picked a Wednesday night game and headed to Toronto to grab our tickets from the scalpers and go watch the game.

We parked near the arena and took the subway up to the Gardens where we could walk off the subway and be right there. It wasn't anything out of the ordinary to see a scalper in a big full length fur coat on each of the city block corners and one located in front of the main entrance to the Gardens. You simply walked up to the scalper, told him what section seats you wanted, he told you the price and you purchased them. Once purchased, you walked into the Gardens, showed your ticket and went to your seat. I don't remember the game we saw, but it was quite easy and very affordable. I want to say we paid $40 each, which was a decent amount of money for sure. We had never been to a game at the Gardens, though, and it was something that we wanted to experience. The seats that we could afford were, as we called them, the nosebleed seats. The seats were in the upper rows of the Gardens, but we were inside the arena watching two professional hockey teams play.

The second time we went to watch a hockey game, it was a Saturday night. We watched the Montreal Canadiens play the Toronto Maple Leafs. Now, this experience was certainly a bit different. We got to learn in detail about the scalping system and the process. As we had done the first time, we parked a few blocks away and took the subway to the Gardens. We found a scalper on one of the corners and asked him for three seats up in the nosebleed section. He said sure no problem, and at the time, it was $150 a seat. That was way out of our range and not affordable for three young guys at their first jobs and living in Oakville.

We thought we were smart, so we walked down to the end of the block and asked another gentleman about tickets for the same type of seats. He responded with the exact same price. At this point, we were becoming disappointed and probably a bit agitated. We walked to the centre of the block, which was in front of the main doors to the Gardens. We stood to the side for a few minutes and watched a gentleman who was in control of both ends of the block. Those guys were obviously working in unison with the main dog in the front of the Gardens. We watched a limousine pull up to the scalper who would walk to the limousine window. You could see tickets were handed inside and cash was handed outside of the limousine window. The limousine would then take off, and at some point, I'm guessing passengers would have been dropped off somewhere and walked into the Gardens. You never saw who purchased the tickets from the limousine.

We were getting a bit more aggravated, so of course, in our youthful stupidity, we went and asked this gentleman for the same tickets. At this point, he didn't even talk to us other than to say to see the same guy at the corner, and that just fired us up even more.

There was a sign immediately in front of him that said no standing, no soliciting, and no scalping of tickets. We thought we'd be big shots because there was a police presence around the front of the garden. We immediately walked over to the police officer and said, "Hey why is this guy selling tickets right there in front of you?" The police officer said, "Mind your business boys, and go on your way." So that did not work out for us. We had one more try at the scalpers, though. We decided to wait until the game started, fully thinking that the price of the tickets would drastically be reduced because the game had already started. So again, we went to one of the scalpers and asked him for the same tickets to which he replied with the same price he gave us earlier. Like fools, we explained that the game had already started, and now we should be getting a discount price. The scalper who was now annoyed said, "Gentlemen, this is the price. Take it or leave it." You guessed it, we walked away disappointed.

We were in downtown Toronto and wanted to see the game, so we had another plan. Across from the Gardens was a bar and restaurant. We left the front of the Gardens and walked over there to watch the game on TV and order some food and drinks. Sure enough, about 20 minutes later, the three scalpers that we had dealt with walked in and sat down at a table across from us and ordered drinks. They had a stack of tickets nearing two inches tall that the two guys at the corner had given to the main man who stood in front of the Gardens. They gave him all the money as he stacked up the left-over tickets. He then counted the money and gave them cash back for what would have been some kind of percentage. The main dog had a mound of cash from the scalpers and left over tickets as they sat there eating their food and having some drinks.

It was obvious that they all worked together and had made the plan not to discount tickets regardless of when the game started. They made enough money doing this every weekend and every home game to make a good living I would suspect. That's how the scalping system worked with the Toronto Maple Leafs. We thought we were three young guys who had figured a way around the scalper system, and we could outthink them. We got to see firsthand at that restaurant exactly how the scalping business works.

It was a fun time, and I certainly enjoyed living in Oakville. I had grown up and had many memorable experiences for the year that I lived there. I again would like to thank Mike and Brian for allowing me to move in with them. I gave them a small amount every month just to help cover some of their costs. They certainly were doing me a favor since the amount they charged me was $300 a month, which I'm sure was certainly less than half of what a one bedroom apartment would be somewhere else in the area. The added benefits were that I got to hang out and live with friends that I had known my whole life through high school and college. It was comforting as it seemed to be an extension of living in Lasalle.

I still see Johnny occasionally, however, maybe only once or twice every few years. He and his wife Tracy live up in the Aurora area near Toronto with a couple of great kids.

The year living with the St. Germain's up in Oakville I would say was a time for me to mature. We had a ton of fun along with our independence. Suddenly, we were out of mom and dad's houses, fending for ourselves, paying bills, washing dishes, cooking dinner, and keeping up an entire household. It was an enjoyable experience no doubt about it, and we still chat casually about some of the crazy stuff that we did. Always included in our chats are our poker parties, sporting events and a couple of nights out at the local bars.

I am obviously still close with Mike and Brian, especially Mike since we're the same age. Brian is a couple of years younger. The whole St. Germain family is close with me, and I am often invited for Christmas dinner and Thanksgiving. Whenever the family gets together in the Windsor area Mike, Brian, Matt, Rob, Diane, and Mrs. St. Germain seem to include me. It's really true that some friendships last a lifetime.

CHRISTMAS TOUR OF THE AHL

Mike St, Germain and his youngest brother Robbie and I did a hockey tour to remember during the Christmas holiday I lived with them in Oakville.

Mike produced a great idea that during the 1994 holidays that we should go for a tour and see how many AHL hockey games and other events we could watch. Mike is the consummate organizer. In fact, just today I asked him when we went on our tour of the AHL, and low and behold, in about five seconds he fired over the itinerary that he had made back in 1994. Twenty-nine years later, and he still had the itinerary saved on his computer. As a long-time friend since grade 11, I would say Mikey is highly organized, the ultimate planner, and he continues to do that to this day.

We decided a few weeks prior to the holiday that we would in fact do it. Using Mike's organizational skills, he planned out the entire trip. We were to leave on December 26th and be back in Oakville on January 1st, 1995.

In classic Mike form, information, key items to do each day were given to Robbie and me to help decide our path and things to do during our trip. Again, highly organized, on day one, we would leave at 9 am. We had a choice of watching a CHL game which was about an hour away or our first AHL hockey game that was two and a half hours away. The third option was six hours away. We were eager to go and picked option number three about six hours away. The teams that we were going to watch were Albany which was the New Jersey Devils farm club playing Adirondack, which was the Detroit Red Wing farm club. Point of note, the Detroit

Red Wings are my favorite team. Mike's favorite team is Toronto, and Robbie's favorite team is Boston. We packed up our clothes, everything we needed, and we were on our way. We made sure we had all our IDs, and we were off to Albany, NY.

The one thing I do remember was that it was a chilly winter, and my mother purchased me a winter jacket. She knew we were going on a tour and wanted me to have a long green winter jacket. To this day, I still have it sitting in my closet. It has a lot of wear and tear on it after nearly 30 years, but I can still wear it.

We used Mike's car, a four door Chrysler. It was nothing fancy and certainly not luxurious. Mike did most of the driving, although I did a little bit, and Robbie may not have been old enough to drive at the time. So, in classic road trip fashion, we made sure to go to the washroom before we got in the car. The driver determines when our next stop would be and who knew what Mike would decide. We learned quickly to have our bladders empty when getting into the car. All three of us were extremely excited to begin our adventure with lots of exploration soon.

We didn't pre-purchase any tickets from what I recall, and the game was at 7:30 pm. We had left in the morning of December 26, and we arrived in Albany near 5 o'clock, having made a couple of stops for lunch and restrooms. Once we got near the arena, we stopped and had dinner. Three kids just recently out of college living on our own and money was not readily available. We knew what we wanted to do, so we just watched where we ate and which hotels we would stay. We got our tickets for the game and did not buy any food or snacks but perhaps a hot dog as we knew concession stands are always expensive. We got tickets, which were not nosebleed seats as we could get reasonable tickets in the middle of the rows of seats for a fair price, which, I want to say at the time, were ten or twelve dollars. There we were sitting in the middle of the Albany arena watching the Detroit Red Wing farm team play the New Jersey farm team. At that time, NHL tickets were somewhere around fifty dollars for nosebleed seats. Purchasing seats for 10 or 12 dollars was a great deal to watch the up-and-coming NHL players. I don't remember exactly where we would have stayed, but after the game, we had to have a hotel. We grabbed a cheap hotel, and we were good until the morning. The funny thing is, we would often only get two beds with the youngest, Robbie sleeping on the floor. That happens when you are the youngest of two brothers, and you're traveling on the cheap.

Our next stop was to watch Providence versus Rochester, which was the Boston farm team versus the New York Rangers team. We woke up, grabbed breakfast, and headed to Providence, which was about two and a half hours away. Now, I remember Robbie being excited because his favourite NHL team was Boston, and we were going to see Providence, which was the minor league team for the Boston Bruins. We jumped in our car and headed on our way for day two adventure. This game was between Providence and the Rochester Americans, which was the New York Rangers minor league team. We arrived early to the game, found a hotel, and did some sight-seeing prior to the game.

Game number two was complete. December 27th was now complete, our first day travel jitters were over, and we were in our rhythm. We have several more days and several more locations, games, and visits to various places to experience.

Next up was game number three. It was back to Albany to watch Providence again, this time playing Albany. Our third day of travel December 28th was in the books, and The Big Apple was next.

Here we are on December 29th, and the start of a few crazy adventures were about to begin. This was the day we travelled towards New York, NY. We were smart enough to realize that we could not afford any hotels in New York, so we ended up staying in the New Jersey area.

The trip from Albany to New York City was about four hours, so we almost cut it in half. We were still about an hour and a half away, but we knew we could afford something in this area. When we got out of Albany that night and into the New Jersey area, it was somewhere around 10:30 pm. We ended up finding a hotel which we still refer to as the Bates Hotel. If you recall, there was a murder mystery movie of a guy named Norman Bates who lived at a hotel and killed a bunch of people. Anyways, it was a horror story, and I will tell you why our adventure at this hotel was remarkably similar.

We rolled up to this hotel, not a brand name, not a big chain. It was privately owned, and we knew that going into the hotel. The sign in the window showed the hotel was open, and there were no reservations made ahead of time. All three of us walked into a ridiculously small lobby with a desk as soon as you walked in. There was nobody to be found, but there was a doorbell on the desk. We rang the doorbell and waited a few minutes. Eventually, a gentleman showed up from down the hallway, and politely asked us what we needed. We explained we needed a hotel room for the evening, and he said absolutely no problem at all, but he only took cash, no credit cards accepted. We put together our American money and paid around $70 for one room for the night. He walked us up to the second floor and down the hallway to our room, which he unlocked. The whole hotel decor looked like it was from the 70's with nothing modern. You could smell the stench of smoke, but it was a place to hang our hat late at night. We had not eaten since lunchtime, so we needed a place to eat. We quickly put our stuff in the room and asked him to have our key. He explained in a matter-of-fact manner that he does not give keys, to just give him a call when we were going out, and he would lock our door. He further explained that when we come back in, you buzz him, and he would come back downstairs, bring you to your room and unlock the door. We said okay, but certainly thought it was very odd.

We had all our luggage in the hotel room with two single beds, so Robbie got to sleep on the floor again. We talked amongst ourselves and thought it was a very peculiar situation, and what did we get ourselves into at this hotel. Mikey was not as worried as Robbie and me, so we set up a plan. We were not as trusting as Mike. We put down our luggage and moved different items to be on edges, setting up a bit of a trap to see if anything got moved or anybody entered our room when we were gone. We walked downstairs and called the innkeeper who went to our room and locked the door. We went and grabbed some food and began wondering. What would we find in the hotel room when we came back? We got back from eating after 1:00 o'clock in the morning and started wondering if we would ever get back into our room.

Sure enough, we walked into the lobby, rang the doorbell. Our new friend came down, brought us to our room and unlocked our door. The first thing Robbie and I did was check the room and determined nothing had been disturbed. The innkeeper was not snooping around, simply crazy thoughts by us, and all was good. We gladly locked the door behind us and went to bed with one eye open anticipating our next adventure on December 29th.

Mike had already pre planned what we were going to do on the 29th, including a few exciting and different adventures. We wanted to see the football stadium where the New York Jets and the New York Giants played since it was in the New Jersey area. The other adventure that was planned was that we wanted to see Central Park. The main thing was we wanted to watch a high school basketball tournament that was being hosted at Madison Square Garden. If you recall, Madison Square Garden is one of the most famous arenas in all of America.

We started with the first stop. Mike had already mapped out how to get to the football stadium. We drove around and found the stadium. A couple curious things. We could drive right into the parking lot, which had the practice facility right beside it, which was a smaller dome-like building. Where we parked, there was a large chain link fence with gates where you could see through a tunnel and into the main famous stadium. Now my personality is not as adventurous as Mike and Robbie. There was nobody around, the parking lot was empty, and it was in the middle of the morning with a gap in the gate.

The temptation was overwhelming for the chance to walk inside of a stadium. Sure, enough Mike and Robbie opened the gate a bit and hustled through the tunnel onto the field. Then they ran to the 50-yard line. I'm not sure if they took any pictures because I don't think cell phones were an important thing back then. They looked all the way around and enjoyed the view and ran back through the tunnel and outside the gate. Now, I am a little more cowardly for sure, but somebody had to get those guys out of jail if they got caught. I stood outside and just peered from the fence inward, too scared to walk through the gate inside the stadium. Now can you imagine that nobody came and yelled at us or obviously arrested us. I don't know if anybody ever saw us. The whole adventure took, I would say, 10 or 15 minutes by the time we walked from the parking lot to the gate, through the gates, through the tunnel, onto the field, and back to the car. I still cannot believe there was nobody around in a giant, fancy NFL stadium. So here I am, 30 years later, thinking wow imagine that scenario now, there would be cameras everywhere. I don't think it would be long before either the police or security would be walking us out of the stadium and to the local jail to explain ourselves and get a big fine for trespassing.

Now we had to make it into New York for the next adventure. Our travel host and organizer Mike drove into New York City. This would lead to an adventure which would never be forgotten. Now, we know a couple of things about New York. We knew areas of New York that we heard about or saw on TV such as the Bronx, Harlem, and Brooklyn. These areas were famous in movies for kids playing basketball, hanging out and doing their own thing.

What could go wrong with three Caucasians driving an older car with Canadian plates through areas which were predominantly rough, tough, mean, and lower class.

Here we were driving through different areas. The one area I do recall was the Bronx. This was very enlightening as we drove into this area and found buildings that were burnt out. Hundreds of people in the middle of the day were just walking around hanging out at the corners. It looked like there were a few drug deals going on in different areas. There were many apartment buildings with windows smashed and garbage cans everywhere, something that we have never seen before in person. As we rolled into different deeper areas of the Bronx, it certainly became a little more daunting. We were in areas where you did not stop at stop signs. You knew because you could feel it, you could see the guys that were hanging out on the streets, on the corner staring at us. I would think they were wondering, who were these three out of country kids driving through their neighborhood. We did not spend a lot of time, but I can tell you the second half of the adventure driving through the Bronx that stop signs and streetlights were very optional. It was a very quick slow down, look for no traffic and keep on moving. A curious thing about the buildings that were burned out, the two first floors' windows and doors were fully enclosed with bricks. I am guessing that it was because they didn't want any people breaking in and setting it on fire and causing any more damage to the building. We did get to see a couple of areas on the drive through the Bronx where there were outdoor basketball courts with a bunch of kids playing basketball, just like in the movies.

Although it was something to do for the first time, I've got to say at least myself and I'm sure Robbie and maybe even Mike were a little bit nervous. Sight-seeing in a foreign country, foreign city in a bad neighborhood and being a tourist was not a good mix. The things you do when you are young and dumb.

Our next adventure would be the high school basketball tournament at Madison Square Garden. Our search for a parking location took a while, but we found a spot throughout the street traffic of one-way streets. We quickly learned about the subway system in New York, a first-time adventure for all of us. We have done it a bit in the Toronto area, but certainly nothing compared to New York City. We found out how to navigate using Mike, our travel advisor. We arrived at Madison Square Garden. I don't recall exactly how we got the tickets; they may have been purchased out of a ticket booth or perhaps purchased from scalpers. We got our three tickets and walked into the famous building for all the championship games and many rock concerts. Entertainers often have a dream to play at Madison Square Garden in New York City. Here we were, inside Madison Square Garden ready to watch high school basketball. Now, this was not just any tournament of local teams. There were the best high school teams across the country attending this tournament. These high school teams had many recruits for NCAA Division One college teams. The tournament was for the best of the best high school teams.

Mike is a big basketball fan. He knew the kids that were being recruited for the various college programs. I do recall a couple of the players that we had watched did end up making a Division One college team, although I cannot remember their names. A few of these tournament players did proceed to a career playing professional basketball in the NBA.

We stayed there for five hours, and it was getting to be near 4:00 o'clock in the middle of the winter. We had one more adventure to complete before we would drive back to New Jersey. Our next adventure was to tour Central Park. We jumped on the subway, found and got in our car, to which we paid $50 in parking fees. At the time, that was a crazy amount but obviously, we all chipped in to share the cost.

We made our way to Central Park, driving through the traffic congestion for over an hour. Central Park is a huge park encompassing hundreds of acres with roadways that you can drive around along with walking and biking lanes. There are different sightseeing areas throughout the park with police on horses, carts getting pulled by horses, people running, people walking in a terribly busy park, but it was all very structured.

We got to Central Park nearing 5:00 o'clock which was just before dusk. We nonchalantly found the entrance and began driving and touring through Central Park. The lanes that go through Central Park go around the perimeter of the park, and it is definitely a few miles around. We were excited as it was something that we wanted to experience. We have obviously never been there; but it was on our hit list to do while in New York. Central Park has lanes for vehicles then bike lanes, and walking lanes beside them. Horse pulled carriages, rickshaws pulled by horses, police officers that ride horses are all throughout the park.

It is typically terribly busy, and in one section, we were stopped for probably about 30 minutes. Now, it was just starting to get dark, and we were talking amongst ourselves inside our car while stopped. We heard a tap on the driver's window, Mike looked up and we all noticed it was a horse with a police officer sitting on it. Mike rolled down the window and talked with the police officer who explained to us that it would be his recommendation that we leave Central Park before it got dark. He let us know that it was no place to be driving around as tourists. We were obviously out of place and the visible minority.

We took his warning very seriously, found the next exit and left Central Park. It was only around 6:00 pm, but it was dark. When we made our way back out of the city, we noticed a curious thing. All the streets are one way. So, navigating them is quite an adventure for tourists. The streets are often three or four lanes wide all going in one direction. The use of car turn signals is optional, lots of car horns, pedestrians walk wherever they want to walk and not necessarily at corners. We were on high alert while Mike was driving to get us out of New York. There you have it, three young tourists in New York City, toured Madison Square Garden, Central Park and walked into a famous football stadium.

There is a little bit of an adventurer in my personality, though I'm typically cautious. Here I am, 30 years later reminiscing, recollecting step by step what we did in New York. I enjoyed the New York tour so much with Mike and Rob that years later, I took my boys who were ten and seven at the time. Their very first trip to New York was great. The next trip to New York was with my two boys and my oldest son's girlfriend when they were 18 and 15 years old. Each time was a very pleasant and fun experience. We found New York clean, the people friendly and I would surely go back. I would recommend it to anybody. The experience of New York is formidable. It is fast moving, it does not shut down, and it's busy 24 hours a day. Wow, what a city.

It is now December 30th, and we are off to our next game. The next game has us traveling to Providence, where Albany will play Providence, the New Jersey Devils farm team playing the Boston Bruins farm team. We head out down the road for another three hours to get to the next game.

So far, we are about two-thirds through our hockey vacation, and it has been quite an adventure. Lots of fun, lots of laughs, and a road trip that will never be forgotten. Again, the same procedure, we get into Providence and spend the night in a hotel. We get up a bit early so we can grab something to eat, grab our tickets and do some normal sightseeing before we watch our next game. Purchasing tickets was not much of an issue each time, one because it's the AHL, and two because it is during the holidays with people travelling. The tour we have been on you notice each stop is 4 or 5 hours from the previous one, which makes it easily driveable between venues.

We grabbed a hotel somewhere in the Providence area and watched the game. Now we have almost completed our tour. The next day will have us heading back home, about 13 hours away. At this point in our tour, it is December 31st. We wake up, grab breakfast, and begin our trip home. Our plan was to go about halfway between Providence and Buffalo.

One more adventure is about to unfold. It's New Year's Eve, and we are on our way home. We are going a bit fast down the highway. Nothing crazy, about twenty miles an hour over the speed limit. It was a four-lane highway, and nobody was around. It was 9:00 o'clock at night, and we got pulled over by a state trooper.

We are in the state of New York, the officer asks all three of us for our ID. I am guessing it was maybe a bit suspicious having three Canadian young guys speeding down the highway in the middle of the evening. Ultimately, we got a speeding ticket for a few hundred dollars.

We all chipped in with money at some point in the next couple of weeks to share the ticket cost. Mike happened to be driving, but it was a team effort, team vacation, and we all agreed to split the cost three ways.

We ended up finding a place on New Year's Eve which was halfway home and finished our trek the next day on January 1st, New Year's Day. We rolled back home somewhere around 2:00 pm in the afternoon, unpacked all our bags, sat down, relaxed, and breathed a big sigh of relief.

There you go. We started on Dec 26th, 1994, and we got back on the 1st of January 1995. I guess officially it would have been seven days, and we saw five hockey games, basketball games, Central Park, NY Jets / NY Giants Football Stadium, received a speeding ticket, and was told not to hang out in Central Park.

Adventure #1 to the New York area was a success.

Here it is. April 15th, 2023, 28 years after our whirlwind tour, and the memories are still vivid. Anytime when I am over at the St. Germain's at a get-together that tour comes up in conversation. Mike, Robbie, and I have lots of laughs reminiscing about our Christmas tour.

Those are how good memories with friends are made, a trip that will never ever be forgotten between us. Mike organized it all, and drove most of the way. Robbie and I tagged along and helped when we were needed. None of this could have happened without Mike St. Germain organizing it. It started with Mike writing up an itinerary, doing all the mapping of it and leading the ship.

Mike has always been the leader of the pack. I just sit back and enjoy what he plans or what he wants to do. Usually, there's not been a lot of disagreement for the last 40 years of our friendship. He figures it out, organizes it, and anybody who wants to be included just jumps in. Birthday parties, get togethers, golf outings are all organized by Mike.

He organizes the function and lets everybody know the date, the time and moves on. A funny thing about Mike. He has had very significant roles over his career as a leader and executive. He knows how to make decisions and how to control the situation, and he does it all very pleasantly.

He is just one of those guys that you know you are well cared for with him. Nearly 40 years later, a big thank you goes out to Mike St. Germain for organizing this crazy trip.

Thanks friend. Excellent job, Mikey.

JOBS

My work life certainly has evolved throughout the years. It's crazy how jobs and careers change. You start one way and end vastly different with many stops along the way. The adage that you don't know what you don't know is definitely true in this case.

My very first job was in a grade 12, and I was hired as an electrician's helper. My brother had reached out to his union, and at the time, the Chrysler Windsor assembly plant was undergoing a major retool. Hundreds and perhaps even thousands of tradesmen participated in the retooling of the local automotive plant. I was hired as an electrician's helper, which meant that I would collaborate with a crew of electricians. If you can imagine the name gopher, well that was my job. I collected all their food and drink orders, walked out to the food truck, placed the orders and brought it back to the guys. I did the same for lunch, and then I was a gopher for the second break in the afternoon. Each time, I gathered orders for coffee, pop, hotdogs, hamburgers and whatever the electricians wanted. The local food truck would have 20 or 30 of us gophers each break. We were all young kids 16 or 17 years old doing the same job. I remember my pay was $6.36 per hour, which was great money and at least double what other kids were making with jobs at a confectionery or on a farm. The job lasted all summer, and I was fortunate to make quite a bit of money, which was great to have for spending during school.

In the next two summers, my sister-in-law Barb got me jobs working at the Chrysler Windsor Assembly plant in various hourly positions. I worked on the line for a few weeks. I worked in the body and white department. I drove cars off the assembly line out into a parking lot. One time, I was a maintenance painter where, directed by the bosses, I painted everything from yellow safety items to offices.

Those were 89-day jobs because, on the 90th day, you were part of the union. So, I worked 89 days in the summer and went back the following year, which worked out great for me. I cannot thank Barb enough for getting me those jobs.

The best job at Chrysler was driving the vans from the assembly plant out into a parking lot. A transportation bus would drive around, pick up the drivers and bring us back to start the process again. I remember sitting in that bus, and these high seniority workers were looking at me and eventually started to talk to me. They asked me how in the heck I got this job because most of them had seniority of thirty-five or even 40 years. It was a high seniority job, and they were sure it was a case of somebody knowing somebody to get me that great job for the summer. There were a bunch of characters who worked that job. I remember one they used to call the Rev because he was a recovering alcoholic. He would walk around the beer store, which was only about five hundred meters from the plant, and gather any empty beer cans and beer bottles. Then, he would cash them in at the end of the week. The Rev was a quiet guy who did his own thing on his breaks and read the Bible after collecting the empty beer cans. There was another gentleman I used to see at the Windsor Spitfires hockey games every week. Many years later, we still remembered each other, and we would shoot the breeze about me working at Chrysler as a young kid. I had that excellent job in 1984. I distinctly remember because many of us drivers were Detroit Tigers baseball fans that summer, and that was the year they won the World Series. The transportation bus driver would put the game on the radio while we were driving back to the plant.

Another college era job I had was working at a local bar around the corner from where I lived on McEwen St. in Windsor. This bar had been immensely popular years before it changed ownership and changed names. At the time of my employment it featured live music. They would bring bands in every Friday or Saturday, sometimes both days. A few famous bands from Canada would play, and the building would be packed. I was a cook in the kitchen and would prepare basic bar food including French fries, chicken fingers and chicken wings. It was a busy bar, and I learned how to be a line cook. When there wasn't a band, the bar would be slow, and I could just study during the week. I do remember some late Thursday nights where once the bar was closed, the bartender would invite us to stay, and we'd have a couple of pops and chat. The next thing I knew, it was three o'clock in the morning, and the next morning I was up and ready to go to college for an 8:00 o'clock class. As you can imagine, a few of those Friday 8:00 o'clock classes were not well remembered, because I am sure I was half asleep.

CAREERS

As you recall, I left college early in my third year to take a job in Mississauga. I was hired as a quality technician. The year was 1985. My starting salary was $19,000, and the job was in the construction industry, a different field than I had studied in college. Construction drill bits and saw blades that cut concrete for highways were produced in our small factory. It was a very messy, loud and dirty job with 10 workers in the shop. My job was to quality check the products being produced in the shop.

After seven months, the general manager I worked for moved on, so he was replaced. I was a 20-year-old kid who knew nothing about career politics or management. I remember they hired a young gentleman who was 10 years my senior, a university graduate with an MBA. He had worked in a similar industry for a handful of years. I specifically remember being extremely upset and disgruntled that they didn't promote me to that position. There I was in the industry for just half a year, fresh out of college with no experience and mad because I wasn't promoted to general manager of what was a $1,000,000 company. What a stupid thought at the time, and what followed was very childish behavior on my part. I remember being so angry that my work ethic completely shifted to the negative, and my work suffered. The new general manager, who was a good guy, noticed and eventually brought me into his office for a man to man talk. He explained to me that there is an old saying that work often expands to the amount of time allowed. Then he went on to explain that my work was taking four times the amount of time it used to take because of my poor attitude. It was a problem, and that I needed to fix it.

I remember just sitting there thinking who this guy is telling me about my work ethic.

In my haste, a few weeks later, I resigned. At that point, I at least had a job to go back to in Windsor. This general manager and I were close to the same age, so we had a bit in common. Once I resigned, he asked where I was going to work and why. I told him I was just moving back to Windsor to be closer to my family. He wished me well, and we went out for a drink to celebrate my new opportunity.

I think now of how dumb it was thinking I was ready for that role. I was twenty years old believing that I was skilled and experienced enough to have that senior management position. It just goes to show you that I was certainly a little bit cocky, thinking I was better than I really was.

I left the Mississauga job and came back to Windsor where I worked at a manufacturing plant that produced diesel components. This plant was a well-established company, in business for 30 years with 600 employees. Even on the first day, I knew this was going to be an exciting job. I was walked around the plant by my boss and introduced to various senior people, including the union chairperson and the safety chairperson for the union. My job was to evaluate the workers doing their jobs, study them to see how many pieces per hour they were producing, and make recommendations. I would mathematically figure out how many parts they should be producing. As you can imagine, I was not popular with the employees.

A young kid coming in to tell veteran workers that they should be basically working faster did not go over well. I certainly wasn't hired to come in and produce studies that would show they were working too fast, or that they should slow down. The company had hired several people before me for this role, and they did not have particularly good experiences. On the first day, I got to meet the safety coordinator who belonged to the union. He then asked me if I was the one who responded to the ad in the paper a few weeks ago, and I said yes. This gentleman would turn out to be a radical, both in the plant and in his personal life. He then chided me saying I was the one who applied for the job that said "asshole wanted." I didn't really know what to say. I was just a young guy who had never experienced this type of mentality. I simply told him I got hired to be a time study, and my boss and I went on our merry way. That was quite a first experience with the union, and it wouldn't be the last.

I worked there for a couple of years doing time studies on the production workers. In my position, once you completed a study, you were required to present your findings to both management and to the union chairperson. The union chair had an office in the main aisle located in the middle of the plant. All he did was deal with union issues all day. He didn't work on the floor. We got along in an amiable manner so I could explain myself. He didn't like a lot of the findings, obviously because his workers had to work harder, but we managed to coexist just fine.

One day, there was a study done, and the findings were posted on the actual machines as required. The union chair had already approved it, but one of the workers went to him and complained. A confrontation began between the three of us in front of his office in the main aisle. He started to scream at me while all his workers were watching out of the corner of their eyes. He yelled that my studies were all bullshit and not accurate, and he was going to go to management to get it straightened out. At this point, my ego kicked in, and I knew I had to respond. There was an audience, and I wasn't going to be bullied by this gentleman come hell or high water.

I raised my voice right back at him, and we had three consecutive shouting matches going on. He would begin to walk away, and I would say something, most likely not very professional, and he would come back to defend himself in front of all his people. This happened three times where he would walk off, and I would chirp something at him, and he'd come back. Eventually, management could hear us screaming at each other, so they came out and broke it up. My boss asked me what was going on, so I explained. He said that everyone needed to cool off. He assured me I was just doing my job, there were no issues with my work, and that the union chair occasionally acted like an idiot. As a recent college graduate, you can imagine my eyes were opened quite a bit to the union mentality in this plant.

I knew many of the guys on the floor, and they understood I had a job to do, and that I would help them out with production rate numbers. My posted numbers were slightly lower than they should have been when I did my study, so they understood that they had been getting away with some crazy low production numbers. The workers and I would often talk about our common interest in hockey. That eventually got back to the chairperson I had battled. Things were different after our shouting match. I had to deal with him daily, and conversations between us were very tense. A few weeks after the shouting match, I was walking down the main hallway, and the plant chairperson came walking toward me. In my mind, I was preparing to do battle yet again.

He came up to me and said, "I heard you're a hockey fan. Would you like to join in our weekly hockey pool with a bunch of the plant guys?" I was shocked, but it seemed to be a truce between us. It cost five dollars to pick our winning teams for each game every week. Once I joined the hockey pool, while we weren't best of friends, we were at least friendly when we talked about hockey. For me, it was a case of standing up for yourself and not being bullied. He respected that I stood up for myself. I'm sure, at the time, the confrontation wasn't the most professional, but at least I stood up for myself. I didn't cower like a little kid and let him bully me. I went on to find out that previous time studies had damage to their cars over the years. Damage such as super gluing their car locks shut and having their car keyed and scratched up. Myself, I never had any issues like that. I had a job to do, and they had a job to do. They respected that I was professional, and we all managed just fine.

Now here goes my ego again. I had calculated, over the course of the year, that I was either saving the company or helping them produce more jobs per hour, which was ultimately additional money for them. I had calculated approximately $125,000.00 of increased production. On one Friday, I was ready to present my case to my boss and ask for a raise. I was called to the HR department on Friday before the long Easter weekend. I thought perfect, they've caught wind of me wanting a new wage, and everything will be good. That thinking could not have been farther from the truth. Instead of a raise, I was laid off. The human resource manager told me they didn't need my position anymore, so they were eliminating it. When he was done speaking, I asked, with a little bit of an attitude, how could he do it. I was saving the company hundreds of thousands of dollars, and that would be a silly move. It didn't matter to him, though. He was one of the owners' sons, and what was done was done.

A curious thing is how you remember milestones in your life. On this layoff weekend, a friend of the family was playing a game out of town. He played Junior B hockey, which was a seriously elevated level. His parents and brothers were scheduled to pick me up at my workplace to drive to watch the hockey game. Here I was. I had to pack everything from my desk, and put it in my car. They picked me up in the parking lot, and for the next hour, I explained how I got laid off. I still couldn't believe it, but I still went and watched the hockey game. The search was on for a job.

The next job that I took was also as a time study but at a production plant where they assembled semi-trucks. This job was a nine month contract and located in Chatham, which was an hour away from my home. At this point, I was still living with my mother. She had sold our house after my father passed away and purchased a mobile home in the town of McGregor.

This was a fun job, and I had a good relationship with the engineers. At that time, I was an avid golfer. I was golfing just about every day, whether it was hitting golf balls at the range or playing a round. I was a member of a golf course less than five minutes away from where I lived. My colleagues at that job were huge golfers, and I got to know the guys so well I still remember their names.

I joined their company's golf league which was fun because I got to play at a different course. Occasionally, we would go over to one of the guy's houses on the water and sit back and relax after a 9-hole game. We golfed at a really cool place that was nearby. It was an 18 hole course on a little island called Harsens Island, with a few houses on it.

My experience working there helped me clearly understand the importance of an education. There were two of us that were hired as contractors for the exact same position. I was a college graduate, and the other gentleman was a university graduate. When the contract came up for renewal, the company only had the funds to hire one of us, and they hired the other guy because of his degree.

The reason I know that is because my boss, who was also his boss, brought me into the office during this process and explained that he wanted to hire me but there was a push to have university degreed personnel in the plant. He had no choice, but he made it clear that I was the one he wanted to hire. I really appreciated hearing that.

A few years after college and three jobs later, I was back to square one looking for employment. This search went on a bit longer than three months. It was now the first time ever being unemployed for any significant length of time and that meant going through the unemployment check processing procedure. I had to fill out forms every couple of weeks to say what I had done to seek employment and if I had any earned income during my unemployment. Occasionally, I would have to go down to the employment office and meet with an employment counselor. They would discuss what I had been doing, how to pursue jobs, where to look and if the agency knew of any opportunities.

Please understand that during this two or three-month sabbatical from working, I was looking anywhere and everywhere for a job, including online to try to get back to being employed as quickly as possible. It was summer, so I did get to enjoy golfing every day just by myself, since my friends were all working. My dues were already paid for the year, so it didn't cost me anything to golf. The unemployment cheque was enough to put gas in my car and drive a few minutes to the golf course.

My life that summer became very methodical; the same routine day after day, and it became irritating. I would wake up at a certain time, have breakfast, search online for jobs, golf, come back home for lunch and then go golf some more. That mundane schedule started to really drag me down mentally. I kept wondering why I wasn't getting a job. Was I doing something wrong in the interview, or was my resume not impressive enough? The longer my dry spell went on, the more my mind wandered. When you have a job, you're making money, but it's more than that. You have purpose and a sense of self worth.

Eventually, I finally found a job. It was through an agency which hired engineers and technologists. I was placed at Ford Motor Company, where I ended up working for three years. It was incredibly fun.

A curious thing is that the last couple of months before getting hired at Ford, I ventured into my first entrepreneurial adventure. My brother had given me an old pickup truck, and I put it to use. I always liked fishing but didn't fish very often. What I did was use that truck to set-up a mobile tackle box. I set up a display case in the bed, and I sold fishing attire, lures, hooks, sinkers, fishing line and a couple of cheap fishing rods.

I then expanded to include a big giant barrel of minnows, bait, and other gear. This adventure actually put a little extra pep in my step. Without any experience, I walked into stores and copied the phone number and address from the packaging of fishing products. I then sent the companies letters and followed up with phone calls. I simply explained that I was starting a business and wanted to sell their products.

When I started, I didn't know what I was doing and didn't know how to run a business, but I took action and did it anyway. The next thing I did was map out the local fishing areas where I could sell my products. I needed to obtain permission before selling in the various communities, so I contacted the local councils, got on their meeting agendas and pitched my business, asking for permission to park my truck at the various properties for a few hours a day and sell my fishing equipment.

I ran the tackle business for two months prior to being hired full-time at Ford. I kept the business going on the weekends for a few months after I started my job. I remember a local news company called me, and I did a phone interview about my business during my lunch break. A small article in a local newspaper was published a few weeks later. My direct boss saw the article and called me in one day. He told me he had read it and wished me all the best. It got to be too much for me, though, so it soon fizzled out. It was simply a few months of a young guy trying to be an entrepreneur during an unemployed time in my life. I distinctly remember one of the statements I made while being interviewed by the paper was, "if you cannot find a job, make a job for yourself."

The three years at the Ford engine plant was quite a learning experience and lots of fun. I got to be friends with quite a few of the guys, often going out for lunch with them. I even joined their golf league. I remember my direct boss had heard that I was an avid golfer who golfed every day. He was a member at a very prestigious golf course in the area. I remember sitting at my desk, and my boss yelling over the cubicles, "Hey Crainer, come over here for a minute." So sure, enough I would walk down to my boss, who was a long-time manager at Ford. He kept a couple of plastic golf balls in his desk. There was another engineer who had a golf club at his desk. My boss would grab his plastic golf balls when things were a little slow and grab the engineer's golf club. He then would ask me questions about how to swing the club. He would pass me the club, and I would cautiously swing the club, hitting the plastic golf balls for probably 20 minutes. This was in the middle of the engineering office at the Ford Essex plant, which was very formal. Here my boss was, trying to get golf lessons from me. We certainly made a connection over golf.

My boss would often get invited out to golf outings at various times throughout those three years. He always made a point of telling whoever invited him, which was usually a supplier to Ford, that he was bringing another guy and to make sure there was room.

He would then call me, and the next thing I know, I was at a golf outing with him and a couple of suppliers. I remember one golf outing in the United States. It was an 18-hole golf tournament at a beautiful golf course. Everything was paid for, and there were prizes of TVs, stereos, golf club sets, golf bags and many other high-end prizes. A fabulous steak dinner and drinks were served after the tournament. I wasn't paired up with my boss at the time.

I was with a supplier for this tournament. We had just finished playing eighteen holes, and we were in the clubhouse getting ready to eat. My boss asked if I wanted to go out again, so, of course I said yes. The next thing I know, he and I are in a golf cart driving around the course playing another nine holes. It was just the two of us golfing when everybody else was in the clubhouse. When we came back in, we ate our meal, received our gifts, went our separate ways, and drove home. That boss lived in Amherstburg where I currently live, and I still see him occasionally, and we chat. He retired a long time ago, but those memories remain. It sure was a fun three years working for him.

I got to know another gentleman there who also lives in the Amherstburg area. I see him two or three times a year at a local grocery store. He owns his own business now, but we still talk about the good old times at Ford.

I guess these last two jobs showed me there is work time, and there's fun time. What I learned is that you've got to have a good relationship with people, respect people, and they will respect you. The one job I was just a contract worker but got close enough to the guys. I was a good person, friendly, did my job with no issues and didn't complain. The second job was at Essex engine plant. It was the same thing where I was just a fun guy, did my work with no fuss, and didn't miss work. I didn't show up late, and I didn't leave early. The next thing you know, I'm in a golf league with my boss and swinging a club in the middle of an engineering office at Ford Motor Company.

At these first four jobs, I developed enough skill to get my next job at a higher rate of pay. My very first job was $19,000 a year which is about $10 an hour with the average of two thousand hours per year. My contract at Ford was done after my third year where I was making $25 an hour. In each of those jobs, I had progressed in my responsibilities and moved onward and upward in salary.

Now, here is the importance of education that stung me on two occasions. During my second year at Ford, I remember a human resources gentleman coming around and asking everybody in the office a few questions. He asked whether the employees were full-time or part time, contract, or in a permanent position. They also asked if the employees were engineers or managers and how many years' experience they had. He also asked the educational status of each employee. Some of the guys were grade 12 and grade 13 education at the time with no post-secondary. Some were degreed engineers while others, including myself, were technologists with a college degree. A few of the engineers had their master's degree while at least two had doctorates. I was curious and started to ask a few questions to the guys. I soon found out that there were numerous engineers with 20 and 25 years at a level because they could not move up any further without additional education. Some of the guys I knew were taking additional courses in the states about an hour away to obtain a degree in business. It was a degree, and it didn't matter what the specialty, it would allow them to move up another level for more money, more benefits and perhaps a car allowance. Hearing that, I knew that my technologist degree, along with being employed on contract, would not get me far.

What I did was enroll in the USA at a college and went twice a week. It was $1500 USF per course, which was huge. I would go on to spend more than 12 grand at night school. Turns out, I didn't pursue my degree soon enough, and the two or three courses I did have at university in the states wasn't enough when they were hiring at the end of my contract. They were hiring many people. I just wasn't one of them.

The boss told me he would certainly hire me, but I was not a degreed engineer. Corporate HR wanted the number of engineers increased along with more doctorates, regardless of previous performance. That was the mandate, so that's what they did.

Again, relationships were a huge factor in getting hired for my next job. Sometimes, it's not what you know, it's who you know. The next job I took was as a project manager, which was another level up in responsibilities and salary. I got that job through a supplier to Ford Motor Company who dealt with me at Ford. The guys at Ford had heard they were looking for someone, and they recommended me. My contract was about to end, and they talked to the supplier about hiring me. Sure enough, I went for an interview and got hired. This company designed and built machinery, and Ford Motor Company was one of their customers.

In my new role, I had to manage and supervise employees, watch the budgets, and get the work done. I would deal with the customer's expected delivery, timelines and keep the project within budget so the company made their anticipated profit.

One of the senior project managers sat me down one day and asked me if I had been a program manager at any time in my career. I answered no, but that I had a background of doing machine design. He explained that, as a project manager, I would wear two different shirts. The first shirt would be a referee shirt, and in that role, I would negotiate, persuade and stop internal battles from happening with different departments within the company all while working in the pursuit of getting the job done on time and on budget. The next shirt, he explained, had a giant target on it. The target was there because the managers and bosses would always point the finger at me if anything went wrong, and the customer would always point the finger at me if anything went wrong. Project management would often have you feeling like everybody was targeting you. It turned out the senior guy that told me this nugget of information was right on the money. You must be able to wear a target and wear a referee shirt at the same time.

Unfortunately, this company had some financial trouble. One day, as we pulled up to the office, we noticed a gentleman sitting in the parking lot. We walked to our desks as the guy came in, changed the locks on the outside doors, then announced that the business was now closed. We grabbed our belongings and left.

The next job I took was with an American company who somehow got hold of the project that was being built by the now defunct company I had just left. The new company needed a project manager to bring it to completion and have it eventually delivered. They hired a firm located in Canada to finish the build, although they were the American parent company. I had a contract salary position and had to hire all the needed designers, and get the manufacturing and build completed.

When the machine was built, it was off to the states for installation at the customer's facility. At this point, I was married with the first child on his way. The job required me to be away for weeks at a time during the installation, which was approximately four months. I would be gone during the week and home on a few weekends. The installation location was approximately two hours away in the United States, so obviously, it was tough on the wife. She had to care for our son the first four months by herself, except on the occasional weekend where I'd be home.

All good things end. The job was installed, and my position was completed. As anticipated, I was once again looking for a job.

THE GENERAL KNOWS TWO THINGS - GM JOB

Another job that I had was again working as a contractor, this time for the General Motors transmission plant located in Windsor ON. Here I learned a few good lessons from a senior engineer who took me under his wing. There were three designers, and we were stationed in a small room isolated from the engineering faculty with a closed door, with three computer workstations and lots of freedom. We were basically by ourselves with no direct supervision, given design tasks, and as we completed them, we would leave the room to go show the appropriate engineer what we had completed. I definitely learned self-control, and that I was responsible for getting the job done.

I was 35 years old at the time. Our small room was located next to a little area that had a fridge and a coffee pot. I wanted to get to know the entire engineering faculty including electrical engineers, process engineers, mechanical engineers, and the managers. General Motors was a huge facility where I only had direct contact with three or four engineers, but I took it upon myself to try to meet as many as possible. At break time, I went next door and suddenly, after not drinking coffee for 35 years, began to drink coffee. At this point, drinking water wasn't immensely popular. Many of the engineers from the different areas of the plant would go to the room and grab a coffee during break and chat casually for a few minutes. I thought that was a fantastic way to meet the other engineers, so I began to go over there and learn how to acquire a taste for coffee. At the tender age of 35, I drank my first cup of coffee for, let's call it, professional development.

It was a fantastic job because you were in control of doing the designs without a lot of supervision. You were expected to do your job, complete it in an organized manner, and complete it on time. The other two individuals that were in my room were also designers but had a different and unique perspective.

The one designer was constantly missing days for assorted reasons, often said to be different doctors' appointments. I would surmise to say that he missed three or four days a month for whatever his reason. The other gentleman seemed to always come in 10 minutes late and leave a little bit early two or three times a week. Now, if you were not disciplined, it was extremely easy to walk up a staircase where no one was watching and walk across the hall and into our room. You would think that nobody would notice your entrance or exit.

The gentleman that I worked with most was a wily old veteran, a nice guy and extremely smart. Out of the things he taught me, I remember two the most. The first one was that he would come in the room occasionally but not very often to give direction, never to check-up. He was not the micro manager type of boss. He told me that the general only sees two things and only cares about two things; whether you are on time to start work and whether you leave work early. That made me think about one of the guys in my room. It wasn't obvious that he came in late and left early because there was no line-of-sight walking across the hall to go into the room. Besides, it was not very often that we had any General Motors employees in the room before my colleague got in there.

I would surmise to say that this gentleman was noticed coming in late and leaving early somehow, either in the hallway, in the parking lot or walking down the stairwell. Whatever the way, that designer did not last long at General Motors. He was told he was no longer needed, and he would have to find another job. All three of us were contractors, so the contract personnel company obviously had to tell him that his gig at General Motors was done. My GM colleague then made a point to let me know, as a friend, to make sure you are on time, and make sure you don't leave early because somebody always notices. It was not directed at me because I was always early and always would stay the extra 10 minutes it took to complete the task. It was just a little reminder mid-career to be careful and smart. Put your nose to the grindstone and just work.

The second thing my GM colleague taught me was also used throughout my career. Curious enough, I just spoke to another designer today that I worked with 20 years ago (I am currently 57 years old). I mentioned the second GM lesson to him as we were chatting, and he chuckled. Here's how it went. There was a design that needed to be done, so my engineer lined me up with the details and gave me the design task. Once I finished, my guy told me they would require thirty-five of the exact same items. He went on to explain that during an upcoming long weekend, he would get the design manufactured, and he would have his guys install one into a production line. Without getting into huge details, the line required approximately thirty-five of these items, and it moved back and forth in a machine. Without any fanfare, I gave him the designs. From there, he told me he would take care of everything. I came back after the long weekend, walked into my room, and noticed the steel manufactured items that I had created and designed were sitting on my desk. The fabrication that I had designed was bent and twisted with huge damage. I looked at it and wondered what went on as I walked out of my room over to the engineer.

He asked me if I saw any issues with the design. He also asked if I ever went down to the machine that was on the floor just one hundred yards away. He then went on to ask if I bothered to look inside the machine to see how it was built and where my item was going to be installed.

I explained that I did not since I had all the drawings from a previous design to which I double checked, and my design would theoretically fit. He went on to explain how that was the critical error in my thinking. He mentioned that, as a designer, you cannot trust a previous designer to provide the correct information to you via a design drawing. He explained that it was my responsibility to go down to the machine and physically itemize where my item was going to be installed. I needed to check myself for accuracy.

He was not upset, but he did make a point of explaining my error. He closed our conversation by saying the following, lesson 2. He said not to worry; a designer becomes the best designer he can be after making his biggest mistake. There was another great role model while I worked at GM. He was a bit younger than me, but smart and a true professional engineer. Mike Powell provided a role model discipline that I still follow today.

As I think about it some 30 years later, I shared that lesson with many up-and-coming designers. I explained to them that scenario, and hopefully, they heeded my words to physically double check all of their designs and not trust previous designs. I told them that once they made a huge mistake, they could be assured that, if they have half a brain, that they will never make that type of mistake again.

I ran into this GM colleague about a year ago as we were shopping. I shook his hand again as we had lost contact. He told me he was now enjoying retirement. Those two General Motors lessons are ones I still recall and live by in my career today. No matter how isolated you think you are, somebody is watching. Whether they tell you directly or not, someone notices you. The next thing to know is if you make a mistake, don't do it again. Learn from it, and correct it. The correction should be as fast as possible, and then move on. It was a great philosophy with great advice that I still am thankful for today. It was great that Dave Easton and Mike Powell were mentors without even knowing they were mentors

ESTIMATOR

My next career move had me doing something a bit different. As I have always been throughout my career, I am up for a challenge and ready to learn a new skill. Here is a quick summary outline of my career so far. I performed time study, then I was a designer, next I was a project manager, and now I would be an estimator.

It's funny that my career followed a close friend named Mark Weigel. Mark and I worked together at three different jobs across our careers. Mark is now happily retired enjoying his family, grandkids, and riding motorcycles.

This latest job involved estimating the cost of welding assembly production lines. It involved calculating cost for the sales personnel so that they could present the price to their potential customer. In this job, you had to figure out the cost of the entire job. First, you had to figure out the process to build the product. I worked closely with the processing department to produce an idea of how to assemble the product. Once you knew how it would be assembled, you could then begin to calculate the cost of producing that assembly. You knew the manufacturing cost. You knew the product costs of the equipment, and you would also estimate design cost. The next item to be considered would be to determine installation cost as well as how long the staff would be at the facility running off the equipment to get it to be functional at the required production rate. As you can see, my design background as well as my experience in program management were both beneficial in this new position.

The final task to happen once everything was calculated was to write up a proposal document, often 30 or more pages, outlining to the customer exactly the process and costs. This document would be given to the sales staff, and they would present the proposal to the customer.

I collaborated with this large integration company in the Windsor area for approximately three years. It was a new department that was being developed, and after three years, the company decided it was not feasible to operate that department, and we were sent on our way. Curious enough, today as I write this book, my boss at that company Rob Grohs, and I are having lunch. It has been 15 years, and we have lunch three or four times a year. Rob is now retired, but we still reminisce about the good old times and the fun we used to have in that newly developed department.

In Rob's department, I not only learned about estimating, but I was also observing and listening to the sales department. I watched and learned how to interact with customers and saw the good, the bad and the ugly of each different technique from the sales guys. I absorbed how they treated customers and how they treated the estimating staff.

Throughout my career, a few of the sales guys seem to be on a bit of the arrogant side while there were a few who seemed to rise above and beyond. I took the best attributes from them all to use in my sales career. I watched them deal with customers daily, and it was a pleasure learning the trade from these experienced sales people. In the best cases, everybody was treated equally whether they were dealing with presidents of companies, engineers of companies or people working on the floor. They were all greeted with a huge smile and friendly handshake. They each would get to know how your day was going, and they knew your family and their names. That was the scenario for customers as well as any peers.

THE CRAIN CHRONICLES A MEMOIR

I learned to have a great personality and be very respectful and professional. Sprinkled in was always a little bit of fun as well as a little bit of casual talk. Overall, interactions were directed in a professional manner. I would have to say, watching each of them led me to my interest in moving into sales after this company department dissolved.

My career follows a very methodical path from designer, program management, estimating and finally into sales.

I was lucky that, after that company dissolved, there was a competitor in the exact same business located a few miles down the road in the Windsor Ontario area. This company had an existing department that was doing the exact same thing that my previous employer had done. Each company was local and family owned.

My new company was around for 60 years and were huge employers in the automotive manufacturing machinery sector. I worked there for approximately 10 years in a couple of different departments, starting in estimating and finishing as a salesperson.

THE BIG CAREER MOVE

At some point during my third or fourth year in my second company as an estimator, I began to develop the itch to be in the sales department. To accomplish this goal, I realized there had to be a plan, because everybody in the sales department were veterans who had come up through the ranks at this company. Over the years between companies, I got to know many engineers at various manufacturing plants. I took it upon myself and on my own time to have conversations with various previous customers from these other companies I worked for prior to this one. These were customers that we were not doing any business with my current employer. I believed they could become customers with a bit of an introduction and proper handling.

I reached out on my own time to talk with them and explain exactly what we did and ask them for an opportunity to give them a quote. It took a few months for them to be comfortable with us, but I won them over. I went to my boss and explained the situation and told him they were interested. The customers that I talked to would provide requests for quotes in an official manner to the proper sales guy. My current employer would pass on the request to me since I had the relationship. I would proceed with processing, quoting, and presenting some preliminary costing to the customer. At the same time, I was always keeping the salesperson of that potential customer in the loop. I was highly successful in bringing in new customers. Although I was not the salesperson, I was the direct reason that new customers were brought onboard. I was successful in bringing in a few new customers that are still there some 10 or 12 years later and have brought that company millions of dollars in revenue.

After about five years of working at the company, I approached the vice president of sales and scheduled a meeting with him. I let him know my intentions to get into sales. I mentioned to him that should there be an opportunity, I would appreciate being considered. We had a friendly conversation. He told me there were no openings, but that he was glad I had stepped forward and showed interest.

Approximately six or seven months later, he came to me and let me know that a position in sales was open. The position was not in the division I had mentioned to him but in another division. We had a conversation where he explained what my responsibilities would be and asked if I had any interest in moving over to the sales department in that division. My interest in sales had me jump into that side of the business as I felt confident, although not having any exact or direct sales experience. My previous jobs, along with my knowledge of estimating and what I thought was the way to sell, created belief in my ability. It was an exciting opportunity, and I said yes.

I was moving up the ladder in my career as this vertical move had me enjoying my own cell phone, a company car, company paid expenses as well as a small raise in pay. The position was salary with no commission and lots of responsibility. It was a very fair salary, and I was excited to begin. Although I was moving into a new department that I was not familiar with, and selling a new product that I was not familiar with, I was eager to learn as fast as possible.

As you can imagine, moving to a new branch of the company required me to meet with staff and personnel with whom I never had any dealings with prior. My reception in the new division as well as in the sales department went well. A couple of funny things happened within the first month.

I remember they were transferring a current client over to me at the same time the previous salesperson received a call from this same disgruntled customer. This customer requested an immediate meeting at his facility.

The current salesperson told me that I should attend this meeting, and that it was an urgent matter that we had to leave immediately to drive to a plant that was about an hour away from our facility. We jumped in the car along with a couple of backup people from the quality department and manufacturing to help address the situation. As we raced to the customer meeting, my mind was scrambling thinking about the situation. The current salesperson explained the situation and gave me a heads up of what was about to happen. I walked into a meeting with a veteran account manager and some of his support staff. The customer was very disgruntled with the product that he was currently using.

I watched how the salesperson interacted with the customer and listened as our back up people and support staff went on to talk. They told the customer that, in fact, it was not our product or manufactured by us, that we had purchased the product, re-labeled it, and sold it to the customer. As you can imagine, that did not impress the customer, and the meeting was over shortly after. During that week, that customer went directly to where we purchased the product, and the account went down to zero sales.

The event the following week again had me and the same salesperson going to a local plant, where again the customer was not pleased with the current product. I had prepared a presentation along with upper management, and we both went to deal with the situation. I had a brief background about some prototype products that were at the plant that we had given them to use. Since I figured it was best to take it head on and deal with the situation promptly, I let them know that the product that we had loaned to them would now be theirs for free. We were able to resolve the situation, give them bonuses of new products, and maintain the customer in good standing.

We had monthly sales meetings with all the sales staff. As a joke, I was awarded a golden cup for losing one client and giving away $40,000 worth of product to the other. The golden cup was a welcome aboard gesture by the sales department, and everybody cheered and had a few chuckles.

I worked at this company for about 10 years, first starting in estimating and then moving into sales. I learned lots of skills at both positions and certainly enjoyed my employment. There comes a time in your career where your age starts to become more of a factor, and you realize that there is one more career move available. Things were fine at the company, however, I was frustrated with some things. It started to feel like the support that was required for me to be ultra-successful was not necessarily there when I needed it.

I did what I thought was the admirable thing and met separately with a couple of senior managers. I told them I was not happy about getting absorbed into office meetings and waiting on support. It seemed I was waiting an abnormal amount of time getting engineering completed, and it was not conducive to selling.

Eventually, an event sparked an impromptu but very quick decision, after months of contemplating. An internal meeting was scheduled with key personnel from my company. It was in preparation for a customer meeting where we had to answer some significant questions about our product. A few hours prior to the internal meeting, a couple of key people cancelled, and yet again, I felt unsupported. That was the final straw. I quickly wrote up my resignation and emailed my boss to let him know we needed a meeting just after lunch. My decision was made. I met with my boss, handed in my resignation and explained to him that I was done. I turned in my car, my phone, my laptop, along with any property from the company, and I went on my merry way.

The following Monday, I started with a new company to which I am still working for today. I have spent approximately eight years here, and I've been successful. I have the same responsibilities this time with a commission and base salary. In sales, a commission certainly drives you to be a go getter even more so than I was normally. As I quickly learned, the commission checks are a direct correlation to the challenging hard work.

I still see many of the folks that I used to work with at the other company. They are now customers of mine, so our relationships are still amiable. I work an exhausting day for good pay. Sometimes in life, you need to move on to grab a new adventure as you get a little bit stagnant and may need to try something new.

I've also seen a few of my previous colleagues at different social gatherings or on sales calls competing for the same customer's business. I've been truly fortunate in my career that I still have relationships with many of the people that I previously worked alongside.

THE BEGINNING OF A NEW LIFE

I should begin to explain an incredibly huge portion of my life. These paragraphs will be primarily information for my two boys. I figured I would throw it in here, and we'll see where it lands. I have mentioned one of my best friends who ended up being my brother-in-law only to be back to friends once we got divorced.

This would be the beginning of a courtship and eventually getting married. It had all started with my friend, Mike, finding himself a girlfriend and eventually announcing their marriage. I was fortunate enough to be asked to be a groomsman. There are multiple times when all the bridesmaids, the groomsmen and the entire wedding party get together to rehearse what must be done at the ceremony. I remember the first meeting was on a Thursday night, which was the very first time I got to meet my future wife. I remember being in awe of this fine young woman.

I was 30 years old at the time and still living with my mother who was in ill health. Although I wasn't there 100% of the time, it was always a good feeling just to be around her for any care that she may have needed. At this time in my life, though, I was ready for a relationship, so I asked her out.

It was a couple of weeks later that I took her on our first date. I had done some research and decided to go to a steakhouse in the Detroit area called Sinbad's. I picked her up at her condominium, and we went across the border and drove 15 minutes to the restaurant. At the time, I was driving what I thought was a cool car; a Crown Victoria with all the luxurious options in it. We had some enjoyable conversation, got to know each other a little better, and had a nice meal.

I was brought up to treat women in a respectful manner, but I could tell that no one had treated her this way. We went for a walk on the pier, since the restaurant was located on the Detroit River. I specifically remember it was a bit of a chilly night as we walked, and she was looking a bit cold. I did the proper thing, and let her use my coat. At the end of the date, I drove her home, and she went on her way.

We went on to have multiple dates and conversations. At six months into dating, we broke it off because she just did not seem interested. After a few months. I still had feelings for her but did not contact her. I remember as she broke it off that I had told her goodbye for now. Those were the words that I used, and sure enough, a few months later, she reached out, and we started dating again. This time, we kept everything moving forward, eventually moving in together in an apartment on the west side of Windsor.

During our engagement and a few years of our marriage, another adventure took place that I have to describe. At this time, my ex-wife and I had already moved in together. We had rented an apartment in a low-income neighbourhood. To save money for our first house, we ended up signing up to be superintendents of the 20-unit apartment complex.

We were both working full time and managing this apartment complex. We did that for a year and a half. We were responsible for evictions, bringing in people to rent and minor repairs to the entire facility. This was a huge escapade for us; never knowing what was around the next corner as far as the dealings with the tenants. The renters were mostly low income, often on welfare or social assistance or some form of government assistance. We were seen by the tenants as lucky people who were wealthy as we both had cars, and we both had jobs.

We were vastly different from the tenants. A few were retired who had no jobs and on social assistance. Others were unemployed with no interest in getting a job. I would say that we were slumlords taking care of a building with tenants who had incredibly low initiative. Some of the things we saw as tenants moved out or got evicted were quite shocking and ridiculous.

One such instance was when a liquid was dripping down from a balcony on the third floor to the second floor. The tenant called us to complain, which meant I had to go check it out only to find out that the tenant immediately above was letting her full-size German shepherd urinate and defecate on her balcony. What was dripping down was urine. Here is a full-size dog never being taken outside to grass, living in a one-bedroom apartment with a small 8-foot-long balcony. Eventually, this tenant was evicted because they were not allowed to have pets. The eviction process is quite lengthy with governmental procedures including the sheriff coming in, locking the doors, and changing the locks. At the final eviction stage, the tenant has a few hours to grab their belongings, which was usually limited, and leave the apartment.

The next event that I recall was after yet another tenant moved out in the middle of the night without rent payment. We eventually found out and had a locksmith open the doors because the tenant didn't bother to leave the keys. I walked into a bedroom after the locksmith opened the bedroom door, and I shockingly found a snakeskin and a cage from the ceiling to the floor. It was obvious that this gentleman had had a huge snake living in the bedroom. The snakeskin was near 10 feet long, so it was a massive snake.

One of our many responsibilities as superintendents was repairing any damages, repainting, and shampooing carpets in the vacant apartments. One time I walked into a two-bedroom apartment that was vacant, and one of the bedrooms was painted black. I mean walls, windows, ceiling, inside the closets and back of the bedroom door were black. I'm not sure what went on in there. It took several coats of paint and long hours to get that room looking back to normal. Scraping the windows to get black paint off was quite a tedious and time-consuming task that took hours of labour.

I would have to say that year and a half was quite an adventure. We learned a lot about dealing with people. Sometimes, you felt bad for people, and other times we recognized they were just plane idiots; very rude and ignorant. In each case. we got through it, and we achieved our goal; saving enough money to buy our first house together.

While living in this apartment, I purchased an engagement ring on the sly, which is typical for me, keeping my emotions close to my heart. I remember purchasing it from a local jeweler in Windsor and made monthly payments on it. Eventually, I had it paid off and was keeping it hidden somewhere. On the anniversary of our first date, we went to a local park named Jackson Park. I had placed the ring in my pants pocket, and we walked around chatting, looking at the beautiful scenery. Eventually, towards the back of the park, I finally gathered up the courage and got down on one knee and proposed to her. She said yes! At that point, we were off to the races, newly engaged, and planning our future together.

We were already living together for a few years at that point and began to make plans for the wedding. We announced the engagement to her family and obviously to my mom, brother, and sister-in-law. A year after the proposal, we got married. She was Catholic, and we wanted to get married in the church, but I was not Catholic. We planned on having our wedding at Jackson Park. Her idea was that one of her uncles, who previously was a priest and had turned to be a reverend, could marry us outside. She reached out to her uncle who attended, and we hired a Lutheran reverend to be head of the service. We invited our families and had a beautiful outdoor wedding. There were 60 people there, Including a photographer who happened to be a friend of the family. It even sprinkled just after the wedding, which was supposed to be good luck.

Our first thought was to have a small wedding with ten people. It grew to double, next 40 friends, then 70 and finally ended up with about one hundred guests. The reception was at a local Knights of Columbus. We were lucky enough that her uncle could supply the alcohol, and we made all our wedding table ornaments ourselves, along with the wine. I remember one of her cousins was very drunk and passed out in the washroom at the end of the night. He was underage at the time, and I had to drag him outside to have somebody drive him home.

We went to Las Vegas for our honeymoon, which my brother and sister-in-law graciously gifted us. We stayed at the Venetian in a beautiful suite. We did the usual tourist tours, including Lake Mead and the Hoover Dam. We then flew home to Windsor where we had previously purchased a house, thanks to a great down payment from her mother and stepfather. A year later, we had our first child. Fast forward, and here I am today with 23 and 20-year-old grown sons.

Our first house was in more central Windsor, a four-bedroom house in the downtown area across from a popular high school that had closed. It was a wonderful experience owning a house. For reference, we paid under $100,000 for our very first home. Within the next year, we had our first child, Linden Lloyd Crain. Two and a half years later, we had our second son, Nolan Gregory Crain while living in our second home.

MARRIAGE AND DIVORCE

We lived in our first house for a year and a half, and then my wife wanted to live in the country. We started looking and found a great little place just outside of the town of Essex. We purchased the house, sold the first one, and moved a few months later. It was a smaller house but had an acre of property, and the neighbors were much further away. The curious thing is that it was 10 minutes away from where I lived with my mother in my late 20s. When I was single, I had joined a golf course, and now with this move, I was four minutes away from the golf course where I was a member. The previous two years, because of the distance and time, it was often difficult to go golfing for four or five hours. Add another half hour commute each way, and I would spend a half a day golfing. As you can imagine, and will certainly learn, time away from home and parenting two babies never goes well in a new marriage.

About a year into this second house, my mother fell ill and passed away. My oldest son, Linden, was a year and a half old at the time. In the midst of all of this, what brought us added joy was the birth of my second son, Nolan Gregory Crain.

We lived in that second house for a couple of years before we started to outgrow it, and the ex-wife was complaining that her family never came out to visit because they lived in Amherstburg, which was about 30 minutes away. Prior to our house three purchase, we investigated doing an addition or a basement. It was only a single-story house, so adding on or doing some kind of renovation was a viable option. The amount of money required to do what was needed to increase our property value, though, just did not work out as far as financing.

Eventually, we made the big move into Amherstburg, closer to the ex-wife's family. She felt that for her family to visit her more we should be closer. She had grown up in that town with her aunts, uncles, and cousins with many of them still living there. Crazy me, I thought, at the time, a happy wife meant a happy life.

She had an excellent job at the time. I had a respectable job at the time, so we decided to make the plunge and double our mortgage payment. We purchased a much newer house that was 15 years old at the time and much bigger at 1800 square feet. A beautiful raised ranch on a great piece of property with a pool and fresh landscaping. We were off to the races in our third home in less than five years.

Although it's often easy to see some signs of a marriage in decline, sometimes when you are in it, either you don't see it, don't want to acknowledge it, or you just continue to refute it. That was the case the last six or so months in our second house. The marriage had started to fall apart slightly, so we did a bit of marriage counseling for a few sessions. It didn't seem to be of value or interest from either side of the table. I would go on to mistakenly think that if we moved closer to her family, closer to her work, she would be happier, and everything would magically heal up and be fixed.

Of course, the first few months in the third house everything was okay with no issues, so I thought perhaps the situation had been resolved. Suddenly, there was a strike at her place of employment, so a new level of stress started to creep in. One income caused the financial burden to amplify, since it now was entirely on me. I understood the situation but did not necessarily agree with it since it was affecting our household. I don't recall exactly the length of time, but two or three months of a strike put a burden on our finances, and stress on the marriage was beginning to show rapidly. A month before my 40th birthday, six months after purchasing our home, the writing was on the wall. The ex-wife announced that she was done with the marriage, it was not going to work, and she wanted a divorce.

My first initial thought was why now. My second thought was, if you wanted out of the marriage, could you not have said that seven months before we decided to double our mortgage expense? That was a real punch in the face. You never really know why things happen, but there are a couple of factors that probably contributed.

The first one was our 11 year age difference. Because of it, we really had no common friends or interests. I think my sports involvement was also a large issue considering it took up a huge amount of my free time. It was important to me, but during those first years of marriage, I made the decision to drop my involvement in hockey to alleviate some stress on my marriage. That topic could be a different story and a different paragraph or chapter in this book. I don't know if I was an up and comer in hockey coaching, but I had advanced myself at the right time and had a few connections in the higher ranks.

The next single reason for my marriage failure was the large amount of bills and debt. The single household income would also push the inevitable much faster. The selling of the $300,000 dream home was a gut-wrenching feeling for me. It was one of the biggest homes in my family next to my brothers and sister-in-law's. It was a sense of accomplishment having that home.

I would learn, after many mistakes, that one of the things to not worry about was where you live, but more importantly, concentrate on how you live. How smart was it to go into a home that was affordable only with two incomes? Obviously, that decision is made every day by thousands and thousands of couples, and it works out fine. In my case, when there was only one income, it didn't work.

There was a lot of bitterness at the beginning of the divorce process. The biggest hurdle was how to survive and where I was going to live. At the beginning, we decided to both live in the house until we could sell the home and move on. That scenario lasted close to six months. Of course, there was a huge issue living in the same house trying to coexist with someone who no longer wanted to be married. We immediately put the house up for sale with a long time high school friend of mine. He had done other real estate deals for us in the past. Well, because of our looming debt and only having one income, credit cards were being maxed out, and lines of credit were beginning to grow. The solution was to put the additional debt onto the selling price. You are hearing correctly. We put the house on the market overpriced. Although we had a few showings, the real estate contract was for 90 days, and immediately, the ex-wife did not like our usual agent. She did not like the number of open houses and didn't like how he was showing the house. It was an attack on me and my friend who was trying to sell the house. I am not sure if she thought there was an inside deal going on or not, but the bottom line is the house was for sale for too much in hopes of covering our debt.

The last month of the three-month contract was very hostile to say the least. After three months, I let my friend know he was no longer going to be the real estate agent. I told her to find an agent that she thought would be a super-agent, the magic seller of our home. Of course, she took me up on my offer. The new real estate agent came in, made a minor adjustment on the price, and began the selling process. Again, open houses and viewings, but no offers and no sale.

Obviously, this was an issue since it went on for about six months. The whole selling of the house, large debt payments, divorce looming and living in the same household scenario was taxing on emotions. Something had to change, and it would turn about quickly.

At this point, any monies in a joint account and all joint debt were now put on the burden of myself. Although our demise was inevitable even if we sold the house quickly, it was another thing that irritated me.

At this point, living in the same household did not work, and I decided to move out and to live with a friend. It was a huge ask of him, and I lived downstairs, where with his help, we set up beds as well as a small kitchen area. We made the arrangements at least livable for the time being. I had the kids two weeks on two weeks off, so the boys had a place to sleep and hang out with me. You guessed it, Mike Janisse came to my aid.

All in all, it was an awkward living situation. I didn't want to intrude and was very conscious of that, so I kept to myself down in his basement. Occasionally, we would chat casually, but I didn't want to disturb him or his lifestyle at all.

He was also single at the time going through his own divorce. We married sisters, and we also got divorced near the same time within a year or so of each other. Very odd dynamics to say the least where he had two boys, and I had two boys. However, he kept his house and his ex-wife moved out. Within a month of my ex-wife living in our dream house, I was pushed into a corner myself.

I still had a full-time job, but I sheepishly walked into the bank and asked for the person that created the mortgage and handed them the keys to my dream home. I explained, apologized, and walked out of the bank without my house. Everyone had finished moving out, I thoroughly cleaned the house and handed the house of my dreams to the financial institution. I don't exactly remember where my ex-wife went to live. I think, at that point, she had a boyfriend, and she moved in with him. I was living in the basement of a friend's house trying to keep my life and boys together.

After a few months, I found a small place that I could rent in the Amherstburg area where I could begin the rebuilding process. It was important that my kids were back to a situation that was normal, including living in the town where they were growing up. The boys were in grade school at the time, with the youngest in junior kindergarten while the oldest was in grade three.

I was very appreciative of having a house now. I was renting a three bedroom home in Amherstburg. It was a clean small place, ugly on the outside and ugly on the inside. At that point in my life, it was what I called home, and I was determined to make it work. Obviously, this time in my life was very emotional and certainly stressful. The attempt to sell the house, deal with an ex-wife, have lawyers involved with separation agreements and manage a full-time job, I was kept busy. The busy schedule and craziness helped me as there was no time to debate or think about things and sulk. I was of the mindset I just had to get through it with the priority number one being the well-being of my two sons.

My boys were with me during the week attending school. I had a full-time job, and the ex-wife was also back to work. In my situation, I needed before and after school day care. My job started at 7:00 am, so the plan was to find a daycare that was open at 6:30, so I could drop the two boys off and go to work. They would be at daycare before and after school. They would be picked up at the daycare by bus, go to school, and come back to daycare by bus. When I was done with work at 5:00 pm, I would race to their daycare to pick them up on the way home.

Many times, through the next 10 years, people would ask me exactly how I got through this crazy time. In my mind, it was what it was, and I just did what was required. There was no whining about it, no complaining about it, we just did it. There were late nights and early mornings here and there, but at the same time, goal number one was to have the least amount of effect, complications, or interruptions for my two boys. All three of us still lived in Amherstburg, so they participated in many different activities. They were in music lessons, soccer, baseball, and hockey as well as their grade school activities.

Eventually, agreements by both sides were made with our lawyers, and we came to an agreement of shared custody. That meant we would share any expenses for the boys and share custody of the boys equally. I will admit that their mother was very gracious and very accommodating during this entire process. It was especially important to me that there was no separation between her family or my family and the two boys. Although her family was much bigger than mine, any events that they were asked to attend were never an issue with me. The divorce was between their mother and I, not them. In fact, I encouraged the boys to stay close to the grandmother and her husband as well as others in my ex-wife's family. Many thought that was crazy, that there should be bitterness between all the parties and a huge separation between the father and the mother's family. I never agreed with that, and luckily, the ex-wife didn't either.

I would say the divorce was amiable. Both sides understood that the kid's well-being was the number one goal. Nobody was trying to take money from the deal. We figured it out between us without having any obvious emotional damage done to the kids.

Now, there were times that were rough between the ex-wife and me. I often didn't agree with decisions she made on a personal level for herself. I wanted to always make sure that those decisions did not involve or affect our two boys. I lived at the new home I was renting for six years. The entire goal was to purchase a home and to move on from the divorce.

I remember trying to save a few dollars here and there by cashing in RRSP's until I finally had enough money to purchase a small house. It was a great feeling to shop for a house where I could raise my children properly. At the same time, the ex-wife moved around various places in Windsor and Amherstburg. It was always important that the kids remained in a stable environment which meant keeping them in the same grade school and high school.

At different times when the ex-wife moved into Windsor, we would make different accommodation schedules. During the summer, they would live with her and with me primarily during the school year.

Eventually, when I purchased our home. I made sure to have them involved to make them feel included because it was truly going to be their home. It was an enjoyable day when we got to move into the home that I currently am sitting in as I write this memoir.

I have to say that this divorce business scarred me, and that is the strong word I'll use. I have never bothered to ever pursue dating anyone. It was never a goal to have someone else in my life. My entire focus was to raise my two boys as best I could and to give them the time and attention that was required for them to be successful in life.

The boy's mother and I got along after the divorce. In fact, I'd say we get along better now than we did when we were married. She has settled down and lives in Windsor with a steady partner. As I write this, the boys are 23 and 20 years old. They are adults now. No supervision is required anymore. They both have their own cars and their own lives.

I often heard two things from friends and family when the boys were young. The first is would you ever get married again, and how to heck did you balance all the different balls you were juggling at the time. I never did think it was juggling. it was just doing what was required, when it was required to keep the boys stable and happy. When you think about it, being raised in a divorce household was terrible for everybody involved.

Even to this day, the boys bounce around from my house to their mother's house. They can come and go as they please. That flexibility is also convenient for them as they work and go to school both in Amherstburg and in Windsor. I live in Amherstburg, Nolan works in Amherstburg and goes to the university in Windsor. Linden works in Windsor and is a councillor in Amherstburg. The daily question nowadays is where they are hanging their hat for the night.

Obviously both the ex-wife and I love our kids and would like to see them 100% of the time, but we realize that they have their own lives. They both are now carving their own path to success. The only thing I ask is that they give me a heads up so I can prepare dinner. Those requests with kids often go unanswered, which in the whole scheme of things, is something small.

I am very thankful that they have grown up into fine young men. I am sure they are scarred or tainted because of just being in the situation of having two households and a mother and father that were married and then divorced. I think you would be foolish to think the situation is not going to affect them some in their future years. Although incredibly sad, it is what it is, but I know my two boys will battle through any adversity. If anything, hopefully they have seen some unusual ways of dealing with stressful times in situations that are not necessarily favourable to everybody.

My future, as far as relationships are concerned, is to remain single. At this point, I'm too old and set in my ways to even think about entertaining a partner. My freedom and stubbornness would be a bad mix for a relationship. I have no issues with being single. I am happy and content. I know my boys are well on their way into adulthood, and it won't be long before they have both fully left the nest and are married, perhaps with their own children.

I wouldn't wish divorce on anyone, especially anyone with children. It's a rough road for the kids no matter how it appears. I've been fortunate enough that the boys' mother and I have gotten along. I would say our communication is above average compared to other divorced couples. I'm always concerned about the boys' being a product of divorce and how that will play into their own relationships, but unfortunately, the statistics show one out of every two marriages end up in divorce.

I admit there were some mistakes made during our marriage. To pin down one thing is impossible. It was the accumulation of a multitude of factors that caused my relationship to sour quickly. I think I was better off to be divorced than stay in a relationship that was breaking down further each week. I don't really know if I could say I would do it all again and not change anything. I look at my two boys daily, though, and I see the products of that marriage. They're both damn excellent products of that marriage, and that's enough for me. I am so grateful our two boys have grown up to be great gentlemen. I know that they will be very productive members of society throughout their adulthood.

On the selfish side, I do harbor a bit of bitterness. One of my resentments is my hockey coaching career. Any aspirations of coaching hockey at any significant level were squashed at the very beginning of the marriage. It didn't really work when we were just dating, either. At that point, I was coaching a minor hockey team. I was often away on weekends and at practices and games during the week. This busy sports schedule definitely reduced relationship building time with my girlfriend. Her comments here and there regarding being absent in the relationship, even as we were dating, may have been red flags to the future failure with her. I battled through that part probably because of stubbornness and blind love you would say. I had offers to move up to junior, which I accepted with excitement. In my very first year coaching junior C, she was pregnant with my oldest son. The comments, the stress and relationship pressure would occur every time I would leave the house to coach hockey. Suddenly the hours, the excitement and the fun of coaching junior hockey was fading under the stress. I found myself often having to race home or leave home at the last possible minute to join the team for practice and for games. The hard part was that I knew what was required, yet I couldn't do anything about it. In a new marriage, I didn't realize how quickly it was breaking down. I often found myself thinking it was just growing pains, and that the wife would learn to accept and tolerate it. The second year of junior, I resigned from my position at the end of the year. I couldn't and wouldn't be able to come back because I needed to work on a marriage that was rapidly deteriorating. The third year, I foolishly moved up to the junior B ranks as another stepping stone. I coached with a close friend of mine in his inaugural junior head coaching season. It was not long before the same stress of maintaining a relationship now with a child began to be magnified daily. Near the end of the first year of my junior B career again, and for the final time, I announced to my close friend that I would not be coming back. There was a serious crack in my marriage, and I needed to try to fix it. Those were my first three years of marriage, and the writing was on the wall at that point. Although I tried to never dwell on it and certainly never spoke about it, it was a given that I was not happy about it. I was willing to take the bullet and sacrifice personal gain to try and maintain a marriage, and it still fell apart.

The whole marriage lasted approximately seven years. The first three were full of turmoil because of hockey, and the next four full of resentment because of the anticipated inevitable divorce that was looming. We tried two or three marriage counseling sessions, but that did not seem to work. We had no common interests, and without a doubt, a sports guy marrying a non-sports partner while trying to remain in sports was not a particularly good mix.

I think about it 25 years later, and obviously the entire paragraph above shows the resentment starting to ooze out. Sometimes, I do wonder what might've been had I pursued my dream and remained in junior hockey. I did one last year as a scout in junior, thinking that it was less of a time commitment. It turned out that, to do the job of an amateur scout, your time on the road increased. Time away from the family also increased and again caused stress. My contract after one year of scouting was not renewed. When I compare myself in my role as a scout to what my fellow scouts at the time were doing, I'm damn lucky to have participated for a full year. My participation was watching a bare minimum number of games, and that was quite embarrassing.

You never know where things could have ended up if the situation at the beginning were different. I do think about it occasionally when I see other scouts, or I see other coaches behind the bench. I wonder if I focused more on my participation and excitement than the acceptance from my partner, where it would have led. As they say, I guess you can't cry over spilled milk.

I have never really expressed these thoughts to my ex-wife. I am resentful of the way my hockey career ended, but I'm excited to be back in hockey in a different role as an owner of a junior C hockey club.

I would think that this chapter with me writing about a failed marriage and some internal thoughts will be shocking to a few, including my ex-wife as she reads the book. I have mentioned to my two boys, in a pretty matter of fact manner, that they should never let their partner control their happiness. Some would say that was very rude. It is certainly direct, but I don't want them to go through what I went through. What I put my two sons through in a failed marriage was awful in so many ways.

I hope, if they learn anything from my failed marriage, that they can learn to be amiable and still maintain a friendship with an ex-partner. The second thing I want them to learn is that you need to be happy in a relationship. If you are not happy at the beginning of the relationship, it doesn't get better. Now, to be clear, the ex-wife was the one that initiated the divorce. In one way, I'm thankful for that because I know my stubbornness would have never asked for a divorce. Instead, I would've just wallowed in this situation and put the happy face on daily even though the happiness was no longer there.

I do recall being separated and not officially divorced for five or six years, having just separation papers. There was still some obvious bitterness. Although I never planned on ever being re-married to my ex-wife, I would not grant the divorce. I simply told her if she wanted to be divorced so badly, then she needed to find out how to do it, because it was very costly. Eventually she became responsible for all the leg work since it was her initiative. We did it all online with the final papers being signed by a justice of the peace. The divorce papers were finally signed seven years after we separated.

If she chose to do so, she could finally get remarried. She was going through some crazy times and was trying to settle down. My goal of not granting a divorce early on helped her out in a few situations where she may or may not have gotten into different marriages with some undesirable partners. I think she would agree when she reads this.

She continued to ask for her wedding rings along with her family ring. My stubbornness and obvious bitterness would never allow me to give the rings to her. Finally, the situation started to settle down, and we began to tolerate each other and communicate after the separation and finally the divorce. It was many years later I returned the wedding rings and the family ring. I am sure I probably made a snide remark when I gave them to her. Giving her the rings, especially since we were no longer a family, meant more to her than they did for me. They were not my rings, but I just felt very odd handing them over.

Financially, emotionally, physically, and now symbolically, the marriage was done and the divorce was official.

TOUGHER

I regret not being much firmer during my marriage with my wife. I seemed to think doing everything that was asked of me and answering all her questions was the right way to respond. My thinking was still that a happy wife meant a happy life. It certainly did not turn out that way. I never could create enough happiness. Even she mentioned that I should have been much firmer with her. I did what she wanted way too often and accepted what she did more often than disputing it. I should've not felt guilty about different things, which would have been a better way to have a marriage. I was always thinking that you give and take, but now that I look back, I did way too much giving.

Marriage is a crazy balancing act. Just because someone wants something or asks for something, you shouldn't feel obligated. If you don't agree with it, you should say that I don't agree with it, and I am not going to accept it. My thinking was always that if I don't agree with it, I will not vocalize it, but I am going to give in to the situation.

It was not the best way when I now think about it. The confidence and the ability to say no is especially important in life, marriage, and business. In your career, you must find a way to say no respectfully. Sometimes when you say no and you disagree, the conversation is not going to end well. You cannot go around your life being a pushover and just accepting each situation just because you don't want any confrontation.

I would say my biggest regret was that I was not a bit more questioning and opinionated. This would have led to more confrontation, which for me is uncomfortable. That's not a concept just for marriage. In life, I am very easygoing, and it is my belief that if it is not a life-or-death situation, you can always get through it. I think over my lifetime that there are many situations where I should've said no. I did not agree with whoever was proposing the idea or situation, but instead I just went with the flow.

I have mentioned before that I was smart enough to know right from wrong. I am speaking of all the other situations where there could've been a happy compromise. Often, I would choose not to have any confrontation in a situation because I never wanted to disagree with the other person. I tried to always respect their opinion. I would never bother to push out my opinion and would just accept their thoughts. So just in saying that, there is quite a conflict for me in regards to pleasing others or pleasing myself.

It's important in life to stand up for what you believe. You do the right thing, and sometimes you will hear from the masses that you're wrong. It's also important that you're not an idiot and disagree, whine and complain about everything. I have always believed that there are two things,and now with this day and age, three things that should be taboo for discussion. Especially in my career and often in my friendships, you always had to know to whom you are talking. The three things that I have chosen to never debate about in depth are religion, politics and now COVID. People are very opinionated, passionate and firm in their beliefs when it comes to these three topics.

I have always been of the belief that it's not important that everybody knows your opinion on everything. There is just no value added to those conversations. Be firm when you need to be firm, and provide your opinion when you are asked. Make sure you are making proper decisions backed by data and facts.

I think, personally, that I could have been closer as a friend rather than a father at times with my two boys. It is a fine line when I needed to be firm, or when I should've just listened without voicing my opinion. My two boys are different in what I try to convey to them. One I often talk to as an advisor more than the other. One I speak to more as a father. I know they both will do well throughout their lifetime. All the best, my sons, and I love you no matter how I speak to you.

NAMING OF THE BOYS

My first son's name is Linden Lloyd Crain, and my second son's name is Nolan Gregory Crain.

Those who know me have mentioned that their names are based on hockey players. While those who don't know me have always seemed to mention that they are incredibly unique names. During each pregnancy, we did not know the sex of either of our kids. Of course, the ex-wife did all the testing and picture taking and birth stuff, but no one could ever tell what sex either were prior to their birth. We didn't care about the sex. We only wanted a healthy child.

Once we found out we were pregnant with our first child, the name game started. Off the very top on my side, I wanted the name to be a bit unique but not weird or obscure with crazy spellings. I realized that would cause issues later in life for the child.

I have a few names that my boys continue to remind me that were for consideration at one point. They laugh about the names that they could've been. For my first son, we threw around a bunch of names, however I cannot remember any names that the wife picked out.

Three of the names were Cooper, Bauer, and Sherwood. Now, for all the athletes reading this, yes, those three names are hockey equipment manufacturers. I always thought they were unique and different, but they would have had to be for a male child. I don't recall what all our name ideas were for a girl. I believe one of the names would have been Corinne, which was picked by me. The crazy thing about that name is that, in grade 3, there was a girl in grade 8 named Corinne, and she was super cute. That name has always stuck with me since then.

Now back to the boys' names. The truth of the matter is my first-born son Linden's name was a combination of thoughts. I remember driving down Front Road in Lasalle, listening to the radio. They mentioned the name Lyndon Baine Johnson who is known as LBJ and the 36th President of the United States of America. I was not a history buff, but the name Lyndon, for whatever reason, caught my attention. I also recognized that the spelling of his name was a bit different. At the time, when my first son was born, there was an NHL hockey player named Trevor Linden. He played for the Vancouver Canucks as the captain of the team. So, my first son's name is a combination of a president's name with a hockey player spelling, and my father's name as his middle name Lloyd. That created the name Linden Lloyd Crain for my first-born son.

Now, my ex-wife did not have a problem with that name. Obviously, there was a lot of discussion once we found out the sex. I remember searching through books and looking online for different male names. Popular names and historical names and stuff like that, but for whatever reason, the name on the radio caught my attention. Me being a hockey guy, it made perfect sense to spell his name after a good hockey player in Trevor Linden.

As we were veteran parents just three years prior, we had gone through a bunch of names for our second child. My next son's name had various name options rolling around in our heads. When we found out at birth that our child was a boy, this one was simpler to choose. Again, a hockey player influence came to my mind. As a hockey coach at the time, Nolan's name is an exact spelling of Owen Nolan, also a great leader and professional hockey player in the NHL. Nolan's middle name, I guess in an egotistical way, is named after me. So, the name Nolan Gregory Crain is a combination of a hockey player's last name and his father's name Gregory. Fast forward 20 years, and a curious phenomenon is occurring with my sons. Linden, with his presidential name influence, is a municipal politician, and Nolan is developing a personality and mentality remarkably like myself at a young adult age.

Those are the facts of the naming of our two boys. I got my wish and had two boys, and I was also successful in having a considerable influence on naming them. Should they have been girls, I'm sure the ex-wife's names would have been chosen for our kids. So, this is just a little bit of history of the boys' names. The names come up multiple times during conversations when people are introduced to them. When questions arise regarding two boys' unique names, the truth is sitting in the above paragraphs.

THE FIRST BORN

The next few will be an exciting couple of chapters since I get to talk about my two boys. My oldest son, Linden Lloyd Crain was born August 1st, 2000. This young man has been a definite inspiration throughout his entire life. Linden was born close to a year after we were married. Even though we lived together for a few years, we wanted to be married prior to having our first child. I wish I could recall the time of birth and his weight and length. It didn't matter at the time, and it wasn't written down by me. I'm sure his mother would know exactly all that information as mothers typically remember, but for me, it was just the proud moment of the birth of my first child.

I was in the room when Linden was born, and it was quite a feeling to have your first offspring. In my memory, the labour process was lengthy. I think her mother was in the room at the same time, but I could be wrong about that. I just remember how excited I was that my child was a boy. We never really cared whether it was a boy or a girl, but the way it turned out was awesome. Here I was with my first child being a little boy. It was such a proud feeling to have a young Crain added to the family. Linden is the oldest son by two years and nine months.

As of the writing of this book, Linden is twenty-two, soon to be 23 years old and well on his way with his career. Linden, I would say, is a bit more serious than his brother and certainly a focused young man. Linden has the nature of being a person that worries about many things. He worries about his family and about his brother. This may be a product of being brought up in a divorced home where often it would only be himself and his brother for a few hours while I was on my way home from traveling for work. When he and his brother stayed with his mother, it would be the same kind of worrying. In that situation, it was more worrying about his mother's partners and their behaviours and habits.

Linden's grade school years were great. He never had any significant issues in grade school. I do seem to remember somehow him getting suspended for a day because of fighting or pushing a kid down in the schoolyard. I would say Linden is very gentle, and I would label him as athletic. Linden did all the usual athletics. He played baseball for at least one year, hockey for many years as well as soccer in grade school.

In high school, he ran for the cross-country team, played on the soccer team and in his last year, for the first time ever, he played football. Here comes Linden's caring part. The senior football team did not have enough participants and needed players, or else they would have to fold the team. Now, here is a young man at the time 5-foot 8" 125 pounds with zero football experience. He took it upon himself to approach the coach and told him if he needed more participants, he was willing to play on the football team and that he did. Although not the most talented player because of experience and size, he gave it his all, and ultimately, the team had enough players to play their season. In Linden's eyes, it was all about allowing his fellow students to play football because he knew that was their love. In this and many cases, he just did what had to be done to help and support others.

Beginning in grade six, Linden showed interest in becoming a lawyer. I would say that interest was sparked by a chance meeting on Canada Day with a friend of mine who was an entertainment lawyer. We were casually walking by each other after not seeing each other for many years, and Linden noticed his T-shirt of a famous band. We struck up a conversation and went on our way.

Linden thought it was peculiar that an older guy had a T-shirt on of a rock and roll band and asked me about it. I explained who the gentleman was and that he was a lawyer for the band that he was wearing on his t-shirt. He handled the business relationships for that band and many other singers, entertainers, and bands. That is where I believe the interest in becoming a lawyer started. That interest went throughout high school and even into his university days.

Linden started to show interest in politics in high school. He was on the student council beginning in grade nine as well as various event organizing initiatives. In Linden's grade 12, he took it upon himself and gathered a team to run for Prime Minister of General Amherst High School. He learned how to campaign and organized fellow students to run his campaign. He won by a landslide and became the Prime Minister of his high school. He even had local restaurants hanging banners with a sign to vote for Linden.

I would say Linden is very social. In fact, I remember one incident at a local restaurant. It was me, my two sons, and the owner, who happened to be our server at the time. She was so impressed with the boys' maturity and politeness that she asked Linden if he wanted a job. He took the job, and his brother, who is three years younger, also had a job offer which he took a few months later.

I would say the maturity of both my sons was a by-product of their environment. As babies, I never understood parents' reasoning when talking to their children in baby talk. We always chose to talk as adults. The other factor I would say that helped with their early maturity was being raised in two households. We were a busy family on both sides. Although we did not run a super tight ship, the boys were taught to be polite and to always behave.

Growing up, if there was any visiting to do, or if we ate out, there was no concern about bringing the kids. As a single parent, you usually have no choice but to bring your kids to everything. Anything I did they did. They got to see real estate negotiations, rental agreements and everything in between.

Linden's social life was busy throughout high school, but I would say that he was not a partier. I do remember him and his girlfriend in grade 11 went to a couple of prom parties, though.

I believe he may have had a couple of girl acquaintances, although they were never referred to as girlfriends. He met his current girlfriend in grade 11, working at the local McDonald's restaurant. They worked there together, and eventually, Linden took another job and so did his girlfriend. It was always preached to Linden by me that he was going to go through university and graduate with some version of a degree. Linden was not very technical or mechanically inclined, and the reason for that was solely because I never bothered to teach Linden any of the hands-on skills that I had learned from my father. The thought process there was a bit selfish, but I never wanted my children to be in the hands-on workforce. I never showed him any of the hands-on skills required to be in the trades. It was always my plan or thought that they would be white collar workers.

Some of that had to do with the fact that, with all of our schedules, there was not time to teach them any of those skills. Often, I would have to hire mechanics, plumbers, or electricians to do work that was required. At the same time, I could do many of those functions. I just didn't have the time. Linden, I knew had the ability, it was just something I didn't bother teaching. The hope was always that they would earn enough income that they could simply hire others to do those tasks.

Linden was fortunate enough, worked hard, and volunteered enough to get an incredibly significant amount of scholarships coming out of high school for his entrance into the University of Windsor. This was one of many situations where Linden understood that you needed to apply for scholarships and obviously, he got some counseling from high school peers. He filled out every application, wrote every letter and applied without my assistance.

I have always tried to let my sons be very independent, standing back and only directing traffic when required. I did give them ideas and tell them what needed to be done. I always made a point of not doing everything for them. Instead, I told them what I would suggest needed to be done and how to proceed.

His graduation from high school was an immensely proud moment for both me and the ex-wife. Listening to him be announced with his awards as well as his scholarship, and him standing centre stage was quite a proud moment as a father. He walked up on the stage as the Prime Minister of his high school, and left the stage 100% ready for the University of Windsor.

He enrolled in the business administration program. As Linden typically does, he immediately jumped into student council at the university. He eventually became the chair of a couple different councils during his university days. As I've mentioned, Linden has always been very social and has never had any issue with simply introducing himself to anyone. He has walked through life with no fear or hesitancy meeting people, regardless of their title, importance, salary, or wealth.

Throughout his four years, at multiple times, Linden had two and sometimes three jobs. He had a job working at a small local retail store as a host and also did social media and marketing for companies in the United States. Somewhere between his third and fourth year, he made a major decision. He decided, after many hours of contemplation, that he was not going to enroll in law school as previously anticipated.

Linden's initiative is unmatched by anyone I know at his tender age of 22 years old. In his second and third year of university, Linden took it upon himself to apply and was selected to be a director and board member of two charity organizations here in his hometown of Amherstburg. Here is a 21-year-old sitting on the board with well-established and much older members. Again, his eagerness drove him to volunteer as well as to help his community, laying the foundation for future aspirations that we'll later discuss. He's never concerned about his age or experience when pursuing a goal. He's always been driven to do exactly what he wants to do, despite what many would think were hurdles.

That is an attribute in life that will lead him to success. He recognized early on that every person, regardless of fame, fortune, or power wakes up like he does, puts their pants on just like he does, and goes about their day. Whether they sit in a fancy high rise in a corner office or they're a local small business owner, everybody at the root is the same.

I've always believed, and I'm certain he has the same thinking, that anyone can be a good person regardless of your fame, fortune, wealth, or status. It's the same for an egotistical person. They can be average, wealthy or important. It's more about who you are than what you do.

Linden, from what I can tell from watching as basically a spectator, has a plan at this point in his career. It's quite fascinating to watch the path he has chosen and the direction and process he is travelling to get to where he wants to go.

In Linden's fourth year of university, he decided to run for counsel of the town of Amherstburg. Here he was, a 22-year-old, campaigning against 15 other candidates to become a council member. Many of those were well established business personalities with previous experience as counselors. He was the youngest by at least 15 years. This was all his own doing, his own thought process and his own success earned. Linden was announced the winner in October 2022, becoming a counselor and gaining more votes in the community than anyone, including the new mayor and vice mayor. It was another proud moment as a father to watch your son organize, use experience, and never back down while proceeding to go after his goal.

I would say Linden is highly organized, driven, volunteer orientated and cares about his community. Here's a prediction of things in the future for my oldest son. I would anticipate he is first going to marry his sweetheart, Julia sometime in the next three or four years. He is currently a self-employed mortgage lender working under the tutelage of some successful guys with strong business acumen. My prediction would be that he may not have children, and I think he's trending to be a successful mortgage lender. It seems he has a burning desire to be an entrepreneur, and that may mean eventually having his own mortgage brokerage firm. In his first two months of being hired, he was learning the knack of being a salesperson as well as understanding the work ethic required to be successful in that industry. As far as politics goes, I think he may do his four years as a counselor, and depending on his success and earnings as a mortgage lender, that may be his last hurrah as a politician.

What I do know, without a doubt, is that he will be extraordinarily successful at all the things he does due to his strong work ethic. I would like to think that he has watched me throughout my career and learned a few things. The most important characteristic is the never quit attitude and that you must work hard to get paid philosophy. I certainly wish him all the best in his future. It has been a crazy ride the last four years of university watching his growth, desire, and work ethic. It will be fun to see his success story unfold because he can already author a remarkable story. All the best, young man, I love you.

THE SECOND BORN

Nolan Gregory Crain was born May 3rd, 2003. A crazy thing...as I write out his birthdate is that back in the day when we had a phone at home, our number in order was 8153. A curious little note is that August 1st is Linden's birthday, May 3rd is Nolan's birthday.

Nolan, many say, is a perfect likeness to me in both looks and personality. Nolan is 19, and, as I start to draft this book, he stands at 6' 2" and weighs 200 pounds. So, in those regards, he is not like his short fat father. His hair does tend to be curly which I had as a young child, teenager, and young adult. As far as those looks go, I would say we are similar. Nolan, as the second child, mimics the memes and articles you see on the second born, carefree and easy going.

Nolan is very generous. I have seen him at various times take money out of his pocket and give some to a less fortunate person standing on the corner asking for money. I have also seen him use money he earned to buy food for people. Nolan's great bubbly personality attracts conversation from anybody, and it makes me proud to watch him. I've had strangers praise his great personality and his proper manners, even as a young kid. At 19, he is now officially a man and certainly looks like a man, with an awesome temperament to go with his good looks.

Nolan is very athletic and extremely smart. Through grade school, he would concur that arduous work was not required for him to bring home great marks in both grade school and high school.

I specifically remember sitting down with him after his sixth-grade year, explaining that he would have to pick up his pace of homework and studying. He needed to be much neater writing notes, too because, in the next couple of years, he would be going into high school where marks would be much more difficult. He listened to what I said and increased his studying and neatness a considerable amount. I would watch and hear about tests coming up and then casually just watch his study habits. Occasionally, I reminded him that he needed to study to get good marks. He commented that he was studying, or he had studied. I would make a mental note of when I anticipated the test or assignment would be graded. I would then ask Nolan what mark he got on that specific exam or assignment. Nolan's personality would come out then. He would produce some story that he did not do very well and that he should have taken what I had told him more seriously. He was sorry, and told me the next test would be much better. At this point, he would pull out his grade, and with a sad face, show it to me. Endlessly, I would be fooled by his sad story about getting a terrible mark because, in fact, often he had high nineties for tests and perfect assignments. Upon showing those results to me, there wasn't a lot I could say. I would go into the test thinking that he should have studied more perhaps, but obviously with his impressive results, he did study and was just a very smart individual.

Nolan's high school was much the same as grade school. He didn't have to work hard to get high marks. He did the minimum and still got high nineties and made the honor roll for four years in a row with about a 95% average.

As I've mentioned, I'm of the belief that lessons need to be learned so they can be corrected. As far as education goes for Nolan, it is obvious that he has a brilliant mind, and he'll be able to go as far as he would like to in schooling because of his intelligence. Now, I must admit his second year of university where he is studying human kinetics with future aspirations to be a chiropractor, he has changed his study habits. He has learned the skill of arduous work and studying and by using the two together, his great marks will continue to be the result. Nolan was also truly fortunate to have earned thousands of dollars in scholarships because of his great marks and applying for these scholarships on his own. I made sure to do a little bit of follow up to be sure that he was applying, though. We always say that getting things done around our house is always on Nolan time. That simply means that Nolan is a bit of a procrastinator, doing the tasks but often at the last minute and after a couple of requests.

I would say Nolan is organized when required regarding school and work. Day-to-day tasks, household chores, cleaning his bedroom and his keeping his car tidy and well-kept is not at the top of Nolan's priority list. Again, that may very well be a learned skill from his father. I would say that although clean, my housekeeping is not always tidy all the time. So again, he is following me and my behaviors.

Nolan's personality is very casual, not necessarily on the shy side, but he comes off quiet. He is very laid back, not aggressive and extremely caring. Throughout high school, one of his summer jobs was a camp counselor, and his helping and caring characteristics came flying out. He also worked at the local McDonald's where I would hear stories of him paying for customers whose card was broken, or it was obvious the customer did not have enough money. Nolan would simply pay with his bank card and send the customer on their way without any fanfare.

I believe Nolan has felt the effect of his big brother Linden due to the latter's volunteering and board membership in the community. I would have to say that Nolan had felt tremendous pressure to keep up with his brother's popularity. I recall in high school, I had asked Nolan if he was going to be on student council and going to follow in his brother's footsteps as the Prime Minister of the school. This was my first insight that yes, in fact, I had either purposefully or subliminally placed a lot of pressure on Nolan to be just like Linden. When I had that conversation somewhere around grade 10 with Nolan, he snapped back that he was going to do his own thing and that he did not have to do everything the same as his brother. I was taken aback by those comments, but at least I was smart enough to understand that this was an obvious exhausting of some feelings because he felt pressure, and it was clearly from me. So, at this point, I would like to apologize to Nolan because he certainly felt unneeded persuasion from me. It was never the plan for him to be exactly like his brother, but obviously, he would constantly hear his brother's success stories around the household. He would hear about it from a local paper, or he would see interviews constantly. I think he's taken it to heart that I would have expected him to be the same, and that's my fault.

His mother and I would often have conversations regarding the two boys, and how they were both different. She did an excellent job of always reminding me they were two different kids with two different goals with two different personalities and that we needed them to grow in their own specific way. There's no book on parenting that I could follow to be a father correctly. I was making a huge error in how I was dealing with Nolan. I quickly realized and thought about exactly that situation where I may have previously made a comment or was thinking about making a comment that compared him to his brother. Those kinds of comments can be construed as very hurtful, and I've tried to refrain from making those comments or creating the illusion of any comparison between Nolan and his brother.

It's not fair to Nolan that I was comparing. I look at my own situation where I'm not necessarily like my brother. We have some of the same attributes while others are drastically different, including my personality which is much different than my brother's. It is not fair for me to expect my two kids to have the same personality, the same drive, the same athletic abilities. It's ridiculous, and it's not correct to think in that manner. Comparing your kids to each other can do nothing but harm. If one doesn't think he's successful because of the other one's success, suddenly you have a personality that is damaged.

I would say in Nolan's high school years the adventurous side of him began to become more apparent. Nolan is a very social individual, and his experimental and venturesome nature came out over those four years. Nolan was more of a partier than his brother as he enjoyed hanging out with the guys as well as going to parties throughout his high school years. I would say Nolan, in many ways, was more mature than his peers at an early age. I would say that it was because of his brother that he grew up a bit quicker. Nolan, I would think although not confirmed, probably experimented with drugs, sex and alcohol as a high school student.

Thinking back as I write this book about my years in high school, I would say Nolan's path was remarkably like mine. I just always worry that because of Nolan's personality, he could easily be taken advantage of by friends and foes in an intoxicated state. Nolan is a big teddy bear by nature, however, being a six foot and two hundred pound lean friendly partying machine can lead to a few different situations. Nolan does not have a mean bone in his body, and as we just mentioned, this young man would give you the shirt off his back along with a few dollars. Nolan's attitude is very bubbly, friendly, and funny. Although the bubbly and friendly can often become very irritating to myself and his brother, he means well. He knows when it's getting us fired up then continues to go down that path. I would say Nolan and his brother get along well, however, sometimes I sense that Nolan feels that he may have two fathers, one in me and the second one in his older brother.

It may be just a fact of being an older brother, but it can lead to some verbal exchanges. As a parent, you don't ever like to see that, but siblings corral amongst themselves often over the dumbest things. Linden is a neat and tidy person while Nolan, not so much. An obvious night and day when you walk into their rooms. Nolan has things scattered for weeks and weeks on the floor, bed unmade while Linden's room does not even look like anybody has ever slept or lived in his room. Yes, my room is similar in the decorating department to Nolan's.

It's fun to have two kids that are different in so many ways. As they get older, you see more differences, and you wonder where each of their paths are going to lead. Nolan's adventures and free spirit has come out a few times throughout university. He had mentioned that he would like to go away for university when he first came out of high school. I did not feel confident and certainly could not afford for Nolan to go away, even though he had earned many scholarships. Nolan had to continue to mature and be organized in his first four years of university before I would be comfortable with him living anywhere for school. I look back at my first years of college and recall they were of zero value, so much waste that I had to return for a fourth year to graduate. There was too much partying and no focus for me during those first few years. Hmmm, I am sure with our similar personalities I was avoiding any potential of the same fate for Nolan.

I do realize that should he choose to become a chiropractor there is nothing at the University of Windsor, and he will need to move away. Nolan will be 21 years old when he completes his undergraduate degree in human kinetics. We will cross that road when it's near, but I believe he'll be leaving the nest to pursue post graduate school, if he chooses. He has also mentioned doing a co-op as one of his friends did last year. It's called an exchange program where he would go out of the country, typically somewhere in Europe, for four months to attend university. That scenario as an exchange student, although expensive, would again be quite an adventure. I stand back and worry that Nolan's friendly personality may lead him to a little more exploring and partying than his marks would accept. Although Nolan's never let me down with his schooling, always having high nineties, you wonder when he is away from the eyes of mom and dad which way he would go. I think the answer would be that he would be fine, and for sure he would go exploring.

Well, not a terrible thing, my father instincts cause my worries to come out. I don't know if at 20 years old I would have ever taken that adventure. Going to a new country not knowing anybody, going to school, and adventuring on weekends across Europe. It would be a wonderful experience, but based on my college years, I know personally, I certainly would not have the discipline to maintain any marks that would allow me to graduate.

Nolan is certainly very much smarter than me. When I think of my college years and all the wasted time that I had doing the stuff that I did then, I often wonder if that would be Nolan's path. Nolan's attitude and personality also shines through in his athletics. He won a few awards as a football player, including one for being a no quit type of player despite any injuries. Nolan is one tough kid. I have seen him twist his ankle where his entire foot was black and blue and swollen up the size of a football. He could barely walk, but within two days, he'd have the trainers tape up his ankle so that he could practice. Nolan is competitive and has athletic ability in about every sport that I have ever witnessed him playing. He loves playing basketball. He's not playing football in university, although it would not surprise me if he suddenly came home and told me he's on the football team. Just a spontaneous kind of thing with his athletic ability. His never quit attitude also comes out in sports. He plays right to the very finish and certainly enjoys winning. I would say Nolan is very patient, and as mentioned numerous times, a very caring personality. Nolan has recently taken on a role as a co-op student in the medical field as a massage therapist's assistant. This year he was also part of the football squad as an assistant trainer. He's a quiet personality where he keeps to himself, but at the same time, he's very social.

In various conversations, I feel Nolan has felt a lot of pressure by me as far as athletics, education, and career. Athletically, socially, and educationally I have always tried to work on Nolan to be confident. At a youthful age, I don't believe he had any confidence in his abilities whether athletically or educationally. He never thought he was good enough to make a team or smart enough to have great marks. I have always tried to boost his confidence. I always seemed to talk to him as a coach and not enough as a father. That is 100% on me, and it's not fair. Although I've always tried to do my best, multiple times while Nolan was growing up, I am sure that I placed undue pressure on him. Whether I was trying to or not, it's all about how it was received. It was received too many times as pressure by his dad. He has never wanted to disappoint me, but I do believe a few times that dad has overwhelmed him and stopped him from having as much fun as he should. He knew or anticipated that his dad would not be happy regarding his play or outcome. Nolan, I am sorry that I was not smart enough to realize the situation sooner.

He is now 20 years old and a man with a great personality that is mixed with great intelligence. He could get into any field that he chooses, that would include being a chiropractor, a doctor, a scientist, or an astronaut. Whatever Nolan wants to do and applies himself to do, he will succeed. There's no question in my mind that his marks would be phenomenal as they have been in his first three years of university. Although he has mentioned being a chiropractor, it wouldn't surprise me if ultimately, he went into another field upon graduation. It would not even surprise me if in the next couple of years, he changed his major.

Nolan is not a hands-on individual and all for the same reasons as Linden. There was never any plan or any concern of teaching Nolan how to fix things. I always wanted Nolan to have a great enough job that if things were required, he could hire somebody. Now I would say I am somewhat hands-on, and my brother is very hands-on. I don't know if it was a good decision for me to direct them to be less technical.

Summarizing Nolan would be as follows. I will say to Nolan to be sure in life that your caring personality is never mistaken for weakness. That would mean that, because of your big heart, be sure that you're not taken advantage of by friends, girlfriends, or family. The next thing I will mention to Nolan is that you can be anything you would like to be if you apply yourself and realize your abilities. Have the confidence to do what you want to do, and keep being you. Have fun with everything within reason, make sure you're doing the right thing. You know right from wrong, and be sure you go down the correct path when making decisions and enjoying yourself. Nolan, I love you with all my heart.

VACATION WITH THE BOYS

My boys have been fortunate enough to have had vacations with me every couple of years. We have done a cruise, a trip out east to Newfoundland, a couple local trips to Niagara Falls and a few trips to New York city.

I'd like to take some more trips as the boys are getting to the age where they are doing their own travels. My 22-year-old and his girlfriend recently went to Los Angeles, and my youngest 19-year-old has gone for weekend trips around Ontario. Vacations are a great way to relax and enjoy new scenario, and culture. I believe too many people, including myself, become too absorbed in their work for 24 hrs a day for 365 days a year. Too often, I am of the belief that no one else will be able to complete my task accordingly; thinking perhaps the company will stutter without my presence for a week. Facts be told we are all easily replaced, and our companies will survive without us.

The first exciting trip was to New York. We drove there one summer when they were ten and seven. We stayed in New Jersey and commuted on a train each day into NYC. We did quite a bit of sightseeing where we got to enjoy and see New York City. We went to the Empire State Building, Wall Street, Times Square and a few other places. My first memory of the trip there with my two boys is still vivid. We got into New Jersey and checked into our hotel around 8:00 o'clock in the evening. The boys were so excited they wanted to get into New York the same evening. It was probably around 9:00 o'clock when we were ready for the adventure. I did not know the lay of the land and along with having two young boys, it was a little bit daunting, to say the least. We took the train into what turned out to be the twin towers station. This station is adjacent to the location where the airplane bombing of the twin towers sadly occurred. It was still very recent. In fact, the train station in that area was still blocked at different areas for further clean up.

That first night we arrived in New York around 10:00 o'clock. We walked around sightseeing, with our first experience being very pleasant. There were police officers at many of the corners while we were walking the area. We asked one officer where there was a place that we could grab something to eat. He gave us directions to a famous hot dog stand. We safely walked there with no issues at all and walked in and grabbed a hot dog, pop, and a fry. Lo and behold, there were a few police officers that frequented the hot dog stand. We finished and just walked around the town getting ready for the next day. We got home that evening around 1:00 o'clock, which sounds a little bit scary.

We did a horse buggy tour of Central Park where we saw famous kid movie landmarks that we recognized. That was a wonderful experience. I would say New York's has to be one of the best places to visit if you're into the hustle and bustle. Obviously, many landmarks, the lights, the action does not stop. It runs full speed 24 hours a day.

The next memorable trip with the boys was out east ending in Newfoundland. The boys and I took a couple of weeks off. We jumped into our car and were off on the next adventure. We drove to Ottawa and spent a full day touring our nation's capital and then spent the night. Our next stop was Quebec City again for a day and a night. Eventually, we got to Nova Scotia, where we met my boss and his family and stayed on his property overlooking the ocean. We got to meet with his family and friends for a day. We then traveled to Prince Edward Island where we spent a couple of days and nights on the island.

We commuted back on a ferry to the mainland and the next day took off for Newfoundland and Labrador where we met one of my current customers. We got to do some whale watching and experience the history of Newfoundland and Labrador.

It was a great and broad experience for the entire vacation out to eastern Canada. The boys met some friends on a 16-hour ship ride from the mainland to St. John's. Nolan is still in contact with those friends at various times throughout the year through casual text and social media.

Now, there is a spontaneous meet up approximately eight years ago on a ship 1500 miles from home. I give my two sons kudos for not being too shy, adventurous, and courageous. They walked around the ship meeting different people all night while I just relaxed. I walked around, listened to the live band and a comedian at one point during the ship ride to St. Johns.

On the way back from our eastern vacation we only stopped for one overnight stay at a motel. The whole trip was very much a spontaneous adventure. We had only planned the first stop in Ottawa and that was it. Linden and Nolan figured out the next city where we would stay. They called ahead to see if we could get a hotel and planned amongst themselves any sightseeing while in each city. Each night, they would decide where we were going to try to stop next. If we wanted, we would stay another night or two in that city. A vacation with no timeline and only a rough destination. I just knew we should be back in about 14 days and not the usual way families typically organize a vacation. They typically know exactly what they are doing the next day, where they're going with full timing and agenda. It becomes very regimented, and I did not want that experience for the boys. I just wanted to just see what happens and wherever we landed each day is where we were spending the night.

The entire trip had exceptionally beautiful landscapes and memorable views. We travelled to Prince Edward Island as I did at the same age as the boys. We made it to Newfoundland and Labrador, which I did not get to do as a young kid. It was an awesome trip with lots of history in Ottawa and Quebec. Lots of fun and stuff to do on the east coast and in Labrador and Newfoundland. On Prince Edward Island, they got to jump off bridges into the ocean with the local kids and experience the friendliness of the residents. Vacations are important for families to do if they can, or are lucky enough to be able to afford it. It was great to pass on some knowledge of our country we live in and bond with the boys.

A very structured vacation we enjoyed was a cruise. We flew from the Detroit airport to Miami, Florida. We rented a great big SUV and drove to South Beach for a day. We would eventually take the cruise from Miami. The first day we landed, we put all our luggage away, and we reached out to a social media personality the boys and I followed. We contacted him just on a whim through Facebook Messenger. The gentlemen named Dave Robards responded, and the next thing you know, my two boys and I are shaking hands with this gentleman that works for Grant Cardone, a wealthy real estate investor and sales mentor. Dave toured us through the office, took some pictures with him and the CFO of the billion-dollar business, which was quite a thrill. Hopefully, there was a bit of a life lesson in this type of meet up. Famous people, ultra-rich people are human, if you want to meet them be sure to reach out to them in a polite manner. The worst they can do is not answer, the best is say yes. If you don't ask, you'll never know their answer. Be courageous and ask to meet, ask for the sale. You could be pleasantly surprised.

I was lucky to have my sister-in-law Barb prepare the entire trip, flights, hotels, and cruise. Basically, she booked everything and gave me an itinerary of where to be at what time. I have always done my cruise traveling with Barb and Gary and never had to worry about anything. I just tagged along.

Taking this kind of adventure with my two boys was exciting and slightly nerve wracking, but obviously, as a parent ,you cannot show that part. We had an exciting time on the cruise with the social aspect and the excursions. In fact, once we got to our room, we walked around the ship for a little bit and then the boys were on their way. I was just there to relax, sit by the pool and in different lounges. At that point, I was writing my first book, and I just sat there and wrote many of the chapters for the next week. The boys did what they did, came and went as they chose. We stayed connected and occasionally, I would reach out, and we would all meet and have a quick lunch or dinner, touch base and everybody would go on their way.

One crazy story was on our very first excursion. I don't recall what island, but man was it an adventure. I specifically remember Barb and Gary telling me to always book any excursions through the ship. In this case, if there were any issues while you were on an excursion, the ship crew would know where we were and help us get back to the ship on time. Well, I did not heed the warning for our very first excursion. The boys and I got off the ship and walked down to the end of the ramp where there were people advertising tours that we could book.

Everything was great during the offshore tour that we had spontaneously booked. We got to see the island, the culture, landscape, and architecture. We got back to the cruise ship dock approximately 1.5 hours before departure. We were in decent shape for time to do some local shopping on the dock. On our way through the dock area, there were ladies that were giving distinct types of hairstyles including dreadlocks and weaves. There were several souvenirs stands selling local pottery and trinkets. All three of us were walking through, with Linden and I noticing different things, talking to people, and looking at each stand. At one point, we turned around and Nolan was nowhere to be found. He was in a chair getting his hair done. We went over to the chair and asked him what was going on here, and he quickly answered he wanted to get his hair braided, which was no big deal to him.

There he was in the chair, and we had about an hour to jump on the ship. We had to be on the ship by 4:30 and then departure would be 5:00 o'clock. We had just over an hour to check out the local shops. Linden and I sat down after we were finished walking around looking at things while Nolan was getting his hair done with a big giant smile. We happened to sit where I could see a price list, I am sure Nolan never even thought about paying for the braiding. I looked at the price list, and it was $5 for a braid.

A little bit of a back story to the upcoming adventure. We were told by the cruise ship to always carry a small amount of cash, credit card and to carry photocopies of your passport. So, I had $100 in cash, no ID for anyone, credit card and we had photocopies of our passports. Linden and I were looking at the pricing and Linden mentioned the braids were $5 each, and it looked like he was getting many braids, and I didn't see any electronics to take a credit card.

I sat there, but it didn't really dawn on me, but I started to look at Nolan's braids and casually count the number of braids and did some math in my head. It was going to be about $160, it looked like to me. I went up to the lady and told her that I didn't have $160 in cash, and she didn"t take credit cards, so we should probably just stop the braids. She explained it was no problem, she would give me a good deal. No problem, no worries speaking in her great accent. It is now about 4:00 o'clock, and we needed to be on the ship in 30 minutes. Now the panic is starting to set in. The hairdressers were less than halfway done completing the braids. I went over to the lady again and explained to her we needed to be on the ship in 20 minutes. She again explained, no problem she got another hair stylist, and they worked fiercely and got it all done by about 4:20. I asked her how much to pay, and she said it was $130, which would have been, in her opinion, a savings. I explained to her quite adamantly that I had $100. I didn't have any more cash, and this is what I was giving her. She went back and forth and said no it was $130, and I basically said, lady here's $100 and we're out of here. I gave her the money, thanked her, and we walked off to get into the turnstiles to the ship docking area. Getting onto the dock through the turnstiles you need to show your ID, which was not a problem. We had photocopies of passports, and it was just about 4:30pm. The government lady at the turnstile asked us where our passports were. I showed her what we had, and she said no, those are paper copies of them. She told me that she did not accept paper copies, to which I explained that the ship told me to take paper copies and to never bring the originals onto an island. She said no, sorry sir. Now the panic had set in, it was 4:30pm and we needed to be on the ship. Another government gentleman came over and saw the panic. He pointed and said to go to that other gate. We ran over to another gate that had just closed and been locked, and I explained to the gentleman on the other side of the fence that we needed to get on that ship. I showed him my ID, and he said they were locked up and secure, and we could not come on here, it was now a security issue. We ran back to the first gate and someone else came out, and I explained to him what was going on and that we needed to get on the ship. It was now about 4:35 at this point, and we were supposed to be on the ship at 4:30. He explained to follow him back to the second gate again for the second time.

We ran over to the gentleman at the second fenced gate, and he said, "I've already told you that you cannot come through here, you're wasting your time, and you're not getting through the fence gate." We ran back to gate number one for a third time where a gentleman who must've been a supervisor came over, had a quick look at our passports, and let us through.

We had to run approximately five hundred yards, across the front of three other ships to the far ship which was ours. If you want a bad visual, you got an old fat guy in flip flops and shorts trying to run. Two young boys, who were 16 and 13 at the time of this cruise, were running ahead of me. I am running down the dock panting and trying not to fall on my face. It was now 4:45, and we continued to run past the first ship, past the second ship, and I could see the third ship, which was ours. A gentleman on a golf cart came wheeling down the dock as we continued to run. He told us to jump on, and he drove off toward our ship. He took a turn and was now running parallel with our ship. As I looked, the dock ropes were off the ship. And only the far loading ramp was down with the captain at the very bottom of the plank. We continued on our golf cart, jumped off the golf cart, raced up the plank and got onto the ship at 4:55. The cruise ship had waited an extra 25 minutes.

Now, if you remember me telling you that if the excursion is not booked through the ship, the staff will have no idea how to track you when you are off the ship. What had happened is that there was another couple a few minutes ahead of me and the two boys that had booked an excursion that was late returning. It was 100% luck that two people who had booked an excursion through the ship were also late returning. Otherwise, that boat would have sailed 25 minutes earlier.

We got to our room where I told Nolan to just find something to do, that I didn't want to talk about anything. I took a huge breath and walked out to the deck to watch the ship sail. I began to think of the protocol if you missed the departure of a ship when you're on a cruise. You must find a way to meet up with that ship at the next stop at your own expense. You'd have to find a private plane or somebody on another boat to get you to the second destination. Now, here we are on an island where we could've been stranded on that dock. We had no cash money, a credit card with a small limit on it, no identification and paper copies of our passport. That would have been one heck of a situation for myself and my two boys to be standing on that dock if that ship had sailed.

I can say that it must have been one hell of a scene to watch an old fat guy and two boys running down the dock hoping that we were going to make the cruise ship. We just kept on running, and I did not fall on my face or pass out. That is an adventure that will never be forgotten.

The next three or four stops on the cruise were fun, uneventful, and always a wonderful time. The boys got to do their own thing, and I got to relax. I would often go to bed at 10:30 at night, and they would roll in around 1:30 pm. They met a bunch of different teenagers, and they just spent time together and did their own thing.

That was quite an adventure we got to experience. We tried many different activities such as swimming with stingrays, snorkeling, swimming in the ocean, we rented jeeps and went on a tour around a different part of an island. We took a bus tour to a small village where we got to see how they lived with outdoor plumbing and outdoor washrooms. We stopped at one area where they produced cigars, went through, and got to see a kid's school and how poor the school was where they were being taught.

You know, with all these islands we were seeing, it was not like North America. One curious thing that you always see is that all the residents, all the kids, were all smiling. There is something to be said about the islanders. They didn't know what they didn't have. They were happy with what they did have in their life. They had a version of a roof over their head, they had food, they had schooling, and they just enjoyed their life. All the different islands that we visited, you could tell that they were immensely proud of what they had, and they didn't worry about not having. Too many people nowadays worry about what they don't have instead of all the important things they do have, including cars, medical hospitalization, jobs, homes, safety, and normal politics.

Now, that is something to be thought about a little bit more. When we start to get down in the dumps thinking about poor me, and why we don't have this or that item, we need to rethink. To think and just experience and watch life on those islands is very humbling. They are incredibly happy to have anything and nothing fancy in our eyes. They had what they had, and they were satisfied with it. Perhaps we can learn from these cultures, be grateful with what you have, family over items. In family and in life, you get what you give.

RESPECT WHAT YOU HAVE

I think about work ethic, and it is a mindset that would work for anybody. In life, you need to work hard to obtain your life goals. Everyone is not given a golden spoon and born into wealth. Most of us have had to work hard to obtain what we currently own. On that note, you must always be grateful and respectful of what you have earned.

In fact, to this day, my kids kind of laugh at me in a fun way with some of my old childhood habits. When I come home from work or meetings where I am dressed in a nice fashion, I immediately change. I head to the bedroom and get into what they call comfortable clothes, and my other clothes are hung up and put away. It is something that was always instilled in me growing up as a young child. In grade school especially, when I came home from school, I would put my play clothes on. Now your play clothes sometimes had a couple of rips here and there, a bit tiny, a bit too short, a little bit raggedy, but they were not your school clothes or good clothes. It was just a case of respecting your items that were new. You tried to keep them as long as you could and in great shape. The other thing I used to do as a kid is that when I got new running shoes, I always wanted to keep them clean. When they started to get a little bit scuffed up or dirty, I would wipe them off to keep them clean. I used to apply white polish for leather type running shoes and hand buff to keep the shoes looking new again. It was just a habit that I did as a kid to keep my clothing and shoes clean and tidy. Obviously, nowadays kids just obtain new ones, or get mom and dad to buy new ones at a price of a few hundred dollars. I remember in my day, Converse Chuck Taylor style shoes were $15.00, and the most popular basketball shoes of my youth. Regular running shoes I would call off brand, or no name brand were $9.00 at the time. These Converse Chuck Taylors which are now popular again 45 years later, are near $125.00 dollars in price. The deal at my house was, if you wanted the fancy brands, I had to save my money and then go to the store a couple of blocks away and buy a new pair of Chuck Taylors. It was just part of learning about money and its value and importance. If you wanted something, you helped your parents, you saved up, you worked, did chores and you got a chance of getting what you wanted, within reason. Today, the children get their chosen items without any fanfare, and in turn, don't learn any money management. My sons, although I would purchase their items, had to wait for their birthdays, Easter or Christmas.

PARENTING THOUGHTS

One crazy phenomenon I don't recall as a child is crying. After the passing of my father, though, I became very emotional at distinct functions and situations. The birth of my children, the graduations of my boys and any of their public successes they had would see me holding back tears and whimpering quietly. I would surmise that what is happening to me at that moment is that I am reminiscing. A flash of a second has me looking around and thinking, man, do I miss my parents. How I wish they were around to watch the accomplishments of my two sons.

Obviously, not having your parents around is a huge void in my life and a disappointment. Not having your parents around to enjoy the accomplishments and growth of your kids is very overwhelming. At different points and milestones throughout their lives, it would be great for them to have my parents direct influence and conversation.

It is a crazy world out there as I have turned into a very emotional father at different points. It certainly always comes back to thinking about my father and my mother. They say that different situations make you stronger, but I could have done without my parents passing away at their tender ages of fifty-seven and seventy-one, when my mother passed away. I look at the future of my two boys and what they are on the brink of accomplishing. It sure would be nice to give my dad and mom a hug while watching this stage of my sons' lives. They have many other events in their future including marriage, graduation, purchasing houses and perhaps children.

I want my children to continue to have their mother's mom and husband in their lives. It is important that the kids get to enjoy their grandma and grandpa. As you get older, it is especially important that you pass on your knowledge to your kids. Even though it is a different time throughout their life as compared to yours, it is still similar. Often, when you're passing on your knowledge, they don't want to listen to it. Sometimes, it's not as easy as just sitting down and chatting. I must admit, sometimes it is yelling and screaming at them. In most cases, you're doing it for the right reasons, and that you're trying to spread your knowledge and experience to them, so as not to repeat the same type of failures you may have seen or endured.

Now, that being said, you do have to watch your kids fail throughout their life. I have always said that unless it is a life-or-death situation, you can let them learn. They can experience failure or success on their own. Obviously, if they were about to make a crucial mistake that is going to cost them jail time or physical harm, then a parent should step in firmly. A wise man once told me that the situation is never as good as you think and not as bad as you think in the heat of the moment. When you're young, and I would say hyper and impatient, situations seem to require you to act right away. As you get older, you realize there is more time in making that decision. You can be more calculated. If the decision doesn't get made, it's not a life-or-death situation. Some decisions are meant to be calculated and thought out, and others are meant to be done right away. Once you have the data and information, you can certainly make a good decision. Other times, it's just not meant to happen because of many different reasons. Sometimes, there's emotion in a young person's decision-making skills, and often that emotion is very, very costly in many ways. Patience has always done more good than harm in my life.

THOUGHTS OF THE KIDS

I sit here at home all alone, 57 years old and writing my memoir. I am not sure why I'm writing the memoir other than to give my boys something to read about their father.

Overall, I'm not necessarily secretive but not the kind of guy to spill all his back history for no reason. I guess one reason would be I never wanted my kids to believe that just because their dad did it, that they should do it. Obviously, as a parent you always want the best for your children, and I always thought that teaching them the positive would be the best for them.

Although I did some crazy things, I was certainly not too wild. A few of my friends were much wilder, and a few of them are remarkably successful. Unfortunately, a few I hung around with in my high school and college years have passed away after continuing their crazy lifestyle. You wonder if their demise started from their casual use of typical high school drugs. Beyond that, they got into serious drugs and a poor lifestyle which eventually led to them passing away way too young.

It was always a debate concerning which side of the fence you could live on, whether you can go to the wild side, the serious side or somewhere in between. I was somewhere in between, probably closer to the straight and narrow side then the wild side. It was always fun to watch the wild siders and their antics in high school. I took a bit after my mom, being there to help them in a few situations; situations where you had to get your friends home safely and make sure they were safe.

There is one thing about raising two young men that is always in the back of my head and always will be in my head, wanting them to be safe. In my days, obviously there were no cell phones and no social media, so none of the craziness that we got into occasionally was ever recorded. Nowadays, you see everything. You can barely even look at somebody without being on social media. Should you have any type of popularity or celebrity status, it's even worse. Growing up these days would be a little bit different for myself and my friends. I guess the same could be said for our kids living in the days when I was growing up. It would be different for them.

Overall, you always want to be a good example for your kids. They knew that I wasn't the perfect angel for sure, but they also realized that I was also serious about important items and always tried to make the right decisions. I have always told them that no matter who you're hanging around, you always have an option to get out of a situation one way or the other. Whether you just leave and drive away, walk away, get away or make up some kind of excuse to get out of the situation at the immediate time, do it, if needed. You certainly didn't want to be caught in anything stupid just because your friend was being an idiot. As the adage goes, you're often guilty by association.

If you look around with young kids these days, you certainly see that relationship where the one kid is trending towards the wild side, but his friend may not be on that trajectory. You always assume he is because of the one kid that the other may follow to the wild side. It's certainly not fair to categorise the innocent kid just because of who he hangs around with, but unfortunately, it's the truth and it's how society is today.

ENGAGE WITH FAMILY

I wonder the whole purpose of writing this memoir or whatever we're going to call the book. The reason is to let my kids know about my life and thoughts in written format. They could learn what I did as a child, what I did as a teenager, as a young adult and grown adult.

Maybe this is my way of having a conversation with my kids. I would say I keep to myself primarily, but hopefully my kids can find a happy medium between being by themselves and being with friends and family. If there is a choice to be made, I suggest getting to know your parents and your friends and family.

Deep conversations with parents may find you surprised at the stuff that you don't know about a parent. They may or may not want you to know some of those things. There is always the conflict of telling your kids how you were as a kid and telling them not to do things that you very well knew you did as a kid. It's a teeter totter where you speak out of both sides of your mouth; basically, don't do as I did, do as I say.

I don't know if that's meant to cover up anything, but it's from a voice of experience when you tell your kids not to do things. You've experienced it yourself; you've seen it, or at this point in your life, you know the outcome. You don't know when your parents are going to be gone, so get to know your parents as much as possible. They may not want to disclose everything they did. Sometimes, it was just plain embarrassing. Sometimes as parents, you wonder if I tell them what I used to do as a kid, will they think it's acceptable, and then they do it as a kid?

Obviously, nowadays life is much different, although many things are the same. The internet and social media have shown the size of the world. The younger people have it tough as anything they do or say can very well be posted on the internet. As we all know, if it's on the internet, it never really goes away. Anything foolish they do as a young kid can be on the Internet for all to see, including future friends, and employers for each of them to comment on and use to formulate an opinion..

I would have to summarize my father as a 5'-9" hardworking labourer with a stocky build. Obviously, I've mentioned his work ethic being second to none. He still maintained time to do things he liked such as raising animals. He worked hard and earned a living, so he could raise and support a family. My mother was a bit shorter at 5' 6" and a slight build as a body type. She loved gardening and raising and supporting her family. That summary is embarrassingly short, so engage with your parents as much as possible. Ask them questions and encourage them to share stories with you. You'll be glad you did.

The one thing I didn't realize until it was too late was how distant, at times, I was from my parents. Once a parent is gone, it's a lingering regret. You don't seem to be close to your parents at the time growing up because one, it wasn't cool or two because you had other things you believed were more important. I don't know if these thoughts were provoked by both my parents having passed away and the writing of this book. I do know that I wish I would have spent more time with them. I would say that the time that I did spend with them set my mind and personality for the remaining years of my life.

The never quit attitude and the work ethic attitude were instilled in me by my father. There were no big giant lectures or anything like that, I absorbed those characteristics just by watching and learning. My mechanical aptitude, although not as good as my father's, is somewhat present. I did learn how to put things together, build things, perform minor repairs on cars and do some plumbing. I knew enough to get by, and if anything were more extreme or complicated, I would have the ability to hire somebody to complete the task. Things like small renovations, painting, a bit of dry walling here and there were all in my wheelhouse and done in my current house.

My caring and philanthropic attitude were passed on by my mother. I watched her helping her family over and over throughout the years. It wasn't until my mid adult years that I began to volunteer on various boards throughout the community. The sense of helping and caring is a great attribute that appears to have been passed on to my sons. Her home cooking and simple lifestyle is certainly remembered each Sunday at dinner time, but that talent was unfortunately not soaked up.

I believe in this fast-paced world with its various distractions, present reflection is good. I know it sounds like incorrect wording; I will leave debate for the scholars. Here is my meaning of the sentence above. Reflect immediately and not 30 years later. This type of thinking may allow you to be in the moment. Build a bond with your parents now so you will have memories forever. Parents, realize your teaching moments and build a closer relationship with your children.

This one I think at this point in my life can be corrected, although I believe the foundations have been set. I would say Nolan has had the drugs, sex, rock'n'roll talk with his mother a few times.

I constantly comment about cleaning his room at the age of nineteen and to be careful and be smart when he is out with his friends. Over the years, there's been some friends of his which I have commented very strongly on their habits and behaviours. As

I think deeper, I realize that sharing my opinion all the time may not have been the best way for me to communicate with Nolan.

Obviously, he still loves me and respects me. Perhaps I placed too much pressure on Nolan, and it very well could have started in high school. His older brother Linden was starting to get a little bit of success and acknowledgment from the community and his school. I'm sure early in his high school days, I compared him to Linden, a crucial mistake in my relationship with Nolan. At this point, as a father I truly apologize.

Linden, at this point in life, has the business acumen of sales and is currently a mortgage agent. I think he and I have a little bit more in common as far as those items in discussions. It's a great feeling when Linden and I communicate where he does ask me my opinion on different things. He will ask me my opinion on what to do or exactly what to say in different situations. It's a great feeling to have your son reach out to you for your opinion. It's a fact in life that as you get older you know, or at least should know more about situations. You've heard about it, read about it, or perhaps even experienced it.

I think Nolan has always suspected that I'm not quite the angel that I come off to be in people's eyes. My lectures to him about making the right decisions perhaps come off a little bit different. Two different kids, really adults now, take my comments vastly different. As I've mentioned one hundred times in this book, Nolan is very easygoing, while Linden is more serious.

I have often been considered the funny guy, so Nolan tends to come to me with conversations that are filled with humour. Linden and I have serious discussions about topics such as business and politics. I love them both dearly and hopefully they know that both can come to me for any advice as a father and as a man. If they're getting sound advice from either myself or the ex-wife, it's all good. They are both going to be phenomenally successful in their adulthood. I obviously love them dearly and wish them all the best.

Each of my parents have passed along their philosophies and character to me. I'm hopeful that I too will pass along characteristics to my boys. Perhaps they'll take my good traits and discard the foolish and out of date ones.

I'm on a tangent, so back to the chapter title. The internet and social media have become a distraction from old school communication. Years ago, it was more common to talk to your parents, one on one in an old fashioned conversation. Today, a text or DM is the mode for both parents and children. Unfortunately, I believe this lack of conversation has often widened the gap between kids and their parents. Do yourself a favour, and reach out to your loved ones and start a conversation, trust me it will be worth the effort.

In reminiscing about my years, I need to heed my words and remember in life **_You get what You give_**.

WISH VACATION

If I had all the money in the world, and maybe not even all the money, but at least a few big bags full, there are some trips we would surely take. I've previously written, vacations are awesome as you get to unwind. Right now, the boys are at the age where if we are going to go on another vacation together, we should do it soon.

I would like to bring my boys out to western Canada, and one stop would be the Rocky Mountains to view Lake Louise. Another place we would visit, and I have never been, would be to British Columbia and then over to Vancouver Island. I think that would be a great trip and lots of fun. I like driving, but I don't know if that would be feasible right now. It's a long, long, and boring drive, but it certainly could be done. This writing might inspire me to start to investigate this vacation. It is about a 30-hour drive, so we would take three or so days to get there and enjoy a few weeks touring.

I think the second place I'd take them if I had lots of money, would be Europe. I was fortunate enough five years ago to be able to fly to France with a colleague of mine on work related duties. While we were there for 13 days, every night after our work was complete for the day, we would travel as far as we could to sightsee that evening. It was not unreasonable for us to travel two or three hours on the weekend to sightsee. I would like the boys to see the culture over in Europe as well as the architecture. It would include visiting many of the castles and churches I saw with my colleague.

If you've never been there, it's amazing to visit buildings, churches, and castles that are 2000 years old. Over here In North

America, if you had a building over one hundred years old, it would be very surprising. The boys would be able to see the culture and nuances and just experience things that are different from North America. Obviously, the scenery is much different over there with mountains and hills, narrow streets, small cars, and their lifestyle is much more relaxed. They have full lunches, typically and late dinners starting at 9:00 pm or so. Each meal is served with wine and often they last an hour and a half. In general, their lifestyle is much more relaxed, and people are in better shape over there. Walking and bicycling are much more common throughout the cities and countryside.

I was lucky enough to experience many different things while in France. It would be awesome to be able to share these famous areas with my boys. Places including the Lemans racetrack and the Eiffel Tower. A visit to an incredibly famous museum named the Louvre, Da Vinci homestead, and various castles that I don't recall their names but each of them different. The other thing is to walk into a big giant cement church, often two or three blocks in size with various wings to the church. When you're standing inside, it's higher than you can believe. There's not a lot of wood other than the pews. Everything is cement with the details, both inside and outside are phenomenal. You can walk inside some of these churches for hours and look at the detail of the masonry. The sculptures that are built are often one hundred feet up in the air. It's just breathtaking architecture in my opinion.

Those would be two of the areas that I would bring my family to visit. Western Canada and France only because I know those two areas. Just thinking of a third place where I've never been and haven't experienced might be another place in Europe. I don't know exactly which countries, perhaps even maybe some in Asia like Japan, Tokyo, Korea, or Vietnam. I think that would be a great vacation because it would be different. Meanwhile, the boys and I have experienced North America, we have experienced a little bit down south in the USA, some tropical islands, and big cities such as New York and Las Vegas. I don't know if we're going to do another vacation, but if so, we should do it quickly. My oldest is set to continue his life on his own with his girlfriend soon to move out in the next six months or so. My youngest is nineteen turning twenty, so he won't be hanging around dad much longer. I do know there's nothing quite like a vacation, and who better to share it with than my two sons and their significant others.

REGRETS

I'm sure everybody will be racing for this chapter to see what Crain regrets in his life. There are a few regrets, although I have always been a believer that you make your choices, and you live with them. Sometimes choices, whether right or wrong, are not known at the time you make the choice. You don't know how it will affect you later in life. The one thing that I have always strived to do is decide. Now, many have said that I contemplate and analyse too long before making a decision. I do believe that you need to have all the facts and make sure you think about everything. There's nothing worse than to make a decision only to find out there is something obvious you never thought about, and now you get to live with that decision. Whatever the decision, I would always take my time and think about things, and I agree, sometimes a little bit too long. Other times, I've just made quick decisions and lived with those results.

The first regret I'll speak about is post-secondary schooling. Although I was certainly never a scholar in high school, I do regret that I never went to university. That comment is made because at least twice during my career, I was told specifically that I could not be hired or promoted because I only had a college diploma. Both of those positions were in engineering type positions at Ford Motor Company and at General Motors.

Now, I'm also a believer that institutional education does not make you magically better than someone with no education. I also believe that just having a university degree does not make you smarter than a college or high school graduate. Each situation is different, however, I think one thing in common that we would all agree upon is the value of work experience. The experience is one of the key factors in success. What the educational process does is give you an opportunity to get that experience when you're hired. I have run across way too many university and college graduates who, upon leaving their institution, immediately believe that they are entitled to a high salary and a better job than the next guy. That next guy, in fact, could have more experience and more knowledge.

The next regret would be my career path, and it certainly came out with my oldest son. I began to live my life through his education, enthusiasm and thought of being a lawyer. I certainly would change my engineering type career to law. Obviously, a significantly different path would have been required. First, it would have required me to apply myself in high school. Second, it would have required me to go to the university. Third, I would've had to go to law school to become a lawyer.

I'll never know if I was ever smart enough to go through that process of university and then law school. I do find myself watching many law movies, stories, and documentaries and just enjoying their process. It was always thrilling to view how they operate, and I certainly enjoyed seeing the fruits of their labour including their cars, houses, and vacations. The ones you see on TV and read about are the high-end lawyers, but most of the lawyers are not making millions and millions of dollars. I just like watching that kind of lifestyle, dressing nice, helping clients and being important. I would have liked to be a trial lawyer applying my trade in a court room, questioning the opposition as far as where they were, what they did, and why they did it.

Another regret would be that I was not close to my father. You really don't know how your relationship is until one of you is gone, and that would be my case. My father was around for my first 20 years. The next 37 years he has been gone. He has imprinted a few things in my life, including the never quit attitude and splendid work ethic. I'm sure there were many more lessons that I didn't bother to grasp onto at the time. It was never cool to hang around with your dad as I grew up. You always had other things to do, people to see and places to go. Never much of an effort, care, or interest was made by me in sitting down with my father to chat. That's what I'm facing now with my two boys. There is never just a good old-fashioned sit down with a hey, how's things going, what are you up to, how's life treating you, how is your girlfriend, how's school, how's work? I do reach out to both of my boys, but it is not an in-depth conversation. My father worked many hours, and when he was not working he relaxed with his animals as that was what he enjoyed doing. I would say occasionally, two or three times a year, he would go out with the guys at his shop and have a couple of pops and come home later in the evening around ten o'clock.

He had a decent size family and growing up, we visited them at Christmas. I would spend time together with my cousins in the living room. They would spend time together in the kitchen area and have a coffee and casually chat. That would be one thing I would recommend everyone pay attention to and get to know your mother and father because one day they are no longer going to be around.

I guess another regret in my life was not hosting many social events. I remember how important it was to my parents to have meals at the table with the family. Often as I was growing up, large Christmas dinners or Easter dinners with family of 10-12 people were a frequent occurrence. I remember many homemade meals with our family, my aunt and her two kids.

Family meals were always a wonderful time, but as a married couple, it never seemed to attach to our lifestyle. When we were married, I think more get-togethers at our home would have been good for the kids to see. Now for the last 13 years, it remains the same dinner scenario. My boys and I often eat at separate times and very seldom at the kitchen table. We never have anyone over for a nice full meal. I don't recall any times where I even invited my brother and sister-in-law over for dinner. I'm not exactly sure why I didn't, whether it was a case of not thinking I had the right equipment or a nice enough house. It was just not believing I had enough ability to cook a large meal for everyone. If I were to do it all again, I would have more social events. I don't know if you'd call them parties but something similar for sure. I see my friends often, having couples over for an evening playing cards or board games. Just a social event at their place with some wine or some drinks and finger food. Just an evening of being with your friends.

The next regret was not fully pursuing my real estate sales career. A few years after college graduation and moving back to Windsor, I obtained my real estate license. You can say it was ridiculously hard to do as it took me a year at night school attending various courses before I finally obtained my real estate license. I always had thought about real estate, but quite frankly, I never had the stones to become a full-time agent. I did it part time for two years, holding an engineering job during the day and dabbling into the real estate sales market part time at night. I had a no name real estate broker hold my license so that I could sell. Although I never sold anything, I was beginning to enjoy the process of finding the hidden gems to put up for sale. I did have a couple of family members list their properties with me. Thirty-five years later, I sit back and think and wonder if I had stuck with it and was brave enough to do it full time, where I would be today. Now, the curious thing is there are two other guys I hung around with in high school that got their real estate licenses right around the same time and remain in the industry. They're both doing very well, and I would like to think that I could have been in the same type of position as far as success had I continued to be a real estate agent. I never jumped in full time since it meant leaving a full-time job with a steady paycheque. That would probably be a large regret that I never stuck with real estate. I do know there are thousands in the local area and most of them are making just a sufficient living and nothing glamorous or with multi-million-dollar incomes. You never know how it could have been, but I'd mark that down as a regret.

The next regret I would say would be not being an entrepreneur and owning my own business. I would say I have always had great admiration and respect for business owners. Most of the companies that I work for were private companies owned by one or two people. I was always of the mindset that yes, they were making money off me, but I was making a wage while working for them. Many people become very agitated by business owners and their success. Often, the employee has the mindset that the owner is not sharing as much as they're making when they see them driving fancy cars or having lavish vacations. My comment to them was always that, at one point during their life, they put everything on the line, including mortgages, marriages, and family to become a successful business owner. Now you see the stories of all the glamour of business owners, but you also see the stress on the owners. They are required to pay bills every week and to employ many as well as making payroll as their employees depend on their income to raise their families. The sleepless nights wondering whether you can make payroll and support your staff with a paycheck every week could become very daunting. I'm not sure exactly what type of business I would have opened. I continue to look around and see success stories, and it runs through my mind that what if I had made that decision years ago to be an entrepreneur? If I owned my own business, I think one of the important things would be to be able to have employees that you could support. Sharing business success with employees would be a great feeling. The ability to give a bonus to an employee knowing they worked hard and knowing that they appreciated it would be fulfilling. The giving, helping, and sharing philosophy is from my mother's side of my personality. One thing I do know is if I were a successful business owner, my two sons would not be raised with a silver spoon in their mouth. They would have been involved in the business as they grew up. It would have been great to be able to offer them the business as they grew older and became knowledgeable and age appropriate to own a business. I would not just give them everything without them earning it. You often see that happening, and you know it's a harm to your kids just to give them everything that they want without them earning it. That's what we're facing today. Kids in the next generation believe they are entitled to have the best of everything. Really, they never bothered to earn it, learn it, or experience it.

Real estate investing would be another regret that I have as I look back. My mother and father owned a duplex while we lived in LaSalle. They also owned a farm in Bothwell ON while living in another house in Windsor. So, although not educated, they were smart enough to know the value of owning real estate and to rent it out as an income producing revenue stream.

Although I have always been very curious about purchasing real estate, again, the situation never came to fruition. I can remember hundreds of times saying that would be a great property or great parcel of land to buy. I never had enough guts to ever put it all on the line to purchase it. Over the last 37 years. I have seen others that have had enough guts to purchase property, and now I get to see the rewards of them owning investment real estate 35 years later.

I would say that I have always been on the very conservative side. I would think it was from growing up as a middle-income family or perhaps it was just not having enough of the risk gene in me to risk failure. I now find myself preaching to my two sons to make sure they get into the property-owning market as early as they can do it. I've told them at an early age that if they got into owning property young and it failed, that they would have their remaining lifespan to regain any loss of money. I hope that they heed my words and get themselves into the investment of properties. I'm a firm believer that although the market does go up and down, it seems to always trend upward in the long haul. During that long haul trending upward as a rental property, it's producing an income every month. I just hope my two sons have enough ambition to do it and not be like their father and think about it for 37 years, knowing that he should have done it, should do it or could have done it.

Sure, everybody is waiting for this section. I would say undoubtedly that getting married was not a regret. The product of that marriage is two beautiful sons. Although there were many difficulties that obviously resulted in a divorce, there were some pleasant memories of the marriage. The next question would be, did I regret who I married? Again, I would say no. I loved her at the time of marriage, however, we did seem to grow apart quickly. I would have to admit that it was love at first sight for me. She is 11 years younger, so I wonder if that was a factor in the divorce. Perhaps she was still in the process of maturing, while I had already grown. I would say one regret would be the age difference. If there was not an age difference, would things have turned out differently? Obviously, you never know, but I think that the daily challenge of having common interests would have been eliminated.

Although the marriage did not turn out how they're written in all the fairy tales, 15 years later we continue to communicate both as friends and parents. I would say that we get along better now than we did for the last part of the marriage. As you can imagine, during a divorce many things are said and various things are assumed, but it's all water under the bridge now. I would admit that I probably did say some things that, although I felt were very truthful, should have never been voiced.

I'm fortunate that I have a good relationship with her entire family. I can have a conversation when I see my ex-wife with no problem. Her mother and her mothers' husband are the grandparents of my two boys. I have always believed it is important that they have that relationship. Many times, during the divorce proceedings and even now, her side of the family would invite me to outings and functions to which I would respectfully decline. It was a nice gesture to include me, but it just felt very awkward. I don't believe the ex-wife had any issues with me continuing to have a relationship with her side of the family. When the ex's family and I meet, we never talk about the marriage or the divorce, it's always idle talk about the two boys. My two sons were the common denominator amongst my family, myself, my ex-wife, and her family. The ex-wife and I were smart enough to understand that it was all about the well-being of our two sons.

An addition to the regret list would be that my two sons had to go through a divorce. They have been very courageous and certainly extraordinarily strong throughout the divorce. They have had to balance back and forth between living with their mother and living with me, weeks at a time, every other week. Before they were driving, it was up to myself and my ex-wife to bring them back and forth between the two different households. Now that they are driving, it is much easier and provides more flexibility to their living arrangements. Since they are both adults, they choose where they are going to sleep. Although divorce happens and was ultimately inevitable, the divorce for me is not a regret as I have moved on, and I would say I am a much happier person.

Any regret of the divorce is solely with my concern for my two boys. On the outside, they have gotten through the divorce part. I would anticipate that their opinion of marriage or divorce is probably skewed from the norm. While watching their mother and father go through it, I hope with all my heart, that they have learned something valuable. I truly aspire that my two boys will never have to experience it. If they do have children in the future, I would wish that their children never have to experience their parents going through a divorce. Divorce is something you don't wish on your worst enemy, but it is quite common in our day and age. I do believe that couples should certainly put more effort into remaining as a couple. It is way too easy to get a divorce, and it is too quickly decided upon by the two parties.

I would say one other item that I regret is participation with my two boys. As I peer out the window and watch kids and their fathers playing, I would say that is a huge regret. I was certainly a good chauffeur driving them to and from their own activities with their friends. As I look back, I don't believe I participated with them directly as much as I should have over the years. Yes, every once in a while, I would play basketball, a little bit of catch when they were young. I think overall I watched them far more than I participated with them in their activities, including any sports. I taught them how to skate at public skating but never really went public skating with them once they learned. I certainly never played hockey with them, although I coached both for a year.

I don't know if it was because I was in my early thirties when I had my boys. I don't know if that's an excuse or a reason. I think of me and my dad, and I would say he certainly didn't do any sporting events with me. Perhaps that's where I learned it. I would help them with different sports or different activities and then let them continue to learn by themselves or with others. In one aspect, I anticipated I was going to be too critical and that it wouldn't be fun for them. Having their father always critiquing how they threw a ball, how they shot a puck, or how they ran. Although I think over their life, I've chimed in too much about what they were doing and how they were doing it. It was always very frustrating to see that they were doing something wrong or incorrect and could've been better. I would help them learn this skill properly which I think is part of being a father.

Overall, I did the unimportant things like sitting and watching TV with them, watching a movie with them sometimes, and playing board games with them. I did all that, but it was at a very bare minimum. I watch these kids going down the street now with their parents and going for a walk, perhaps headed to a park. They are younger children, maybe four or five years old. This view certainly has spurred a few memories and regrets that are running through my head. Did I participate in their activities enough, or was I more of a spectator, mentor, and chauffeur?

CONFIDENCE

There is another thing that I think about now that I should have done differently. I don't know if it's a full regret, it would be to have more confidence in my youth with girls. I seemed to have quite often gotten into the friend zone quickly as a teenager. I have always been proud of acting as a gentleman and certainly have told my boys to treat women and girls properly; not as objects but as humans with value.

As a teenager, my confidence level was low. I would say my maturity level was there, but the confidence factor never had me pursuing girls much, and that was 100% all about confidence. I had a good relationship with everyone and had a good relationship with the girls; no real enemies that I can remember. There were no serious romances in my high school days, but I sit here and reminisce of how many opportunities I passed on. A few nudges and some wink winks that I often received, but I didn't bother to finish their pursuit. I was more of a social guy who felt more comfortable just hanging out with the guys at those parties than getting close to the girls. Forty years later, there are a few what ifs that I think about for sure. Would those opportunities have ended in a much more unique way had I pursued them. It's always a question.

Finding the love of my life was not a huge pursuit for me. Growing up, it was never a real thought. As I got older into my late 20s and early 30s, I do recall thinking, you know what? What does the world think of me as a single man, living with his mother? I was always being social but never really had a full-time girlfriend on my arm at functions. I often wondered whether the world would think I was just a freak, or it wouldn't matter to them. Obviously, no one ever said anything to me, but when you go out socially by yourself, and you go to parties by yourself, it felt odd. Periodically, you start to think of how you're being looked at perhaps as a weirdo or just a normal guy that didn't have a full-time girlfriend. Many decades later, I sit here as a single man; a full circle moment I would say.

KID FUN

As kids 45 years ago, you played outside as your form of entertainment. You walked down the street to your friend's house, walked up their steps, knocked on their door and asked for little Johnny, who would come to the door. Next, you would ask if he wanted to come outside and hangout or play road hockey, tag, catch or strikeout, and you would play wherever you wanted. We often played on our street, local park, playground or in the school yard. Nowadays, I don't remember any kids ever coming up to the door knocking, asking for any of my kids to come outside and do something. You know, at the very most, they may use their cell phone to call each other, but that is very rare. Nowadays, all they seem to do is text each other on their cell phones. They text each other, figure out what to do, and they take off from the house and meet each other. The personal inquiry of going over to their house and seeing little Johnny has all faded away. The elimination of the personal part is sad, not even a cell phone call anymore. It is just a text with words on a cell phone screen that they look at and communicate.

We did fun things like smash up derby with your bikes, where you had a bunch of friends, and you rode your bike to smash into each other. How about the old classic of hide and go seek where you would go and hide around the neighborhood, often when it started to get dark. Whoever was the seeker would have to find where you were hiding while the others tried to stay hidden. The other similar game I remember playing was called kick the can. I remember trying to explain it to my kids. Basically, you took a pop can, and everybody would gather around it. The person who was the last seeker would run and kick the can somewhere, and during that time the person that was the new seeker would run to get the can and bring it back to where it was and stand it up again. Everyone else would scatter and hide while the seeker would run around and try to find you. In the meantime, everyone hiding would be watching so you could run to where that can was and kick it again. Everybody who was found previously would scatter and the seeker would start again. He would have to run all the way back from where he was looking and grab the can to put it back in place. We would play it for hours and hours just hiding around the neighbourhood.

The other game I remember playing as a kid we called it chicken. Basically, it was like a bike jousting scenario where you would be opposed to each other approximately 30 feet apart. You would start to pedal your bike towards each other prepared to have a head on collision. One of you or none of you, or both could veer off to avoid a collision. If you were stubborn enough, you just ran into each other and smashed into the other bike rider. Each rider might fall off and scrape their knees and elbows and sometimes bend your handlebars or break your rims on your bike. Yes, exciting times with a bike.

The other thing I just thought of were bike pedals which were steel. Yes steel, meaning if your foot slipped from it, you would carve up your shins. Nowadays, all the bike pedals are either rubber or plastic, so if your foot falls off it would be no big deal on your shins. In my day, you read it correctly. If your foot came off or your chain came off and slipped, those vicious steel pedals would carve you up for some blood.

The other thing I'm just sitting here reminiscing about is the other thing we did when I lived in Windsor as a 10 or 11-year-old. We would build bike choppers out of our bikes. You would have a normal standard bike, not a 10 speed or 18 speed like you see these days, more old fashioned bikes. They had forks that would go around the tires. What you could do if you had an old pair of wheel forks from an alley or if you found an abandoned bike, you would cut them off somehow with your father's tools. You could place the newly cut forks onto your forks that were on your bike to extend the front end. You'd put the tire on the extended portion so that you would have a big, long front end. Obviously, the steering and the safety part was never thought about because if you leaned too far back, you would flip the bike over. If you ran over anything big, you would bend the new extended forks that you just placed on your bike.

The other thing we used to do that I was not particularly good at was riding a wheelie on your bike. You pull the front end up and ride and peddle only on your back tire while the front tire is in the air. There were guys in my neighborhood in Windsor that could do a wheelie for miles. I was all excited if I could do that for two or three pedal rotations. There are guys that could pull up the front tire and just wheel down the road with no effort.

The other recollection I had was that I never had a curfew time as a little kid. It was just well known that when the streetlights came on, you were expected to be home shortly after they were illuminated. I didn't have a watch or cell phone where you could check your time, or mom and dad could call you. I just knew the streetlights were starting to come on and you better bust your butt and get home and get washed up for the night and settle in.

I remember in high school was the beginning of the video game era. Nowadays, it's Xbox and PSPs that the kids play against people across the world through the Internet. In my day, there were a couple of systems that were quite basic and simple to operate. One system was called Atari, and it was a tennis game. You had your hand control with a dial, and you would rotate the paddle to move the graphic up and down the screen. You could only move it either up or down to touch what was a ball coming from the other side of the screen. The corresponding player you were playing against did the same, and a ball that would go from the left side of your TV to the right side of your TV. Today, kids and adults are playing all kinds of crazy games like Call of Duty, NFL football, NHL Hockey and many other popular games. It's no wonder the kids are doing everything online where the graphics are unbelievable and look to me like real life.

Occasionally, Nolan will have a couple of friends over, and they'll sit there for a few hours and play against somebody on the internet different games such as NHL, soccer, or basketball.

I sure wonder how the next generation of video games will look, as it is obvious that outdoor play has all but been eliminated.

MY DOG ADVENTURES

This chapter will be about myself and my animals. As you read early on in the book, my father owned many different types of animals including horses, dogs, homing pigeons, fancy pigeons, canaries, finches, rabbits, and even chickens. Each of these as I think about it now, were all in competitions, whether showing the horses or riding the horses in rodeos. Showing pigeons at fairs, racing pigeons for money, or showing canaries and finches, rabbits and chickens for trophies at the local fairs was a pastime.

I could say that his love of animals certainly rubbed off on me at one point in my life. I watched from afar his raising the canaries and finches and racing pigeons. I didn't get to see him with the horses, and I certainly was with him regarding the showing of chickens and fancy pigeons at the local fairs.

The one thing we always had while growing up were dogs. They were always smaller dogs, and I do remember a particular breed that for some reason we always fancied. That breed would be a Chihuahua. These little dogs were about four to five pounds and little, tiny things. They were always in our house as I grew up. I recall them as always being well behaved and would sleep on their little pillows. We would take them on our camping trips because they were so convenient being small. They would jump in the van with us and were never a big deal at all.

I would think some of his acumen on how he cared for his animals certainly rubbed off on me later in my adulthood. My father was very regimented as far as watering and feeding all his animals in every situation and never missing a day. If we went on vacation at the time we had pigeons and other animals that we couldn't bring with us, then arrangements were made. Friends would help take care of the animals with very detailed instructions on how and when to water and feed.

He really enjoyed his animals and certainly would spend hours and hours with them. Just watching and studying them and their behaviours, simply enjoying his animals. He didn't hang out at bars, but he sure would hang out with his animals. I do remember the joy in his face and his relaxed state that he would be in watching his animals, feeding and watering them and taking care of them. It was a very emotional time after the death of my father when we had to find homes for all his canaries and finches.

Now, fast forward to after my dad passed, we still had a small little Chihuahua, and her name was Duchess. Just a little thing, we had a small house at the time, and she didn't take up much room, and when I was gone for work would provide friendship and companionship for my mother.

While we lived on McEwen, we had Duchess, and I got the idea of owning a German shepherd dog. I do recall that scenario because at the time of the passing of my father, he had a close friend of an actual world-famous dog judge. This gentleman would be flown around the world to judge dogs in the confirmation class. These dog shows are the ones you often see on TV where dogs prance around a square ring with the judge making a final decision on who wins based on the looks of the dog. Eventually many different dogs were put into a final ring and walked around with handlers, and the judge would make a determination of the best in the show.

I recall reaching out to this gentleman and speaking with him asking him about looking at dogs that I'd determined I would like to own, including the German shepherd breed. I had gone on YouTube and looked at some German shepherd puppies and decided that would be the dog I would like to own. I invited the professional judge to come out and to look at the puppies with me to make sure I chose well, and there were no issues.

I certainly wasn't a dog expert or knew what I was looking for with all little cute puppies running around. The gentleman's name was Newt, and he came over to the kennel and viewed the puppies. He gave me his opinion that the dogs were fine, they were healthy, and they were good show quality as he looked at their pedigree. The pedigree is the background of both the mother and father, and in this case, any credentials they had obtained through showing in various dog shows.

Shortly after his viewing, I chose a dog, and I now was at the beginning stages of owning a dog. The first thing that was unknown to me is that the kennel chooses the first letter of their official name. The kennel owner told me that the litter would be registered with the Canadian Kennel Club, and the official name of the dog needed to start with the letter R. Somehow, I came up with the name Reba. I have a sneaky suspicion that there was a famous singer around that time named Reba McEntire that my mother enjoyed listening to, and that was the influence of naming my first German shepherd pup Reba. Now, I had a brand-new puppy, and I had a little Chihuahua and my mother all living in a small two-bedroom house in the middle of Windsor.

I had to learn how to raise a German shepherd puppy along with still taking care of a small little four pound Chihuahua. It's funny as I think back, the little Chihuahua certainly ran the household and had no issues barking or doing a little growl at the German shepherd, whether it was a puppy or full grown. Reba certainly understood that little Duchess ran the house, and if Duchess didn't like something that Reba was doing, the little Chihuahua would let her know. If, at night, I was giving Reba more attention than little Duchess, she would come over, jump on my lap and basically demand that she get the attention instead of the shepherd.

The Internet was available now, and I scoured it trying to learn about raising and caring for my German Shepherd. A friend of the family raised rottweilers, and he recommended a veterinarian that I would ultimately take my German shepherd to for nine years.

At 12 weeks old, I understood that it was time to train the dog to be well behaved, properly mannered, and disciplined. Turns out, I enrolled in a dog training class at my college where I would attend classes once a week on the weekends. I got to know the instructor who, by chance, worked as a professor at St. Clair college where I attended school.

I got to have a few offline conversations with him, and he was a rather well-known dog trainer in many different disciplines which sparked my interest. In fact, at one point, he invited me to watch a very advanced class at his house in his backyard which was huge. Here I got to see a different type of dog training.

Over the course of 10 weeks, the participants got to learn very basic commands. The dog needed to be able to walk beside you properly without pulling. Your dog should be able to sit and stay on command. Other drills included having your dog return to you if they were off leash, and you recalled them. Each of the various commands and techniques that we learned were all exercises to put your dog into a canine show in the discipline of obedience.

I remember that he instructed us to practice as much as possible but only for 10-minute segments because as a small three or four month old puppy, they had to learn and be able to use their brain without tiring. This gentleman certainly knew what he was talking about as he had written a few books about dog obedience training. He trained RCMP officers for search and rescue missions and trained the local police force with tracking. This skill is for finding missing persons or criminals, so he knew what he was teaching.

I went for the next 10 weeks, practicing as much as possible every day and often two or three times on the weekends when I had the spare time. I was working full time, so each training session was at night. I used the knowledge that he passed on to the class about how to perform the exercise. The process of teaching a dog how to behave in all circumstances was exciting to me. I remember in week #10 there was an exam to pass for graduation. We had practiced several different exercises that would be the same as showing a dog in an obedience competition.

These included walking the dog next to you, walking your dog without a leash, stopping, and sitting and standing your dog to get examined by a show judge, staying and a recall at 50 yards. One more exercise was walking your dog in a Figure 8 clockwise and counterclockwise pattern around traffic cones, which requires different techniques for the dog.

Now back to week #10 of the training. There was a graduation, and each student would be tested on all the disciplines that he had taught for the previous nine weeks. I specifically recall that my female dog, as they say, came into season, meaning she was ovulating for the week going into the exam. That was not a big deal as she certainly could practice with me. The issue was that when I brought her to be tested there were 15 other dogs including male dogs. Now, you can imagine the commotion bringing a female dog that was in that situation into a group of dogs, including males. Somehow biologically, the females produce an odor that a male dog can smell, and it drives them wild. My female dog certainly didn't behave very well and was driving all the other dogs nuts during all the testing, and ultimately, my dog got a low score but did pass. It was a very low score compared to how she could perform the prior week.

I was very excited about continuing to learn how to train a dog and certainly dove into books and VHS tapes to learn more about what I could do with Reba. I decided on a whim to enter an obedience dog show. The dog show would be an obedience class which means dogs would need to perform various skills based on commands or hand signals given by their owner. These were the same exercises and skills I had recently learned in my dog training classes. This is not to be confused with dogs that are in confirmation shows, which are dogs prancing around a ring with their handlers and only being judged for their looks and body shape.

At this point in my dog show experience, I had never even been to a dog show, and certainly never an obedience trials show. I had seen a few videos of them but never experienced a trial in person. I found a dog show a few hours away from my home, enrolled and signed up, which would be the first show I had ever been involved in. It was probably six or eight weeks in the future when I signed up, and I knew there was hard work to do with my very young dog. Reba was approximately nine months old at the time of going into the dog show. I was up for the task. I recall myself, my mom and my dog Reba jumped into my mom's car and drove a few hours to the dog show where it was being hosted. The dog trials would last two days which would be starting on Saturday and ending on Sunday. The trials have two tests in one day, and the third is on the second day.

There were six exercises that Reba and I had to show a certain level of proficiency to eventually gather enough points to pass. The course I was in was a basic obedience course which would create, if passed, a designation of CD (Companion / dog). The examination of all six was a total of 200 points. You were required to pass three total trials with a minimum score of 175 in each trial to earn the CD designation as a basic obedience course. Although I'm not explaining it very well, pass three trials and then you would be able to have a CD designation. This designation would always be attached to your dog's name. Now, if you remember me talking about pedigrees, that designation of CD would be filed with the Canadian Kennel Club, and should I pass the three tests, then Reba would have the designation of CD beside her name on the Canadian Kennel Club pedigree certificate.

I remember the night before traveling to the dog show I was very nervous. Eventually, I overcame the pre-show nerves and got out of my comfort zone. The trials were in the middle of a rural area in a large barn with hundreds and hundreds of dogs segregated into different areas. I signed into the event, and they gave me a number tag, the show ring I would be in, and the time I would be in that ring.

Inside the event, there were hundreds of dogs of various sizes walking around sniffing each other, barking at each other, and sometimes growling at each other. Just that experience alone would scare many people off from showing dogs. Now you add hundreds of spectators watching their friends or family show dogs, and it was quite a sight to see. I remember in each of the three trials you had to perform all six exercises as dictated by the judge. The exercises included basic commands as well as more complex disciplines.

I believe I scored 185, which was a passing score but on the lower end. I needed 175 out of 200 to get one segment and needed a total of three to get the designation. The next test was sometime in the afternoon, so we walked around, had something to eat and prepared for the next test that was later in the afternoon. Reba and I were more relaxed for the second trial as we both were now familiar with the situation. We were used to the crowd noise and dogs barking. In one of the exercises, you had to walk out 50 yards and have your dog sit, then lay down and then stay all on verbal commands. After the stay command of your dog, you returned from where you came from this time without your dog. You turned around on the judge's command and looked at your dog, while the dog stayed there and could not move for three minutes. I must admit those three minutes staring at your dog and crossing your fingers were painful. Hoping the dog would not just jump up and run back to you, all the dog could do is just lay there and look at his master. After the world's longest three minutes, the judge would finally tell me to recall your dog, sir. I gave the command which was "Reba come." At that point, my dog jumped up and ran as fast as possible to face me then sat down in front of me. I then gave the command to heal, the dog walked around me with great enthusiasm and sat to my left side. We did all the other disciplines, and we had a very good score of, I believe, somewhere in the high one eighties. A great compliment came when the judge came over and gave me my scores and mentioned that she had never seen a dog with as much enthusiasm and love for the recall as Reba. That was quite a compliment from a judge to little old me who never previously showed a dog. I was not a professional trainer, just some guy off the street and his love for the dog and enjoyment of training a dog. It's a compliment that I still remember today some 25 years later. I went on to the next trial the following day and again passed. Suddenly, after my first dog show, me and my dog Reba had the designation of CD, which in the dog world means companion dog. The CD designation simply means that your dog is disciplined, listens to you and is a well-behaved dog. I certainly was very proud of having this designation. Throughout that summer, I went to two other shows and did well. Those didn't give me any further designation as I went into the same class again just for the experience.

The next designation was called CDX which was an extension to the CD which was a companion dog. It required further intense training for dogs to climb walls to fetch items, climb through tunnels and other very difficult exercises. I talked to the gentleman that I trained under at the college, and he allowed me to come over and watch because he was teaching that class, but I never did go into that class. Just having the CD designation was enough for me. It was quite an accomplishment for a guy that knew nothing and a dog that had to listen to a guy that knew nothing. I remember getting a fancy collar for my dog, and I think I purchased a T-shirt that had a German shepherd on it at the dog show. I was right into the dog show scene for a summer, with all the souvenirs and that kind of stuff. It was cool to have a dog that listened and was well behaved. I didn't have to worry about anything and knew the dog would always be there and friendly.

At about 16-months old, I had Reba bred to another obedience level dog to have puppies. The stud's background was Schutzhund which is a protection discipline for dogs. Reba had 8 puppies. I sold one to a friend and gave my best friend Mike Janisse a puppy, however, I could not sell the other ones. Many agreed the puppies had an excellent background, but nobody appeared to be interested in the offspring of Reba and the stud. Ultimately, I had to bring in six puppies to the Humane Society for them to adopt out to anybody who would want them.

Reba was a great dog and certainly provided companionship when Duchess passed away while we lived in McGregor. Reba passed on at about age nine years old. That is one of the saddest days when you must bring your dog to get put down by the veterinarian. She had deteriorated the last year of her life with thyroid cancer. It was terrible to watch her have no energy, internal bleeding and to know there is no cure or remedies for it. She had begun to be in pain just walking around, so I knew it was time to humanely relieve her of her pain. I brought her in by myself and was there as the doctor injected her with a drug that would end her life. When it was over, I walked out bawling my eyes out as I was probably 27 or 28 years old at the time. It's quite an experience losing a dog who basically was a family member for nine years.

Fast forward to being married, and, with my infinite wisdom, I again decided to purchase a German shepherd puppy. My ex-wife had heard about my previous dog and how disciplined it behaved. She basically gave the approval not knowing too much about German shepherds and their tendencies. I found a breeder and talked to him about the backgrounds of the mother and father. I knew I wanted a dog that had designations in the obedience discipline. The ex-wife was pregnant at the time, and I wanted the puppy acclimated to our household before the baby arrived. At the time the wife was pregnant, the dog would follow my ex-wife around, sit with her on the couch, lay beside her in the bed, follow her into the kitchen and living room, and watch her outside through the window. The bond a dog has with a woman that is pregnant is crazy to watch. Dogs can sense there's a change in the female of the house and basically wants to take care of her. Again, I trained the dog by myself. This time, however, there were some minor details where we now lived in the middle of Windsor with a small backyard. I worked, and the ex-wife took care of my son Linden at the time. The issue became when our dog went outside to do its business, we had a neighbor that had two crazy fully grown dogs that would run and torment my poor puppy whose name was Beaudie.

All the training vanished when it came to Beaudie being socialized with other dogs. She seemed to be very afraid and undisciplined, meaning she would lunge at other dogs, bark at other dogs, and try to chase other dogs while you're walking with her. That situation was not acceptable in my house, and it was very hard to take the dog for a walk. I could train her if there were no other dogs around with no issue as she was a quick learner. I trained in the basement in inclement weather as we had an unfinished basement. I trained across the street where there was a large park and in a schoolyard. Unfortunately, whenever she went outside, the dogs next door would torment, and they would bark at each other like lunatics. Eventually, I knew Beaudie had to have what they call socialization with other dogs. She needed to understand that other dogs could be her friends, and you didn't have to be in protective mode or be aggressive with other dogs that would be walking beside your dog. I was working at General Motors then, and one of my colleagues had a young pup. He told me about a trainer that he had used with great success. The trainer was in the country and again a well-known trainer. This training was one-on-one in his three-car garage. He had his own dog which was also a German Shepherd. He trained me and gave me various exercises and then, at some point during the 12 or 14 weeks of schooling, he would bring his dog in, and he would direct me on how to handle my dog during the exercises with his dog just sitting idly beside him. At different points, he would take my dog and discipline and train it while his dog, which was very well mannered and disciplined, just sat there calm as a cucumber. Eventually, after weeks and weeks, our dogs began to get to know each other. He would bring in a friend's dog, so suddenly, as my dog progressed and learned how to behave with other dogs, there would be three or four dogs in a three car garage all mingling. Eventually, I did my training as instructed by the trainer with no interference from the other dogs and no issues with my dog. Suddenly, we had re-schooled and retrained my dog to behave. Fast forward after the 14 weeks of training, there are no more issues with my dog. Beaudie was perfect on the leash, perfect in every sense. It just took socializing with other dogs and to learn how to behave. Beaudie had to learn what was acceptable and what wasn't acceptable in an environment with other dogs that was non-threatening. Sometimes, I had to be stern in the training with nothing mean or abusive, but the dog had to understand that I was the master in those situations.

When Beaudie was about a year and a half old, and my son would have been nearly a year old there was a big decision to be made. My ex-wife and I owned a house with hardwood floors in all the rooms. You can imagine a German shepherd has long hair, and a few times a year she would shed. My ex-wife came to the point where she could no longer stand any dog hair laying around the house. Basically, she said we needed to rehome the dog. What you need to understand is that the house was always clean. There was no real dog hair laying around in huge mounds at all. Occasionally, because of the dark hardwood, you could sweep up some dog hair and simply put it in the garbage. Nobody ever complained of the dog hair, nobody made comments that our house was a mess because of our dog. Beaudie was never allowed in the kitchen while we were eating and never allowed in the bed while we're sleeping. The only issues were minor dog hair around the house and all the craziness when she was only a puppy with the dogs next door. That was solved with some serious training. The ex-wife was not an animal person and not a dog person, and it was all new to her owning an 85 pound German Shepherd. I was the one that cleaned the yard from any dog remnants, and I was the one that gave the dog a bath and took care of the dog. My ex-wife made it clear that the dog was not welcome in our house.

I called up the breeder from where I bought the dog from and asked him if he would like to have the dog back, obviously at no charge, just to give it a good home. He responded that he had no room for another dog. He had a few dogs himself as he also lived in Windsor.

I searched around for anybody that might want to take Beaudie, to which there were no real offers. As you can imagine, it was very emotional for a couple of reasons. One, giving my dog away after purchasing it, training it, and caring for it was disappointing. Two, because the ex-wife was suddenly giving an ultimatum to rehome the dog.

Eventually, after a month or so searching for somebody, the ex-wife's cousin's husband owned a farm out in the county and took the dog. It was a sad sight giving my dog up to another family. Suddenly, my dog went from living indoors in a beautiful house to now living outside in a doghouse in the middle of a farm.

Approximately a year later, we purchased a house out in the country only five minutes away from where Beaudie lived at my ex-wife's cousin and husband's farm. Luckily, the house we purchased was fully fenced and was on an acre of land. Our new house also had an outdoor dog pen. Now, I certainly wasn't pleased with the outdoor dog pen scenario. However, I talked the ex-wife into a compromise to get Beaudie back. At night and when we were not home, she would live outside, but at least be with me. When I was home I could take her out of the dog pen and have her in the yard to enjoy. The dog wouldn't be in the house to cause any hair issues within the house. Oh, but a short-term reunion was unfolding at the Crains.

Fast forward another two years, and we were on the move again, purchasing our 3rd house. This time in the Town of Amherstburg. This house was larger and certainly fancier, however it had a smaller yard. It was more upscale and certainly more expensive. In fact, the house we purchased in Amherstburg was twice the amount of the previous house. As you can imagine, the next conversation was about my dog Beaudie. Prior to moving, there was again another ultimatum about the dog. This time the dog couldn't move with us because we had a big fancy house with just a little subdivision property. Beaudie would not be allowed in the house and had no place outside and again my poor dog was on the move. At her workplace, she knew a guy, and he came over and again I gave up my dog for now, the second time to another set of owners. Apparently, he also lived on a farm where Beaudie could live the rest of her life. I heard she had the full run of the farm, and Beaudie was loving it there. I don't believe any of that as

I think it was just something to appease me saying the dog was in good hands. I heard rumors that Beaudie had bit someone. Who really knows the full story?

I guess the moral of the story is that when you get a dog when you're in a relationship or marriage, you need to be very sure that both parties fully understand. Each person must agree that taking care of the dog would be two people's responsibility. Two people need to be enthusiastic about owning a dog and would be taking care of the pooch.

A funny thing happened probably a year after moving into our big fancy house. The ex-wife went to the Humane Society and brought home a dog without any conversation with me. She walked in there and grabbed the dog and thought it would be great to have a little dog with our two children. It was a little poodle or cockapoo or something. This breed was hypo allergenic and would not shed. It was only one or two days that the dog showed terrible behavior. In fact, at night when the two children were put to bed, the issue amplified. They were only three years old and a baby at the time. The dog would jump up on the bed of my oldest and sleep. If anybody even walked down the hallway, the dog would jump off the bed and come charging while snapping and barking at the person. You couldn't walk into the bedroom without the dog lunging at you, barking, growling, and trying to bite. I explained to the wife that wasn't acceptable. We tried another few weeks, but the little dog ended up biting two or three of her friends and aunts when they would visit. The dog was just a lunatic and not well behaved. I suspect, at some point, maybe the dog was abused or something because it just wasn't wired properly. This time I said that the dog must go because it is going to eventually bite our kids. I believe she returned the demon to the Humane Society.

Now those are my adventures of owning and training dogs. I would certainly say that owning animals is very pleasurable. I enjoyed the training aspect of it, and hearing the compliments on how well behaved your dog is in every situation whether in public, in a crowd, by itself or with visitors at your house, I must admit, is quite a good feeling.

Fast forward 10 years, and I had purchased my own home long after a divorce. I thought about having a dog a bit. However, the house was not set up appropriately, and the yard was not fenced. The door that we use all the time goes out to a driveway which is wide open to the road. Owning a dog would be very costly due to having to put a fence around the yard. It would be a pain to let the dog out, walk around to the fenced yard, wait for it to do its business, and eventually walk it back inside the house. The house was just not set up, and our lives were too busy. A few times every couple of months, I would be gone for a week for work, often going for days at a time. Other times, I'm gone the full day. It wouldn't be fair to a dog, so I decided that I wouldn't have any dogs because of our house and yard layout. The kids were growing up without animals, and that was kind of sad. Unfortunately, it was also just our lifestyles and how the house was laid out. We couldn't have a dog and feel good about it. The youngest son Nolan is in university and the oldest now moved out and is no longer living at the house.

The next animal owning event was a few years after my divorce. At one point the ex-wife had a cat that she no longer wanted. The boys were living back and forth between households, so I reluctantly decided to take the cat. I have never in my entire life ever had a cat or knew how to really care for one. I decided for the sake of the cat and the boys that we would have a cat.

I must admit the cat named Kiki was a pretty decent cat. Cats are very different from dogs. Dogs you can call, and they will cuddle with you, and they listen to you. Cats, on the other hand, have their own personalities. They do what they want to do, and they go where they want to go. They climb up on whatever they want to climb up on. In my case, at the very beginning, the cat would climb up onto a table or the kitchen counter. I would push it off and even spray it with water. Eventually, the cat understood that it couldn't just go everywhere, it just needed to be a cat and hang out on the couches or chairs. Occasionally, as a big adventure KiKi would jump up on me and sit with me. Overall, cats are just a different personality than I was used to having in my house.

I was never a big fan of any animals peeing and pooping in the house, even though it was in a litter box. In my eyes, no matter how often you clean them, they always smell somewhere in your house. It was never really appealing to me to have a cat bathroom in my house. Comparing cat urine to dog urine, there is no real comparison. Dog urine is mild with a light smell while cat urine is toxic smelling ammonia based. It reeks, and it is just a terrible smell.

KiKi ended up getting sick, and I spent lots of money at the veterinarian because of whatever sickness. She had accidents where she would urinate in the house a few times. As you can imagine my response, the smell of cat urine was awful, but at least it was downstairs in a room that was never used.

I gave the cat back to the ex-wife. I don't know what she did with it. I think ultimately, she had to euthanize the cat. As soon as I gave up the cat, I removed all the flooring, including the carpet in a quest to get rid of the cat urine smell. The urine of a cat is very ammonia based, and it smells strong and awful. I couldn't wait to get rid of the carpet, flooring and the underlay to get rid of the entire smell. Ultimately, I did but it was quite an adventure removing everything and washing the bare cement. I went and refloored the entire basement, just in case.

OL JIM

As I'm setting up my new shed and cleaning out the garage, I ran across an old friend, a clay head sculpture I call Jim. He's been a friend since I was 16 years old, which is 41 years ago, when I lived in Lasalle. There was an exceptionally large ditch in front of the houses along the street; a monster of a ditch at easily 8 feet deep and nearly 12 feet across the top opening.

At one point, the township went down the entire road, cleaning the ditch. They used a backhoe and scooped the bottom of the ditch from one side and placed the remnants on the other side. The entire length of the ditch we owned was approximately 150 feet. The town would dig it out and place the old sogging dirt on the bank closest to the road, where it remained to dry while they cleaned out the ditches along the entire street. Eventually, they would come back and would load it up in dump trucks and take it to wherever it was required.

In the meantime, this guy had an idea. I was never much of an artist, and I certainly never took any art classes in school. As I am finding out later in life, sometimes I do things that maybe were hidden minor interests when I was a young child.

I went and grabbed a huge chunk of clay that was mixed into the pile of sludge. You see as they were digging deeper into the ditch, they got down to good old-fashioned clay. Clay as in grey clay that people would make sculptures and pottery. It was crazy heavy as I remember bringing it down the driveway in a wheelbarrow to the house and bringing it downstairs onto a cardboard covered table. It was probably a piece that was two feet by two feet and was at least 60 pounds. Downstairs in LaSalle was a rec room that never got used very much by the family. I now had this large block of clay which I did not have any idea what I would be doing with it, but it was clay and thought it was cool.

At this time, I was into the band called The Doors and was reading the biography of Jim Morrison, the leader of the band The Doors. The book was called No One Here Gets Out Alive and was one of the first books I had read just on my own, other than in school. So, at 16, it was a grandiose event to read books about your favorite bands. As the story goes, there were various pictures in the book with a few famous Jim Morrison portraits. There was also one that was not as famous but caught my eye for whatever reason.

I developed an idea as I read the book and looked at this giant chunk of clay. I knew I was going to try and produce a sculpture. I decided it was going to be a bust, basically the head portion and a little bit of the shoulders of Jim Morrison. The picture I picked to duplicate in clay would not be familiar to very many people and certainly not the most popular amongst the fans. Jim Morrison had a beard and curly hair at the time the photo was taken but you never noticed him with a beard very often.

I went on not knowing how to sculpt, manipulate, mold, or develop clay. What I had to begin sculpting was a bust of the picture of Jim Morrison with a beard. I had enough clay that I could make it the size of an actual head with shoulders on it. It was solid clay from our ditch out front of our house that was as clean and natural as a piece you could purchase. I figured out how to cut the clay with knives, wet it down to massage the features of the head. Somehow, I figured out how to make curly hair or my version of curly hair and my version of a beard on him. I remember using marbles for eyes and eventually after a week of pounding, cutting, and molding the clay, he was complete.

I guess real artists and people that make pottery do a drying procedure in a kiln, where they heat it, and it hardens. I did not have any fancy equipment like that for sure, however, I would think over the last 40 years the Jim bust has naturally dried. Since I was a 16-year-old, I've kept this crazy head with me. Many moves, I want to say at least a dozen house moves. It was on a piece of heavy plastic at the time I produced it so that I could carry it. It still probably weighs forty pounds, the nose has been bumped off and a piece on the very back of it I just noticed has chipped off, but it remains the same as I created it.

It certainly has been a focal point for conversation throughout the early years. Nobody really knows what it is as I've had it stuck back in the corner of the garage. It's just a memory of when I was 16 years old, and it's not particularly good. I always thought it was cool that it was a natural piece of clay from a ditch, nonetheless.

It's exactly how it was produced and somehow it was naturally dried. It didn't crack, and it has remained how it was created by my hands, excluding a few bumps and bruises. My two sons have seen it here and there and would often ask what it was, but I never explained it. They sometimes would suggest that I should throw it away, just shake their head and go on their way.

I just recently moved it out of the garage from under a table into the new shed. I made a shelf for it and put it up on the shelf. My oldest had carried it for me and put it up on the shelf. Again, he looked at it and just shook his head and said, what is this thing, and why don't you just get rid of it?

Of course, I will never get rid of it. I'm just hoping that one day I'll be able to pass it on to them, but I'm not sure if they would ever keep it in the family. Thinking that I am 57 years old and produced it when I was 16 years old, and it's still in one piece is amazing. Forty-one years with a bust head of Jim Morrison is quite a feat, and hopefully, it will stay in the family. They could pass on a crazy story about how their dad thought he was an artist and produced a sculpture.

Now that I think about it further, I didn't know what I was doing, and I started it and restarted and eventually the sculpture was good enough for me. I was proud of it at the time, and here it is 41 years later, sitting proudly in my shed. The legend should be on a shelf for everybody to see, and it will again be quite a conversation piece with anybody that goes into the shed. A silly story about a man and his Jim Morrison bust.

HELP OTHERS

I just got done driving through Atlanta, Georgia and saw something that caused me to think. The city was terribly busy, and the traffic was backed up bumper to bumper. The road I took was through downtown Atlanta as I was driving back home from a long work week. I was in the middle traffic lane, and at one point, I had to stop at a traffic light. I was ten cars back from the light and over to my right, in the middle of a sidewalk was obviously a homeless person. The traffic stop allowed me to observe this poor gentleman for 10 minutes while the traffic inched forward. It got me thinking of this gentleman while he was sitting down on the sidewalk. He was wearing what would appear to be a winter coat, a winter hat, raggedy clothes and two different shoes in the middle of the heat of July. The gentlemen had a long, scruffy beard, long hair and sat there holding his sign staring out in front of him with no emotion or movement. His hands were taped, and he was holding a cardboard sign that said, homeless, can you spare any change? The words can you and the words God Bless were at the bottom of the cardboard sign isolated on the cardboard.

In front of me was a BMW, an expensive car, to the side of me was a Tesla. The other cars around me were just average cars. I continued to watch this homeless person and began to think of his story.

As I've spoken about in this book, we have many, many reasons to be thankful, happy, and positive in our lives. This gentleman, although not knowing his story, obviously has come upon tough times. I sat there and wondered how long he had been homeless, where and when he previously worked, and what events caused him to be homeless. What was his life like 10 years ago or as a young adult? You wonder if he was just recently homeless. Perhaps he lost his job because of the Covid virus. You wonder if he has ever married, and does he have any children? His white beard had me thinking that he was close to my age, suspecting in his mid-fifties. Perhaps he was self-employed, and business went bad, and he lost all his money and had a mortgage he could not pay. Maybe he was a military veteran who came home with injuries, mental situations where he could not hold a job and bounced from job to job. Whatever the reason, it grew to where he would have no job and no place to live, and suddenly, he is living on the streets of Atlanta, Georgia.

A million things go through your mind piecing together his current state. Could he be a drug addict, was he an athlete, previously a movie star, or musician? I think when we see homeless people sitting there. asking for money we just walk by and think tough luck.

I've always thought about taking one of these gentlemen to have a meal at a local restaurant. Treat him like a person and get to know him for a half hour. Make sure that he was well fed and show a little bit of compassion. Unfortunately, I've never done it because of too many horror stories about being attacked.

You hear and read about them, although I've never witnessed anyone trying to assist homeless people. You hear of restaurants that may have said they are not welcome because of how they look. I would hope and must think that denial of food to a person who may be down on his luck from a paying patron would be rare. You hear the stories that all homeless people are drug addicts and or criminals. I'm sure there are some, but that is the situation for all the population that some are bad people who got into crime. They could not hold a job and eventually declined into homelessness. I would think there is quite a story with many other people who are homeless. Thousands would have quite a different story, although they look different from you and I because of their cleanliness and clothing. We need to remember they are human beings no matter their appearance, living or work situation.

Unfortunately, I did not have any cash on me, and the roads were congested. I drove home and wondered if it would've taken a heroic effort for me to pull aside, go to a local bank, get some American money, walk over to this gentleman, and pass on kindness and compassion.

I believe overall I've tried to teach my two boys to be very compassionate, sympathetic, and empathetic to other humans' situations. You don't know their story. As analysts on TV will tell you, many of us are only a few pay checks away from being in a financial crisis.

I'm proud to say that my two sons are very giving to the community. Sitting on boards of organizations and volunteering several times a year. Whether in the wintry weather or in the middle of the summer, when there's better things to do, I've seen both help others. When we're walking in a different city and see a homeless person as we walk beside them, empathy is often shown. I've seen a few times where my boys have pulled money out of their own pocket without any prompting and passed on a few dollars. I've also seen them walk into a restaurant and grab some takeout food, bring it over to the less fortunate and give it to them. It's a proud moment when your children will simply help others out of the kindness of their hearts. As teenagers and young adults, they enjoy having a huge heart and caring about people.

As I reminisce about what just recently happened in Atlanta, I wonder if there is more that I can personally do to help people. In these types of situations, I've donated money to different societies trying to help people. You write a check, or you give a donation, but you don't really get to see personally how the money is used or who it helps.

This year, I volunteered to help at a Christmas dinner at a mission in our local town of Amherstburg. People volunteered to prepare the food, to cook the food and hand the food to anyone that came through the door looking for a warm Christmas meal. I was there for about five hours, starting with peeling and cutting potatoes. I then moved into the kitchen where I was filling plates with various foods. This is a small community of 22,000 people, and I got to participate in handing out a meal to over one hundred people. Many of the people that came through the dinner line appeared like you and me. They did not have the means to prepare or afford their own Christmas dinner. I got to peer through the kitchen door and watch them socialize with each other. They were dressed up as best they could, you could see by their actions and their conversations that a few of them may have a mental illness. The common thing with those folks was that they were all thankful and grateful for the meal that we prepared for them.

I must say that I've never seen any of those people, I don't think on the streets, begging for money. The homeless that are on the streets that you see are not the only ones in your neighborhood or in your communities that need help. If you look around, there are many that don't have jobs. Perhaps they don't have any place to live and are couch surfing from bed to bed with friends and family. They may be on social assistance where the government tries to help them. When they walked through the door at the mission, you did not know their story. I am quite confident that there was no abuse of getting a free turkey dinner for Christmas. You would like to believe that if they walked through the door, they were in need.

Once the cleanup was complete, I got to talk with the founder of the mission and had an enjoyable conversation. Here is a gentleman that was a skilled welder in the trades and took it upon himself to open a mission to help the less fortunate after retiring due to an accident. There are donations of food, money, and time from volunteers to help run the program. Tim McCallister and his wife spend countless hours helping people in need throughout the community. I walked out of that Christmas dinner with a whole new appreciation of our community. It's quite eye opening to know that there are that many people in my home community that require help.

My two boys are very volunteer oriented and certainly very compassionate to others, which makes me enormously proud. They'll have success and accomplishments, win medals and awards throughout their lives, I'm sure. However, to see their compassion and commitment to helping others and their willingness to volunteer is an attribute that makes me smile with gratification.

As I drive home from Georgia, I wonder what else I can do. Although not flush with money, I do have some free time. How can I have personal interaction with those in need throughout my community? I'm sure I will ponder this for a while, and I'm confident I'll produce an idea of exactly what I can do in the future to help.

I am truly fortunate, although I've worked hard and long for what I have in life. It's not as much as many but certainly more than others. At my age, considering my health, I'm at the point in my career where I'm satisfied. I would say I don't want for anything. I have a job, food on my table, a place to live, a car to drive, and most importantly, two beautiful children. As you read this, I'd like you to think about what you can do for your community. I ask you to get involved. It's one thing to hand money to a charity that is appreciated and often well used. It's another thing to interact and get to know those you are helping. I always try to remember that in life **You get what You give**.

POSITIVE LIFE

It's crazy writing this as I drive down the 401 to a customer. I've mentioned it before, but again, the memories that come out are unbelievable. What you remember for the craziest reasons sure is a testament to how your life was lived. My life has been incredibly positive. Oh, I dealt with the death of my parents, a divorce was a negative thing, but, overall, I've been very fortunate to have a positive life. I've been lucky enough to have had great parents to show me many things. If I had to bring it down to one thing each would be very difficult because they taught me countless lessons. One thing that stands out from my father is the no quit attitude, and the one thing from my mother is her compassion to help others. Those two specific things, from what I've seen with my two sons, have somehow morphed into their lifestyle. The boys both have a no quit attitude and along with that, I must admit, a little bit of stubbornness that they got from me. I've always preached to them that if they started anything, if they enrolled in anything, it was to be completed. They don't want to be known as a quitter. Sometimes, I'm sure it was a bit unfair because there was no reason for them to complete a few things other than a little bird on their shoulder telling them that they cannot quit. In many ways, I believe for both of my sons it has created a very driven and focused attitude towards setting goals and completing them.

Suffice it to say my life has been extremely rewarding and satisfying with many milestones including a marriage and two great children. I've always been extremely fortunate to have a job, and I would also say the jobs have been rewarding, and I've always been paid accordingly. I believe as you get older, you think of these types of things. How fortunate you are to have a home, vehicles to drive and food on your table. At the top of the list, the birth of my two sons Linden and Nolan have led me to being positive in my life. As with many, I've encountered a few bumps in the road and perhaps a set back here and there. It's all normal. Life is not all candy canes and gumdrops. I move forward and think positively because I have many situations that keep me positive.

RELIGION

If I could've changed, or at least learned about a topic, it would be my knowledge of religion. My kids grew up as Catholics and they went to a catholic public school and a public high school. They did participate in baptisms and confirmations as they grew and learned through those processes about the religion. I certainly have minimal knowledge. Whenever the occasion arises to be in a church and to listen to the priest, I always listen to the priest and wonder what he is really talking about during his sermons. There are obviously procedures in church that I never knew, silly things like when to stand up, when to sing and read. The limited times I have been in church over my entire life, the readings and comments the priest would make would often hit home. I often wondered about the Bible itself and what message it really had inside. I wonder sometimes about religions in general. Are they just somebody's thoughts, someone's opinion or perhaps facts? You never really know other than there certainly are those who have a strong opinion. I think having faith in something is important, but at times, I do wonder if it's all real or just made up.

My side of the family was never religious. I don't recall any conversations around the topic of church. My mother and father certainly were not religious, and we did not attend church. In fact, if you were to ask me for 100 per cent certainty if I were Anglican or presbyterian, I could only guess.

Now my ex-wife's side is much different. I would say her grandmother was deeply religious, and she went to church every day. My ex-wife has aunts and uncles that go to church multiple times a week and on Sunday for mass. Now, I would not necessarily say they are holy rollers, but they are strong believers in the Catholic religion. They know the Catholic religion and all that it means.

I always heard rumblings that you were expected to give 20% of your earnings to the Catholic Church, and as a result, that religion is one of the richest organizations in the world. In my eyes, that seems a bit odd, the request for money from the parishioners. It also is very unfortunate that the news needs to report on the abuse in the religion. You hear of all the damage that many different religions cause to millions of people. You hear about molestations by various priests and then monetary payouts to the victims. There are rumblings that priests are moved to different church locations once the rumors start to develop regarding inappropriate conduct. You see and hear about wars that have started because of religion. In those cases, a group believes in this type of God while others believe in another God. In some cases, there is no compromise and thousands and millions of innocent people are killed in a war over religion.

I shake my head when I think about one religion fighting another religion. I wonder if, in these wars, are the religious leaders accepting of the deaths and is the war for other gains? As it trickles down from the leaders to the actual person in the war, I wonder if the participants battle mentally with these thoughts. Why would my religious leader accept his people's killing? Yes, it's one of those things you never really know when you contemplate, and there is often a great debate on both sides.

I do wish I had learned more about religion in school. I know that when I walk into a church it's a different vibe, and I begin to think during full church proceedings. Church is highly personal. Each person can think of how and what they want to think about it. Church is noticeably quiet with different people in different states of being, some crying, some excited while others are visibly emotional. If nothing else, walking into the church I think about my past and my future. I think about unusual things that I have never really thought about sitting in front of a television, playing on my phone, or listening to the radio. I don't know which religion is correct, or which religion is wrong. I do believe in God but would not call myself religious. I wouldn't say I'm faithful to a church because simply put, I don't attend church. I go for weddings, baptisms, and funerals. At the maximum, I would attend twice a year, and the last time was when my kids were baptized and confirmed.

In summary, the more knowledge you have on any subject, the more intelligent your conversations are on the subject. In my case, unfortunately, I don't have much knowledge on religion. I have opinions but certainly wish I would have had additional knowledge. Whether you believe in it or not, I would suggest just broadening your horizons.

OLD VS NEW

This should be a little bit of a fun chapter where I'll be talking of when I was a kid to how it is now 50 years later. The first thing is, I'm looking around the room, and there are no house phones. When I was growing up, there was one house phone for all to use. It was an actual dial phone where you put your finger into a small round hole and rotated the numbers you were dialing. You picked up the talking and hearing portion, which was separate from the dialing mechanism. It had a big earpiece that covered your ear and your mouth at the same time. A fun fact, back in the day, phone numbers were only 7 digits, there was no area code, but as the population got larger they added the area code 30 years ago. I remember that, as a teenager, it was always cool to have your own phone in your bedroom. You had phone wire cords around the baseboards in your house and small phone boxes where you could plug in the phone. I remember pleading with my mom and dad to have a phone in my room. I eventually wired my own phone using the small phone junction box. Not much went on with that phone, but occasionally, I could sit in my room and talk to a friend that would have had the same kind of scenario. As a teenager, it was always important to have your privacy. Fast forward 45 years later where we have no home phone, and my two boys have their cell phones. The home phone is all but eliminated, and now everybody carries a cell phone everywhere all the time.

The next thing is I'm sitting here watching Netflix, which is a subscription network where you can watch movies for $12 dollars a month. Back in my day, just for reference, we had VCRs or videocassette recorders. There was a machine that was five inches tall and the same length and depth as a microwave and each neighbourhood would have a video store where you would rent a VHS tape of the movie you wanted to watch. You would put the tape into the VCR machine that was connected to your television, and you could view, fast forward, rewind the tape, sit on the couch, and watch a movie.

The big treat while growing up at the time was to go to an actual movie theatre. I don't remember the last time I have been to a movie theatre to watch a movie on a big screen. The other option you always had on a Friday or Saturday night as a teenager was to go to a drive-in theatre. You would load up your friends, including the girls and you drove to a big field that had a huge screen at one end of it. Here you paid your money to enter the drive-in with a car full. You would drive to a spot in the lot and park your vehicle. Originally, they gave you a small little radio box that you hung on the inside of your window, and it would play the sounds of the movie. Then technology advanced so you could dial it in on your car radio. As soon as it got dark, the first of the two movies would begin. Usually, the movies would end early in the morning, and you would drive home. For all those who may be wondering, the shagging wagon was always the vehicle of choice when we were going to the drive-in as teenagers.

I happened to be driving around today and noticed the parks where the kids play. In my day, we had steel slides that were probably ten feet in the air. You would slide down the steel chute, and if you were lucky, you would land in the sand at the bottom. Often after it rained, the sand was a mud puddle. The crazy thing was that obviously, during a summer day, or in the mid-afternoon, that steel chute would be blistering hot. Sure enough, though, someone would always try to slide on it. If the kid had shorts on, you would burn the back of your legs and at the bottom of the slide run around like an idiot squealing. Of course, we would do the same the next day, not thinking again. Nowadays, everything is plastic, and you can't have slides that are that height. I see rubber matting around playgrounds now, the equipment is tamer and obviously much safer. The other thing that we had at playgrounds, which you don't see now, is an actual merry go round. This was a circular piece of playground equipment that rotated when pushed. You could put five or six people on it, then a few kids would run in a circle pushing as fast as possible and then jump onto the merry-go-round, and it would spin because of the centrifugal force. Depending on what you eat that day or when you ate, people would vomit off the side. Other kids would jump off into the open to the grass or the sand, perhaps scraping your knee because you hit a rock.

A common piece of playground equipment we had for a bunch of fun were swings. I've not seen any swings around in my neighborhood for years. They were probably deemed unsafe. We had smaller swings and then big swings for the adventurous. I would say the crossmember was twenty feet in the air with the rubber swing portion only a few feet from the ground. You would pump your legs back and forth, or you had a buddy who could push you to start. Next, you would try to see how high up you could go as you were swinging. Man, we did a bunch of silly stuff such as see how far you could jump out while hoping that you could land on something soft like the grass. Naturally, not every landing was executed like a gymnast, and occasionally, you would land on a rock and scrape your leg or elbow.

Now, steel slides are not safe, merry go rounds are not safe, swings are not safe, but the poor kids are living in a safety bubble nowadays when they play outside. They have rubber matting around everywhere on the playground, so the kids don't scrape their knees. Everything is plastic, nothing is as high as it once was. There's no spinning, so you cannot put your hand in anything rotating. All the bars, anything you climb has safety considerations so that you cannot stick your head through and get caught or put your hand through that kind of stuff. The kids nowadays are shielded from any scrapes or bruises as much as possible.

The next thing that's different between when I grew up and when my boys are now growing up is the television. I am sitting here looking at a 42 inch colour TV. When I grew up, if you had a 20-inch colour TV, you were the talk of the neighbourhood. You may have a TV that was built into a large cabinet with a record player, and you might even have a radio that was built into that TV cabinet. If you had all kinds of money, you had a colour TV with a remote. In my family when I grew up, I was the remote. So, mom or dad would say, hey, let's watch a different channel, of which there were probably five or six channels and all local channels. I would go up and turn the channel using a rotating knob on the front of the TV. One thing that the kids these days have never seen was an aerial (antenna) often called rabbit ears; a device that would sit on top of the TV and was wired into the back of it. You moved it around to get better reception so that what you were watching on the screen wasn't fuzzy, distorted, or snowy. I'm looking here while I'm writing this, and I changed the channel multiple times Click, click, click. If there is a commercial, it just takes one click to another channel, all from the comfort of my recliner. No aerials to worry about a perfect screen and hundreds of channels to watch. If you were super lucky years ago, you had your own TV in your bedroom, a much smaller version at maybe 12 inches and only black and white. Just for reference, that TV screen is smaller than the typical computer screen laptops or notebooks that kids are using nowadays.

The next huge difference between eras would be the music industry. When I grew up, the first thing we had were vinyl records. A record was 12 inches in diameter, vinyl they call it these days. They would usually always have cool dust sleeves with great artwork and graphics on the outside package. You would come home, and you most likely played it in your room because all the music that you were interested in, your parents didn't want to hear. That was the first music media, the next generation was cassettes. These cassettes were about the size of your hand, and they had a plastic case. Two small winding wheels would rotate in the machine, and it had a small ribbon that had all the music on it. It required a cassette player to listen, and it could be played at home and in your car if it had a cassette player. That was the next generation. After the cassette, there was the compact disc also known as a CD. I'll try to explain. This was a small disc about 5 inches in diameter with the same kind of idea as the vinyl record but now a more modern technology. Again, you would have a CD player at your house, and perhaps you were lucky enough to have a CD player in your car. You could listen to it in the house and then bring it out to your car and listen while driving around town.

I would say the next generation for music would be just having a radio with a satellite subscription. You have hundreds of stations that you can dial into in your car. With many different genres of music to choose from, anywhere you travel you have access to the exact same stations.

You now can buy small devices that you plug into the internet, and with a voice command, it will play different music that you request. You can hook up multiple speakers to different areas of the house, and you basically tell it what genre you want to hear. A bit of history. Nowadays, you have cell phones that have subscriptions to all your music sitting on your cell phone. You play whatever you want to play sitting anywhere around the world. These are just a few decades of changes that I noticed throughout my years. I'm not sure what sits ahead, but I'm sure some engineer is sitting at his desk figuring out the next invention.

BIG HOUSES

This is a rambling commentary to consider more than anything. I drove around on the weekend to some popular subdivisions in the local Amherstburg area. The first thing I noticed was the unbelievable amount of new development that has occurred in the last five years in this area. There are acres of new houses and more being developed for additional subdivisions of huge houses. The astonishing thing is that these houses are no longer $150,000 or $200,000 houses or even $300,000 houses. I drove around subdivisions that were average 15 years ago, however, in today's market their value would be close to $600,000.

Now these beautiful new houses being built have two and three car garages, four bedrooms and are monstrous in size. I remember back, and my very first house I bought was $95,000 in the city of Windsor. I paid $95,000 for a four-bedroom basic brick home with a 40-foot frontage and 100 foot deep lot. It was very much a typical home in the area. Just blocks and blocks of these types of houses. Three years later, I was excited that I had sold it for $115,000 and with real estate fees, I had profited five or $6,000. I moved out to the country to a smaller house but with a one-acre property. I think about my very first house on my very first wage. I was barely making $46,000 a year, and I was about 15 years into my career.

It's crazy to think of my two boys and how they could possibly afford a starter home when these homes are priced at nearly $600,000. They would be going into a new career. There's no way they're going to be making $150,000 a year. As an example, a $500,000 house, you would need to have a minimum of 5% down, suddenly you need $25,000 cash for a down payment for a 25-year-old house located in the low end of the subdivisions around the area.

I don't know how it's going to be feasible for this generation to get into the housing market. I'm guessing they're going to be leaning on their parents quite heavily and that is only one phase of it. Once they get a down payment, how are they going to be able to afford a mortgage of $475,000.00? I would think, and I'm not a mortgage broker, but some of these payments are going to be twenty-five hundred dollars per month for the next 30 years. In the last five years, my house that I'm living in now has doubled in value. Now that is all good if I want to sell it, I could make money. The issues are after you sell then what, maybe live in a van down by the river. I could take any of the proceeds certainly and have it for a down payment on another bigger house and more money per month for my mortgage. At my stage in life, with a career starting to wind down in the next 10 years hopefully, I want to start accumulating a little bit of wealth and have money in the bank.

It just floors me and amazes me all at the same time how big and beautiful these houses are around my area. I'm curious to know how different it must be to own one of those houses. You must be dual income with each person earning big money. When I first got into the market with my ex-wife, it was with just a single income. We never wanted to use her income. That was extra money just in case of a rainy day and that would be the case until the final marriage house where we got in way over our heads.

I feel sad for my boys and anybody trying to get into the market as the housing prices have doubled in the last five years. As the professionals will tell you, the prices of houses are high, and they are going to stay in that situation. Obviously, they're going to start to creep up again in the next few years and monthly payments are going to continue to be well over $2500 for a house. I don't know the financial numbers, but suddenly you are going to need a dual income to afford your very first home. A couple is going to have to work paycheck to paycheck to afford a decent house, and I am not talking anything fancy. A house with two or three bedrooms and now the normal is to have a two-car garage. Obviously, back in my first home purchasing days, there was no garage. The normal in my area now is at least a two-car garage, three bedrooms and a tiny bit of property located in a subdivision.

It seems to me that couples are going into a very heavily burdened purchasing situation in their first property. It is going to be financially stressful on marriages. It's sad to think that if there are any blips in the road, it could be devastating. If money is required for a rainy day, that couple is going to struggle with having a big house, nice car, and vacations. Trying to have all three of those things, it just does not seem to be worth it or affordable. Old school is meeting new school as far as housing and affordability. In 2008, the housing market dropped, and people were losing houses and jobs left and right. Maybe you can see the upcoming trend. Currently, you don't see very many junk cars out there. You see a lot of new high-end cars. Young couples have new houses, dual incomes, and you hear about them going on great vacations with little care for the future. I just shake my head that these couples don't know what they don't know. It's an old saying, but it's unfortunately true.

I don't know how they're going to do it, but looking around at the number of buildings, the number of properties, and the size of these houses in subdivisions, obviously, someone is figuring out how to afford it. I don't know what the trick is other than huge, magnificent debt load, but I wish them all the best. Hopefully, nothing crazy happens in our market or in the economy, but I just don't understand how many are going to be able to afford to get into this market and that includes my boys. I don't have the money to give them both huge down payments for their very first home. I don't know exactly how new home buyers are going to afford houses other than to go into some serious debt.

My oldest and his girlfriend are about to get into the rental market. They're going to rent a brand-new apartment in Amherstburg for approximately $1600 a month. The one bedroom, approximately seven hundred square feet apartment is being built as I write this, and they're going to spend $1600 plus other expenses every single month. I remember paying less than $700 a month for my very first house I owned. Many items, habits, and traditions are going the way of the dodo bird and housing is following that trend. People cannot afford housing until they are successful, maybe into their mid 30s or early 40s, and until then, they try to save a couple of bucks renting and have at least flexibility in where they live. You sign a lease for a year, you live there and then perhaps your job, or interests take you somewhere else where you can once again lease. I'm not sure how it's going to all flush out, but I'll be very curious and am certainly going to be watching. Good luck to everybody just getting into the housing market.

TODAY'S DRUGS

Unfortunately, kids and adults, including myself, need to be very aware of the kinds of drugs on the streets of their very own towns. Although all drugs are serious, the latest are leading to huge issues in our communities. What we are facing currently are those in the opioid family of drugs, and it is a huge issue in society. The drug called fentanyl is 50 times more potent than heroin and 100 times stronger than morphine. I understand it is highly addictive with an addiction rate in the high 80% after one use. You see these people on fentanyl in videos on social media, and the news recording users acting and behaving very strangely. Unfortunately, the drug users are the ones that you see dancing naked and talking to walls stumbling around and flailing their arms.

Those people are often in a crisis and addicted to opioids. The users often look to be in their mid to early 20s. I don't remember seeing anyone in the videos in their 40s and 50s. I would think that kind of drug use and addiction steals their life very quickly. Those addictions cause serious issues as you could imagine a loss of job, loss of family, loss of lives and loss of their relationship with their children. As I drive around the Windsor area, you see what's commonly known as homeless people. They are often begging for money. Now, I do believe there's a correlation between abuse and drug addiction with some of those people who are strung out on drugs. I would say it is especially important to know that many of those people in those situations obviously never wanted to be addicted. They may have gotten caught up trying drugs which eventually led to serious addiction to drugs. Those drugs, in turn, cause them to make crazy decisions which lead to missing work or school, and eventually, they lose everything around them.

Anyone that cares about them, at some point, pushes them away. Obviously, employers would do the same thing, and sooner than later, in many cases, they are without a job. As we all know, no income leads to no lodging, and suddenly, they are homeless.

You see those situations on the news and videos especially where people are editing the videos adding music to addicts dancing around struggling on drugs. It is all fun and games for the person who has edited the video with music, and I do admit that I've seen some of those videos. At the same time, after watching the videos, you need to realize those people are humans. They had a mother; they had a father, and they may or may not have children. They are certainly in a bad frame of mind, and their situation often is not very forgiving and many times ends in tragedy. I think it's especially important that the world has compassion for these folks, and you realize there is a very addictive state where they can't control their situation. Society needs to figure out a way to provide help to these individuals.

Alcohol and alcoholism are also rampant throughout society, however it appears that it is not necessarily broadcasted on the news or social media. This addiction is widely accepted, and unfortunately has become mainstream. I would think just based on numbers and how long alcohol has been here that there are more people addicted to alcohol. We have created a buzz word called alcoholic and drug dependent users are drug addicts. I'm not a scientist, and I've never done any research, but I have noticed that alcoholism seems easier to talk about than drug addiction. Sadly, alcoholism is accepted while drug addicts are shunned and labelled misfits of society.

DOWNSIZE TIME

My exciting Wednesday night consists of watching one hockey game on TV, and another one on my phone. My oldest and his girlfriend are at a hockey game, while my youngest is off to workout. I sit here all alone thinking.

I'm thinking about all the times and all the fun I've had with my boys growing up. It always made me feel great that I could provide for them in many ways. We enjoyed vacations, cruises, trips to Quebec, and trips to New York. A great vacation to Newfoundland Island and Labrador was one of our highlights. I got to travel a little bit as I grew up, always in a trailer and always camping. Although the boys and I and sometimes with my oldest son's girlfriend travel, we are not in campers; we are in hotels and eating in restaurants.

I've been fortunate enough to have the ability to afford hotels for any vacations that we have been able to enjoy. I sit here at my age knowing that Linden and his girlfriend will be moving out in a few months into a brand-new apartment. The only remaining one will be my youngest Nolan. Although only in second year of university, I do anticipate him moving for his studies at some point. Nolan has always been a carefree young man, and it wouldn't surprise me if, before he graduated, he would move out with a couple of friends into a rented house.

It makes me think about this house where I am currently living. As far as I'm concerned, it's a great house on a great piece of property in a nice subdivision. However, I think about the area that I use as compared to the entire footprint of the house.

I primarily use the upstairs, obviously, the kitchen, my bedroom, and the common washroom. If I go downstairs three or four times in a month, it's only to do laundry. My home has a fireplace, TV area, and an office that the boys and I created during the pandemic years. I must admit that the office looks great and is decorated beautifully. That room for years was just a junk storage room with a weight machine and was painted a putrid green when I purchased it, and I never bothered to repaint it. After a couple of thoughts during COVID, we removed all the junk including the weight machine. We painted the walls, painted the trim, and installed a new ceiling in the room. I purchased a desk and sitting chair, some window blinds and added a TV and bookshelf. It wasn't too long before it was quite a nice office in my opinion, but as I just mentioned, it's hardly ever used.

As far as the outside is concerned, I've hired a person to upkeep the yard, including cutting the grass weekly. It just doesn't excite me anymore to do yard work, and I would rather spend my time doing other things. I just recently, after two years, completed a rustic looking shed. The only remaining item to complete it would be the cement around the shed. I have a small, attached garage which I enjoy using in the summertime, just to sit in there and watch the television that I have mounted in the garage.

This leads me into thinking, at what point do I downsize? Would I downsize into another home? My preference would be a single story home with the laundry on the same floor as the living space. I must say, going up and down stairs to do laundry is not my favorite.

We'll see. Do I downsize into another home or into a condominium? Perhaps I downsize into renting an apartment. The one thing I do know is I certainly enjoy watching the outside and any activity. I guess my preference for an apartment or condominium would be to have a beautiful view and a balcony.

The decision will be made, I would think, in the next couple of years, and we'll see where it goes. I think of all the homes that I've lived in throughout my life, and it's got to be nearly eight or nine. One more move will certainly not be an issue.

I look at my career and see 11 jobs. I guess, as many would say, there is never any grass growing under my feet. I learned a lesson about loyalty from my father's situation of being unemployed for a year and a half from a company to which he worked for over 30 years. Unfortunately, in this world, there is no longer any loyalty between employer and employee and between the employee and employer. Whenever I made moves in my career, I always had the mindset that I had done a fair day's work for a fair day's pay. While I was working for that company, I gave everything I had to the company. I have learned that, at the end of the day, it needs to be all about me. If I had a chance to advance in opportunity, wage, or responsibility, I would think about pursuing a potential new job. If I have given my all to the company from which I've been paid, the loyalty ends at that point. I have seen friends and family in situations where when the going gets tough for a company, the employer doesn't have a problem reducing the number of employees regardless of seniority, title, wage, or ability. It's simply a case that the employee is only a number, so when heads need to roll, the employer makes the heads roll based on whatever is needed at the time. Unfortunately, it's the way of the world. The loyalty portion of society has gone the way of the dinosaur.

THE FUTURE

The other curious thing I've done while going through all of this contemplation, reminiscing and writing is that I've made it a point of finishing a backyard shed that's taken two years to complete. I've hired a second person to complete it, and they've done a fantastic job. I've torn apart the inside of my garage to have it cleaned out and things placed properly in the shed. The next thing that will happen is I'll have the backyard finished as it has looked terrible for the last two years while trying to get a shed built from the first builder. The yard has been a mess, quite frankly, as it just sat there with only the basic maintenance of cutting grass and trimming. My goal this summer is to get all that done, including any new patio area that is required. The cement work will be hired out, and I've now hired out the lawn maintenance including planting grass, trimming hedges and flowerbed maintenance. My conscious effort is to have this house cleaned up including the garage, yard and new shed completed.

The next thing would be to paint the interior of the house and refinish the bathroom downstairs, all to be done to get full value for the house, or a little extra value if it needs to be up on the market. Now, currently there are no plans for me to sell the house, however, based on what I went through the last eight months medically, being prepared is not a terrible thing.

Nobody has really noticed, so everything has been kept under my hat. My thought is that I get the house back in tiptop shape should it need to be sold for me to purchase another smaller house with less maintenance, move into an apartment or in the worst case, the boys need to sell it.

I need to admit that some of these paragraphs and chapters in this book are a little bit morbid. When authoring this book, I just kind of let it all hang out. I am not even sure of the complete plan. Although my thought would be, if possible, to keep this book a secret and have it written and edited with the cover illustration completed. I will need to go to different people to complete the draft editing. I had personal friends and even the ex-wife edit my last two books. I don't want to alarm anybody, so I'd hire somebody else to complete the full editing. I'd love to have it all done completely and then published. I think this time I would not publicize it on social media because really there are just a few people that I would have any interest in reading it. My brother and sister-in-law, my two boys and ex-wife would really be the only ones that would have any interest in it at all. It is not going to be a big, popular book. My first two certainly were not but anyways, enough of me.

I don't want to come off as feeling sorry for myself, but I owe it to my boys to give them a little more history of the old man. What he has done, what he is saying, what he thinks, and then also a little bit about their grandparents and family. Unfortunately, I don't know any in depth information regarding their grandparents or even aunts and uncles, but I have tried to explain everything that I know.

I would think that some of the dates and duration of years may be a bit off, but this is my version. Once I go into editing, I always try to find out a little bit more concerning family accuracy. In the case of different dates, I'll have to be very secretive about how I confirm facts that I do think are important. I don't want to tip off anybody right now that I'm writing a book. Just the thought that I'm drafting a book or a memoir or whatever would lead them to believe that there's something wrong with me. You know what I mean, the whole thought that I'm drafting my last book on my deathbed, which is not true. It's just something I've been thinking about for a few years, and now is the time to complete it.

We'll see exactly how it goes as it's getting near the finish at just over 110,000 words. It will edit it out to approximately 90,000 words completed. As I write it, I'll put it in chronological order, but mostly it's about thoughts and some fun stuff in there and some crazy things not too many people know.

It's a factual book, a collection of memories that are again, just for my sons reading and information, should they choose to read it. It's exciting to draft another book. I would think that this is going to be my last book. I've written two hockey books, something I enjoyed, and now my third book is about my life and my thoughts outside of hockey. I've got two separate lives: one a hockey life and one my personal life. As I think about it, my recent friends and old friends know more about my hockey life than they do my personal life or my history. Either way, we know the 57 years of my life have been exciting and rewarding with the culmination of two great sons.

Breaking news here on the housing front. After much debate, I have decided to move into an apartment in Amherstburg, Ontario in January 2024. The decision was made after many sleepless nights pondering the future, as well as my health. I currently live in a two floor, raised ranch style house with a large yard. Three bedrooms upstairs and one bath, while downstairs has a bath, office, living room and the laundry facilities. At this point, too much house for too few people. I knew I was eventually going to downsize, so I'm basically just fast tracking the inevitable. I think I have probably sped the process up by about five years. My oldest son has moved out into an apartment of his own with his girlfriend, Julia. He moved out more than a year ago. Now, my youngest son has just completed his third year of university locally. After his four-year degree, he will further his education in either the United States, Canada or overseas.

I have always fully realised that Nolan was going to move to pursue his education at the highest level, so that was not a surprise. Moving out for Linden was not a surprise, either as he's at that age and very self-sufficient with his long-time steady girlfriend. His career is moving along rapidly after graduating a year and a half ago from the University of Windsor.

I have visited Linden and Julia's brand-new apartment many times. Their apartment building has a gorgeous sightline overlooking a river. The views had me beginning to think of my possible residency in this type of complex. It's filled with amenities including a pool table, a social room, pool, workout room and golf simulator, which are all very appealing.

After a few visits, I certainly began to seriously contemplate making a move into an apartment. Their apartment building is approximately a year and a half old. The occupancy rate of the complex skyrocketed to 100% very quickly. Next to their apartment building a second one identical to the very first one is currently being built. I understood how quickly the first apartment complex filled up, and I anticipated it would be the same for the second building. I went to a few open houses where I viewed a two bedroom and already knew of Linden and Julia's one bedroom. I also compared the facility to another new apartment building being built in Amherstburg. The second apartment did not have the same type of view of the water, which I've always explained to the boys that I wanted. I enjoy looking at the water. In fact, I don't know if it's a full pastime, but I do spend a few hours a week viewing the waterways around the Amherstburg area. I just find that a water view is very relaxing and something that, at my age, I enjoy.

The time came to decide. If I wanted to have a good view, I had to act soon. The apartment located on the waterfront was the place to go for me. The next issue was timing. Although I've been called an over analyzer throughout my life, now is not the time. Ultimately, after some more contemplation, I made a decision which I'll call phase one of the upcoming process. I contacted the apartment building leasing company and spoke to them a bit more, asking about pricing and availability. They responded that application availability would begin at the beginning of February 2024. At this point, I knew the facts, knew the prices, knew the availability and knew the apartments' layouts and features.

I hemmed and hollered for another week or so and eventually made the call. I asked exactly how I go through the process of renting an apartment. They explained that I would first fill out an application and submit it with all my pertinent information. With that, you either got approved or not approved, and from there you'd pick your apartment, location, size of apartment including one bedroom, one bedroom with a den or a two-bedroom.

Ultimately, within a few hours of my application, I was approved having received the confirmation e-mail. I would call it go time, either I'm going to rent or forget about the idea. This would be the last chance for me to change my mind. A couple more days passed, and as per usual Crain contemplation, I finally committed and said "let's do it." I gave them a deposit for the first month's rent, and I'll be a proud renter come October 7th, 2024. I chose a one bedroom plus a den layout which will give Nolan a place to stay when he is visiting from out of town or out of country. In the meantime, for his last year of local university, he'll have a bedroom.

Now phase two is to determine if I'm going to sell my house, or the idea of renting my house has certainly crossed my mind. Renting obviously, as long as it's more than my mortgage, would allow me to have a small monthly income. Selling the house would allow me to have a small sum of cash after the proceeds of selling. I think right now in April of 2024, my thought would be to sell this house and have a little bit of money in the bank. In October 2024, I will move into a brand-new apartment, with brand new appliances on one floor and a great view facing the water from my balcony.

Well, now the hard part begins for the next eight months. I'm in the process of radically downsizing from three bedrooms, two bathrooms, office and two living areas. A wall full of sports memorabilia as well shelves full of books take a lot of space. I have found the easiest way to reduce is to sell the items. I'm currently listing items on Facebook marketplace where I take a few pictures, provide a brief description, and provide the price. Viewers contact me, we negotiate a price and hopefully, it's sold. Slowly, I am reducing my items, with the next items to reduce being art pieces.

Admittedly, the downsizing effort is quite daunting, having accumulated many items over the years. It also is emotional in many ways, sorting and deciding what items will need to be sold or donated. There seems to be memories attached to articles, often involving the purchase reason, the boys and other thoughts. I need to keep focused on the task at hand and remove myself from the emotional attachment. It's sometimes not an easy task but necessary to begin life in an apartment.

Now let's get into the next chapter of my life.

CONCLUSION

So, drafting this book, which is my third book, has been a bit different than the first two. The first one was about hockey and how I figured it paralleled many things going on in the world and in life. It got into a little bit of my hockey history. It was to be informative to my two boys about my hockey adventures.

The second book was about being a general manager in the Junior C hockey ranks. It chronicled a year as a general manager in the hockey world. I sprinkled a few chapters of my thoughts on the future of hockey and today's players.

The first book had a tagline or kick line, whatever you would call it. Go hard to the net, keep your stick on the ice, put the biscuit in the basket. The second book had the buzzwords of Never Say Never. In fact, those buzzwords were going to be the name of the book at one point, early in the writing of it. However, there is a famous Canadian artist that has a song called *Never Say Never*. I did not want any issues with copyright infringement or anything else, so I changed the title of the book. I'm not exactly sure what title my third book will have, but I'm sure I'll produce something creative.

This book has been a deep dive into my life, thoughts, and philosophies. It was written for my two boys as I've mentioned many times. I don't really discuss my past with anyone, but there is nothing shady, embarrassing or criminal about it.

I would say overall I'm a private person. Many would ask why you would be private with your two sons. I guess it's just the nature of the beast of Greg Crain. I don't want anyone to think that I'm bragging, so I've never really discussed my life. It's just the way that I am in life. You run across many people that will pump their own tires. Myself, I am reserved and very humble regarding my life.

I think many times pumping your own tires in different careers is required. We all know that the squeaky wheel gets the grease. That is certainly true in many careers that I've seen throughout my work years, including my own. If you're an outgoing, friendly person and personable, it's a huge advantage in life and your career.

Nobody really likes hanging out with someone who's grumpy, negative or complains a lot. Although it's extremely easy to go down the rabbit hole of negativity and constant complaining, it's not a good habit. You can spiral into the abyss, where you hate everything. The effect is that nobody wants to hang around you when you don't enjoy anything about life. Man, we have all seen a few things happen to people that spin out in that state of mind. In my opinion, a few things can happen. You could just be isolated your entire life and still function, or in extreme cases, you may start to think about decommissioning yourself. I have always tried to avoid being around negativity or people that complain. If you just look around, there are so many things to be positive and excited about.

As I authored this book, I certainly went into my life, trials and tribulations, things I've done, haven't done and things I've regretted. It was literally a touch base on items I wish I could've redone or done when I had the chance. I recently read that many people on their deathbed regret not what they did, but what they never did.

Meaning, if you want to do something in your life, do it, be smart, enjoy it and often, you will have memories of it for your entire life. Now that being said, being smart is especially important. Making sure it's legal is important, not hurting yourself physically or others is also important.

I look back on events in my life and many times, I wish I could do them over again. There are also those I wish hadn't done as well as those I didn't that I wish I had. At my current age of fifty-seven, I certainly have lots of memories that have flooded the chapters throughout the book. I would say overall I have a great life, with many great experiences. I've always strived to be the type of guy that contemplates far too long. I finally decide after figuring it out and eventually move forward. A wise man once told me that often, in the heat of the situation, at the very moment of happening, it's not as bad as you think, and it's not as good as you may think. If you think back and assess situations you've been in, it really is true.

Sometimes, we all get very extreme with the thinking the world is ending or that we just created a brand-new world. Often, it's in the middle and not as good or as bad as you're thinking. I have always been a big believer in having my mind default to the worst-case scenario.

I find if you're in a situation and think of the worst possible outcome and how you would deal with it, often your mind opens, and you feel relieved a bit. Try this worst-case type of thinking when stressing about a decision or situation, and I think you'll be surprised.

As I continued writing about my journey in life, I had lots of smiles, and like I've mentioned, the memories will remain. If 50 years later, I am remembering something that happened when I was six or seven years old, it certainly has affected me and left an imprint. At the same time, there are millions of things that I don't recall. I brushed them aside, whether negative or positive events.

It's going to be very curious regarding the boys' memories of their childhood. It does come out occasionally, a memory for them that I don't recall. When they mention it, it's usually nothing I would have thought would be a core memory, but for them, it is.

A memory, in my eyes, just happens. You don't go into a situation thinking that this is going to be a memory and make a point of memorizing it. That is not the authentic way they happen in life. Something happens, and suddenly it's carved into your brain and never ends up going away. Sometimes, the details of it change or get a bit fogging as you get older, but the base memory is still there.

I sit back and continue to think how fast time goes. My brother is 68 years old, tapping on 70 years on this planet. I have nieces and nephews who are in their late 20s, one son who is 23 and one son who is about to turn 21 years old.

It just makes you think back to that long tape measure that I spoke about early in the book. You pull out the tape to the average life expectancy number, you mark it, and you now put your finger on your age. The difference between the two marked numbers are the years you've got left on this planet. I'm sitting here wondering about the zero to the magic number on the tape measure tape. Have I accomplished anything? Have I done more good than I have bad? Have I helped enough people? Have I hurt any people? I guess the latest buzzword is as follows, when you leave the planet, have you left the world in a little bit better place than when you were born? And by the way, you have 80 years to accomplish all that you can. Your success can be measured in many ways. Some would measure it by money, others measure it by marriage. Some measure it by the number of kids you have. Others will leave the earth and never have even thought about it. I would suggest anybody reading this crazy book, especially this chapter to figure out what you want to do in your life. It certainly should not be when you're 10 years old, but you may know what you want to accomplish in life at age 20. You need to be ready for the bumps in the road, the stop signs, the haters, and the naysayers. Embrace those who are trying to help you, and discard those who are trying to hinder you. I have learned and watched many successful people, and I can sum it up by thinking, why not you? If you've figured out your measurement for success, the mindset needs to be, why can't it be you? It doesn't matter where you're born or who your parents were. It only matters about how you're going to do it and what you're willing to sacrifice to get there. Currently, too many people grab onto excuses. Once they can grab an excuse, they don't have to continue to pursue what they want. An adage I like to state is this, "If you say you can't, you are correct."

In summary, be a good human, help others and pursue your dreams without any excuses, knowing there will need to be sacrifices.

Remember in life.....**You get what You give.**

APPENDIX A

MEMORIES

The way I determined these memories is by using three criteria:

1. The emotion of the event.
2. The feeling of the event.
3. The excitement of the event.

Here are a few memories from my life adventures:

1. Vacation trip to Lake Louise to see its beautiful colours.
2. The death of my father.
3. The death of my mother.
4. The birth of Linden Lloyd Crain.
5. The birth of Nolan Gregory Crain.
6. The high school graduations of Linden and Nolan.
7. My college graduation.
8. My divorce and how it let down my family.
9. The late night I received a phone call from Linden regarding Nolan.
10. Calling my brother from the hospital regarding the decision to unhook our mother from life support.

NOTE: There are obviously many other memories I could also slide into this list.

These are the ones that came to mind. I think you'll agree, many of them are life changing or brought huge excitement or changes in my life. I hope my boys will have a much larger list of events as they grow old, with their memory list starting when they were young until they're 150 years old. I've mentioned before that memories just happen. It's crazy what you do remember and why, what may trigger the memories, and how sometimes, you don't even know why you remember them. I hope that my two boys have memories that include me, and that they'll share those memories with whomever they choose. Having a memory of their father would be an incredible honour.

APPENDIX B

FAVOURITES AND FACTS

Here is a little fun chapter about all my favourites, habits, and quirky things. Weird things that my kids may have not recognized, or friends and family may have never noticed.

- Favorite colour is red, and my second favorite colour is purple.
- Favorite number is 12, followed by my second favorite 24. The NHL's toughest hockey player Mr. Bob Probert of the Detroit Red Wings wore #24.
- I throw right-handed.
- I shoot basketball left-handed.
- I golf right-handed.
- I write with my right hand.
- I play hockey left-handed.
- My eyes are blue.
- Waist size is fifty-four inches.
- Shirt size is 5X.
- Favorite sport is hockey.
- The sport I don't understand and don't enjoy watching is curling.
- Favorite collegiate team is the University of Michigan. My second favorite college is the University of Notre Dame.
- Favorite hockey team is the Detroit Red Wings.
- Favorite baseball team is the Toronto Blue Jays.

- Favorite basketball team is the Detroit Pistons.
- Favorite football team is the Detroit Lions.
- Favorite food is veal parmesan.
- Favorite drink is milk.
- My favourite car is a Corvette.
- My dream car would be a Lamborghini.
- My dream SUV would be a Land Rover.
- I have one brother named Gary Robert Swope.
- I have one sister-in-law named Barbara Anne Swope.
- My father's name is Lloyd Ivan George Crain.
- My mother's full birth name is Donna Emeline Mackenzie.
- My longest friend's name is Mike Janisse. We have known each other for more than 45 years.
- I grew up in Windsor and LaSalle, Ontario.
- I've had my motorcycle license since I was 16 years old.
- I earned my motorcycle license using a borrowed scooter.
- I've had ten jobs since graduating college.
- I graduated college in 1988.
- I graduated college with an Industrial Engineering Technologist Diploma.
- My college diploma was a three-year course. It took me 4½ years to graduate.
- I kept my college graduation gown for many years.
- I still have my silver high school ring and my gold college ring.
- My mother saved 2-dollar bills to buy my gold college ring.
- I swore in front of my mother for the first time when I was 34 years old.

- My first pair of basketball shoes were white Chuck Taylor Converse that cost $15.
- I enjoy collecting artwork of local artists and have over twenty pieces hanging on my walls.
- I collect watches and pens.
- My favourite fast food is Harvey's.
- I don't like sushi.
- I am an Anglican as a religious denomination.
- I have been a quality technician, a time study, a project manager, a mechanical designer, an estimator, and an account manager throughout my career.
- I once threw up because of drinking too much Sambuca, to this day the smell of Sambuca makes me want to hurl.
- I attended Wrestle Mania 3 in Detroit, Michigan at the Silverdome.
- My first concert was to see a band called The King Bees at an outdoor grass bowl music facility at St. Clair College in Windsor Ontario. The King Bees were an obscure band that got jeered off the stage after one song. Beer bottles were thrown at them from the crowd when we were leaving.
- The only rock concert I have seen was George Thorogood, which was at the Pine Knob theatre, an outdoor event in Detroit, Michigan.
- I have been to Las Vegas three times and once on a honeymoon.
- Although I'm not afraid of heights, it's not my preference.
- My favorite wrestler is Macho Man Savage.
- I broke my left ankle in Grade 7 on a dirt bike.
- When my kids were little, we used to play fight with my closing moves being the claw, the hook, and the hammer.

APPENDIX C

Disappointments

This list was created using criteria like my list of memories.

1. Career choices.
2. Scholastic choices.

Here is my list of disappointments:

1. Never winning a Schmaltz cup as a hockey coach.
2. Divorce.
3. Never owning my own business.
4. Never being a real estate agent.
5. Not being more physically fit throughout my life.
6. Not being more physically active with my two boys.
7. Not taking more vacations.
8. Never owning a boat.
9. Never obtaining a university degree.
10. Not being a lawyer.

When you look at the above list of disappointments, a few of them are superficial, and a few really would never have changed my life to any degree. Others are decisions that today look different to me as a 57-year-old.

Overall, the list contains thorns in my life, of what could have been or should have been. Do you have thorns in your life? Do regrets or disappointments hang like clouds over your ambition? If so, it's up to you to decide which ones are the thorns, which ones are superficial, which really didn't matter at all, and which ones you can still do something about.

APPENDIX D

WHAT ABOUT...

- That time with vodka shots for others and water shots for me.
- The visit to the ballet and the necktie.
- The ice cubes and ear piercing.
- That time with the motorcycle and the no trespassing chain.
- Those bicycle rides with water bottle beers.
- That $40 for a scorpion tattoo.
- That 2 for 1 liquor shots in Buffalo night.
- The neighbour who side swiped you while we headed to the bar.
- The teacher and the wedding.
- The dirt bike rides from Lasalle to the Windsor McDonalds.
- The flipped over golf cart in Blue Mountain.
- A gently rolled golf cart at the tournament.
- The black painted baseboards.
- That Devil's night and the grapes.
- That Devil's night and washing windows.
- Pylons and the Fiero.
- That scar, the spoon, and the bowl.
- The 23" long catfish.
- The competition for credit cards and charge cards.
- The illegal passing ticket.

- The Levi jacket with painted band logos on the back era.
- The white Levi jacket.
- Teachers and parties.
- The Old Shillelagh and the tap on the window.
- Lafayette Coney Island and the wedding.
- The club and the wedding ring.
- The hitchhiker and the police officer.
- The abandoned building and the windows.
- The car engine and pigeon lunch.
- The Honda and the oil smoke ride.
- The flat tire trip to Chicago.
- Skiing on pavement.
- Transporting cement.
- 30 ft of steel tubing and a car.
- Roofing and sunburns.
- Those hockey games while in school.
- 180 in an 80.
- The great motorcycle escape.
- The Maple Bush parties.
- The Matchett Rd. house festivities.
- Summer school.
- The unsafe motorcycle ride from Cottam.
- The garage sale car.
- The 4-door red Plymouth Horizon car.
- The hidden sidewalks.
- Blue Mountain teacher's kid.
- Barbed wire and motorcycles.
- The Virginia bike ride.

APPENDIX E

A Life Poem

Fifty-seven years ago, I was presented to this crazy, vast, and amazing world.
A life with valleys, mountains, oceans and many a swirl.

A kid was born with plenty of energy and aspiration.
Each day full of thought and self-regulation.

I grew up enjoying sports, family, and friends.
Unfortunately, many have passed, and others they too will end.

A few of those friends were close and loyal.
While others have drifted as they were coddled and often spoiled.

High school was always quite a wild adventure.
A few too many nights having a series of quenchers.

Those college years were much to talk about at parties.
The goal was to gather more influence than the front row smarties.

After those years it was time to grow and progress.
Onward and upward to a life of riches and success.

Ol hockey was my love at that point in time.
Perhaps I could make it to the ladder for the ultimate climb.

I dabbled here and there as an enthusiastic coach.
Of course, over those years there were many times of parental reproach.

Then came miraculously the love of my life.
What followed was a few great years of marriage and spice.

Two boys were the outcome of the seven years together.
Too many squabbles to survive the rough, stormy weather.

Gallons of alligator tears to wipe with a comforting soft tissue.
Soon we both decided to move on without hate, fanfare, or issue.

Ups and downs, with frowns and bright smiles
Happy and sad while the mind drifted for miles and miles.

Stability was always the final and ultimate destination.
It was grueling, tedious, and tiresome communication.

Sometimes marriage sucks with a bad and an often-predictable disappointing consequence.
Do this, do that could often damage, bruise this fragile confidence.

The boys grew so fast and delightful.
Never a time where they were ignorant or spiteful.

Over the years I have traveled up-and-down the highway for miles and miles.
Each stop a handshake, info, chitchat, and smiles.

Sales meetings and travel without my two best friends.
Often thousands of miles away from watching their latest trends.

Drive, meet, eat, and sleep.
Present, sell, close and repeat.

This is what I know, this is what I do.
When you do it so often, it becomes like your favorite old shoe.

Now, at this age I tend to want to reflect and ponder.
The future, their lives, to be sure they don't need but also not squander.

Set the boys up for their growth and promising success.
Damn I am lucky, satisfied and yes so blessed.

My life has been full of love, excitement, and colourful bubbles.
Never a worry of loneliness, poverty, or troubles.

I am here to try and pass on some experience and knowledge.
Although at one point it took five years to graduate from a reputable college.

Well for now I will close this little life story with pride.
To all who may read, enjoy your life, love, and endless flowing tide.

In life, You get what You give!!!